MY GREATEST DAY IN
GOLF

ALSO BY BOB McCULLOUGH

New York Running Guide
Washington D.C. Running Guide

My Greatest Day Series:
My Greatest Day in Baseball
My Greatest Day in NASCAR

MY GREATEST DAY IN

GOLF

THE LEGENDS OF GOLF
RECOUNT THEIR GREATEST MOMENTS

AS TOLD TO
BOB McCULLOUGH

THOMAS DUNNE BOOKS
ST. MARTIN'S GRIFFIN ≋ NEW YORK

THOMAS DUNNE BOOKS.
An imprint of St. Martin's Press.

www.stmartins.com

Library of Congress Cataloging-in-Publication Data

McCullough, Bob.
    My greatest day in golf: the legends of golf recount their greatest moments /
as told to Bob McCullough.
        p. cm.
    ISBN 0-312-25259-5 (hc)
    ISBN 0-312-28909-X (pbk)
    1. Golf—United States—Anecdotes. 2. Golfers—United States—Anecdotes.
    I. Title: Legends of golf recount their greatest moments. II. Title.

GV967.M365 2001
796.352'0973—dc21   00-045971

First St. Martin's Griffin Edition: July 2002

10 9 8 7 6 5 4 3 2 1

This book is dedicated to my father, Eugene McCullough, a lifelong golfer whose greatest days in golf will always be among my fondest memories.

CONTENTS

Editor's Note

Most of the interviews in this collection were conducted at the end of the 1999 season, and several were originally intended to be part of a magazine series. As the collection evolved, it became apparent that much of the content constituted a de facto tribute to the Big Three. As a result, the majority of the interviews were conducted with members of the Senior Tour, although an attempt was made to represent golfers from every decade of the last half-century. I hope I have done justice to their contributions to the game.

As I went through the interviewing process, I became painfully aware of all the fine players I was unable to include, simply because of the length restrictions of a single book. It remains my fondest wish that there will be subsequent volumes of this collection in which I can continue to track and update the exploits of golf's greatest players.

As always, the author would like to thank those who participated in sharing their stories—it was a pleasure to meander briefly through the last half-century of the game's history in this fashion, and I continue to be delighted by the surprises, the achievements, and the intimate moments that emerge in their choices. Equally important were the contributions of those who helped set up the interviews—as was the case in earlier volumes, this book couldn't have happened without them.

MY GREATEST DAY IN
GOLF

TOMMY BOLT

During his career, Tommy Bolt was considered a first-rate shot maker, a contemporary of Ben Hogan whose golf skills often matched those of the master, with whom he dueled on several notable occasions. Bolt, who went by the nickname of "Thunderbolt," was also renowned for his temper and his penchant, early in his career, for club-throwing. For his greatest day he chose his victory over Gary Player in the 1958 U.S. Open, and he also gave a brief rundown of his greatest day playing against Hogan.

My greatest day in golf, huh? Well, when I won the U.S. Open at Tulsa, that was my greatest day.

I was playing real good when I went to Tulsa. Of course, I was born in Oklahoma, and I had a lot of people up there that I actually knew. At that point in time I was at peace, I had peace of mind, I was at peace with the world. I had complete control of my emotions and everything I was doing, it was the greatest thing in the world. I just felt like everything was gonna happen good, and consequently, if you feel that way, everything happens good.

I had my ups and downs, and so does everybody else, but this was a good week for me, and that was my goal, winning the U.S. Open. I was feeling good, and after I birdied the first hole, I felt like, well, I wonder who's gonna finish second? That's the way I felt in my mind.

Of course, I made a few mistakes out there, made some bogeys, and I missed some fairways, but instead of trying to go for the green from the missed fairway, which is a mistake in the U.S. Open, I sacrificed a stroke and pitched out into the fairway and went on and took my bogey rather than try to birdie or par the hole from a tough lie in the rough. You have to do that when you play in those major tournaments, because we're all human, and we're gonna miss some shots.

I tell you what I did on the eleventh hole, a par three hole. I missed a green to the right, just hole high to the right. The flag was on the upper plateau, the last round this was too, and there was another trap right over the green. And right over the green to the left there was another bunker, and the flag was fairly close to that, and I had a pretty tough lie in the bunker and just a little bit of green to work with.

Rather than go for the flag from there and trying to make my three, I pitched it onto the big part of the green, out of the bunker, and I almost made the putt for par, but I two-putted for a bogey from there. So I actually sacrificed a stroke rather than putting it in the other bunker and making a five, making a double-bogey. That's the way you have to play to win the Open . . . you're gonna have to sacrifice some strokes. You have to concentrate, because concentration is 75 percent of golf to start with, it may go to 95 percent, that's what a mental game it is really.

I have no idea how far behind me Gary Player was—I'm telling you, I never worried about anybody else. I don't know if we had scoreboards up or not in those days, I can't remember, 'cause I didn't care, it didn't make any difference who was there, or what have you. I just knew that when I started up the eighteenth fairway, all the media joined in the back of me, you know what I mean, to walk up the fairway with me. I knew that I had won the tournament, it was my tournament to win.

The earlier rounds I shot two 71s, and I led it at 142—I was leading the U.S. Open at 142. Of course, that was a very demanding golf course, Southern Hills was, and they had really set it up pretty tough. The fairways in those days were only thirty yards wide, you had to drive the ball pretty darned good to keep it in the fairway. And the heat, it was ninety-five degrees almost every day, but there was a breeze, there was about a fifteen-mile-an-hour breeze blowing.

It suited me to a tee. It was really hard on some of the guys from the northern part of the country, because they'd never been in any weather like that—not just heated up, it was just perfect for me. I've got a little bit of arthritis in the upper part of the back, and I just love hot weather, the looser I get, the better I play. When you feel loose like that, you feel like you can swing. I'm not a wintertime golfer, that's why I live in Florida, so I can stay in this heat.

I played the course before, when I went there the first time. I had a little Indian boy caddy for me, I guess he was about fourteen, fifteen years old, and he was a good kid. I said, son, don't tell me, don't say anything to me unless I ask you. And he kept his mouth quiet, and all he did was clean the balls, and then the clubs, and carry the bags, and he was one of the best caddies I ever had, he never said a word, he was really a great kid.

I had a lot of family in Oklahoma, lot of friends too. It didn't put any pressure on me—let me tell you about friends. You see, professional golfers are performers, just like the actors. The more people you put out there pulling for you, it gives you the incentive to perform, so actually you concentrate better and you play better. Palmer became a great player because the people made him a great player—the public made him a champion. They inspire you to become a champion, to play hard, to play well.

It was the greatest feeling—winning the Open was my childhood dream. You know, when I was caddying, whenever we played on caddy's day we were always playing for the U.S. Open, for the national open. So that was my ultimate dream, to win the Open, and I just felt I had achieved it, that was the greatest feeling that a guy could have, believe me.

My first victory comes pretty close to matching winning the U.S. Open, I'll tell you that. The tournament: The North and South at Pinehurst in 1951. That was the first tournament that I won, that would be pretty close. But the U.S. Open had to be the crowning glory.

I did have a bit of a temper when I played—I've contained myself a lot. Everybody has a temper, golf is a frustrating game, and I don't know of one player that's playing out there that hasn't thrown a golf club. Show me a professional golfer who hasn't thrown a club, and I'll show you a guy that's not serious about the game.

I was reading Norman Vincent Peale, and Bishop Sheen, some sayings by them, every morning I'd read something, and I'd go out to the golf course and I'd try to live by it. And that's the way it happened, off and on, a little at a time before that tournament. I was really playing good when I went there, and I was thinking good, and feeling good.

When I left the golf course out in California to turn pro, all the weight of the world was lifted off me. I thought I wanted to be a club pro, but after one year and five hundred bosses, I said, this is not for me. Every member and all his kids are your boss, so I said, uh-uh, I'm not cut out for this. Some guys are cut out for it, some are not, and I wasn't cut out for that, so that was a lot of weight lifted off my shoulders, and I just felt at ease and free. It was a great feeling.

I never was really a good putter—I'm not a great putter. I won most of my golf tournaments for my play from tee to green. Hogan wasn't a great putter either, he only putted about 25 percent as well as some of those kids putt out there nowadays—they're tremendous putters.

We practiced our long game and tried to learn to play from tee to green—we put putting secondary. Actually, it ranks right along with your golf, all golfers neglect their short game, your better putters are the guys that are always hanging around the putting greens, always chipping and putting. But we always went to the practice tee and hit those long shots, and we neglected that part of our game.

There's fourteen different clubs in the bag, and you have to play one as equally well as you do the other, and so I neglected my short game. Hogan, I saw him practice putting a few times, but not really devoting a lot of time to it. He was out hitting balls, too, and he's the greatest player I ever played with, Hogan was. There's some good ones. Nicklaus was a great player. Nicklaus is right along there with him, but I'm happy to be ranked as a great shot maker, it's a great honor.

I do have a greatest day playing with Hogan, yes I do. In 1960, Hogan and I tied for the Memphis Open at the Old Colonial Country Club in Memphis, which was a pretty good little golf course, a very exacting little course. I shot 65 the last day to tie [Gene] Littler and Hogan, and then we played off on Monday.

I got out there the first nine holes, and boy, I was just playing super, I was making everything. I think I had about a four-shot lead over Hogan after nine holes. Littler, I was six or seven shots ahead of him, I think I got a 31 or something on the front side. That little son-of-a-gun Hogan, at the sixteenth hole, which is a par five, he put it on in two and two-putted for a birdie, and I made my five.

At the seventeenth hole, at the Old Colonial Country Club, there is a par three, about 190 yards long. We walked over to the tee, and Hogan and Littler hit their three-iron shots about fifteen feet right underneath the hole.

I'd been with Hogan just a while back, I'd taken some lessons from him—he was my tutor, in other words. And I said, it's now or never, boy. We were dead even playing seventeen, I put down a two-iron and put that left hand over on top where Hogan put it, and I hit that two-iron, I liked to hole that two-iron.

As we were walking off that tee, toward the green, he says to me, nice shot. That was the only two words he said all day. That's how deeply he concentrated on his game, he has his mind on his business. And I made that two, and I won the tournament, I think I shot 67 and he shot 68.

I won the Colonial tournament in 1958 at Fort Worth before I won the Open at Tulsa, and he and I played the last round together. I was leading him by one shot, one shot with one hole to play. Naturally he was teeing up first on the eighteenth hole there, and he was gonna show me how to turn that thing around that corner, that little dogleg left on that eighteenth hole there. Boy, he put a snapper on that jesse, boy, put it in that rough, and he come up with a double-bogey.

And I won that tournament, 'cause I was leading him by a shot when we were playing that last hole. He could still play back in those days too, he could really play from tee to green, he was good around the greens, but I guess his nerves got to him a little bit, in my book he never was a great putter. He had to have super-slick greens in order to get it to the hole.

The greatest day I ever saw him have was when he shot that 67 at Oakland Hills, and he really played great golf. From tee to green he was unbelievable, and he made a couple of putts, you know, they have slick greens. You gotta have slick greens like you have at Oakmont and Oakland Hills, like they have at the U.S. Open—then he could get it to the hole. He had such a tender touch.

Beating that man, to me, that was the greatest. That was a great achievement, believe me.

BILLY CASPER

Of all his victories in major tournaments, Billy Casper is per-
haps best remembered for the late charge he mounted in the
1966 U.S. Open to overtake Arnold Palmer. But Casper chose
a different major victory for his greatest day—the day he fi-
nally conquered Augusta and won the Masters. It took a mem-
orable playoff to do it, but the hole that sticks out in Casper's
mind was a miraculous rescue shot from an impossible lie that
kept him from the jaws of disaster. It began with a disastrous
drive.

This happened in the 1970 playoff at the Masters. The playoff
was with Gene Littler, we had shot 279, and we had an
eighteen-hole playoff, which was the last eighteen-hole playoff
at Augusta. I had birdied the first hole and had a one-shot lead
going to the second tee, and I hit a drive that was probably as
bad as any drive I ever hit. Dead left, diving hook, hit a tree,
bouncing left.

The ball wound up in a water hazard at the bottom of the
hill where the grass in the water hazard had all been walked
down because of the massive galleries during the week. And
situated behind the ball about two inches was a branch that
covered about half of the width of the ball.

The only shot I had was a nine-iron, where I had to fit the

club over the limb and under the ball and get it up very quickly to get it over the trees to get it back over the fairway. I made the swing, and it came off perfectly—I got the ball back out on the fairway, which was about 130 yards from the green after the shot.

Littler, in the meantime, hit a perfect drive, hitting a perfect second down in front of the green in two. I had a five-iron, I positioned it on the fairway, and I hit it just off the back edge of the green. Littler hit a very bad chip, he jumped it into the sand trap and came out of the trap long and scored six on the hole. I chipped the ball close to the hole and scored a five, and I went on to pick up another shot on him.

This particular shot that I played out of the hazard never resulted in any score, and I consider it the greatest shot I ever hit in my life, because of . . . the whole program. To be able to take a club and fit it over a branch that was covering about half the ball and hit it just perfectly to get back in play, to even have the opportunity was remarkable. I could have made a score of . . . you know, anything.

I then went on to build up a seven-shot lead, and then to lose four shots to Littler from twelve through fifteen and have but a three-shot lead going to sixteen. He, shooting first, hit the ball on sixteen very close to the hole, about twelve or fourteen feet. And then I hit a wonderful five-iron and wound up about six feet from the hole. He two-putted, and I one-putted, and for all practical purposes I had won the Masters with that shot, and also the shot back on the second hole.

I had shot a final round of 71, and it was interesting, in the 1969 Masters I had shot 66–71–71 and led the tournament by one shot over George Archer. I teed off the final day, and I shot 40 on the front side, and then bogeyed ten to go five over. And then I birdied three of the last eight holes, and I finished one shot behind Archer.

In 1970, I shot 72–68–68, 208, the same score I'd shot the year before, and I had a one-shot lead on Gene Littler. And

Gene shot 70, and I shot 71, so we tied and had the playoff. It's interesting that the same two scores were shot two years in a row, and I shot the same two scores two years in a row and had a one-shot lead. I didn't think about that until after it was over.

You know, I got away to such a wonderful lead, I got a stroke on the first hole, stroke on the second hole, I holed a big putt at the third and got another stroke and scored par at the fourth and got another stroke. And I birdied the seventh and got another stroke, and I birdied the . . . let's see, I think I got one at the tenth, one at the eleventh, and I was seven shots ahead. I birdied eleven, I think I was something like four or five under par . . . let's see, birdie first, seven, and eleven, I think I was four under at that time.

The shot that I hit out of the hazard at the second hole was just . . . I mean, it was a dream shot. You know, you would get there in the same situation, and you may pull it off once every hundred times. And I consider it the shot that really won the Masters for me.

One of the things I remember is I walked off the green, I had won the playoff, Cliff Roberts was there, and he shook my hand and he said, thank you. It wasn't congratulations, but it was thank you. He was a good friend, and I guess he had been rooting for me for a number of years—I finally won the tournament after the year before.

And the jacket that they put on me was about three times as big as it needed to be, and I could wrap it all around me. It was really interesting, I had lost a considerable amount of weight, and so anyhow . . . I could now fill that jacket very nicely.

That was the Monday, and the only players there were Gene Littler and George Archer.

I think the greatest tournament there is is the Masters. Many of the media said I could never win at Augusta because of my conservative play, and so I had the opportunity in '69, and I was able to. You know, I always felt I could win at Augusta, because I got into Augusta in 1957 through my play in the U.S. Open at Rochester, New York, in '56. I was able to nearly finish in the top twenty-four every year, so I got back in the following year.

The only time I missed was almost the next year in '58 when I missed the cut and I was out . . . no, it was '59, I did, in April of '59 I missed the cut. And then that year I won the Open, so I got back in. Then I started the stretch where I never missed the top twenty-four until I actually won, and that was my way of getting back into the Masters, so in my mind I felt I could always play at Augusta, and win, because of the scoring that I had going on there.

I've played every year since '57, even though I didn't . . . I was eligible to play in '90, but I accompanied my daughter and a group of high school entertainers to the Republic of China that year. I played practice rounds on Thursday, I left to go to China . . . I was eligible to play that year, but I didn't play in the championship.

I found that I was playing extremely well every year we played at Augusta, I think the year before I was the leading money winner going in there, and I usually played very well in the early part of the year. So we always, and still do, look forward to going to Augusta, and so therefore it just carried over. I finished in the top ten a number of times, and definitely in the top twenty-five almost every year.

I guess winning the U.S. Senior Open at Hazeltine would have to be my greatest day on the Senior Tour, and playing in an eighteen-hole playoff with Rod Funseth in which we tied and then we had a sudden-death playoff where I birdied the first hole, hitting a drive and an eight-iron and holing about a ten- to twelve-foot putt. Just striking the ball, you know, solidly, the three times, having the success of having the ball go in the hole for the win.

Well, of course, the Hall of Fame, the day that I was inducted in the World Golf Hall of Fame, that encompasses your entire career. It's not a shot or a week or a day, but it's being recognized as one of the great players. That is very gratifying, humbling, and I guess what's stayed with me is that one of the leaders of our church gave the invocation for the ceremony.

JIM COLBERT

When Jim Colbert won the Monsanto Open Invitational in 1969 after a two-day rain delay, the national TV cameras were gone after a weekend of coverage, but the win helped launch a lengthy pro career that saw Colbert win eight tournaments on the regular tour. Colbert came into his own in 1991 when he joined the Senior Tour, winning a total of eighteen tournaments, including his second greatest day—a dramatic comeback after at Napa in 1999 after a bout with cancer.

That would be 1969 . . . it was my first win.

A little background—it was a $100,000 tournament, there was only one other tournament that year with that same purse . . . I mean, everybody played. There were golf pros there I never heard of, coming out of the woodwork to play in a $100,000 tournament.

To preface this, the tournament before that was in Orlando at Rio Sonara, and I had played real good there, but I putted so horrible, I mean I really putted terrible. And in those days I was traveling with my buddy Dean Beman, and staying in a Holiday Inn. That was a Sunday night and we were gonna drive over to Pensacola on Monday morning.

And Sunday night it just rained, just a downpour. And you know, staying at the Holiday Inn you don't have your car protected or anything. I had a couple of golf balls in the room, the only club I had was a sand wedge that I hadn't used in the tournament, that and two balls. And I was so bugged about this putting, because I really, really played good and just couldn't get anything done on the greens.

I couldn't sleep, so I ended up putting all night. I was putting into a glass, you know, one of those glasses they have in the room? And I was putting with a sand wedge, into this glass. And I did this all night, because it was raining too hard to run out to the car and get my putter out of the car. So before the night was over I got pretty good at putting into that glass.

So we were gonna meet at Rio Sonara and leave for Pensacola the next morning. We were gonna leave by eight o'clock. Well, I got out there about seven o'clock, it had quit raining, and I mean, there's not a soul around, everything's closed. I just grabbed my putter and two balls and ran out to the putting green, threw the balls down on the putting green, and there was a hole right close by. And I picked the farthest distance from the hole I could find and knocked the first one in. I mean, clear across the green.

And I never hit the second one, I just walked across and sat in the car, waiting for Dean to get there. I figured I'd solved my putting problem. I don't know [what I was doing in Orlando when I played], I was just putting awful. When you're putting with the sand wedge, you have to keep it off the ground to stay connected, you have to hit it right on that point, I just leaned into the sand wedge. I was just missing 'em.

So we get over to Pensacola, and I played pretty good in the practice rounds. I was starting on the tenth hole in the tournament, which is a hole you can drive, it's probably one of the easiest holes on the golf course. And I drive it right down to the front of the green, then chip it up about twelve or fifteen feet, and I three-putt. I hit the first one too hard, I hit the second one too hard, both of 'em hit the hole, but I hit 'em both too hard, and I start out with a five.

I was playing with a couple of guys. I remember I was playing with Grier Jones and Fred Murray. And they both birdied the golf course, and I made five, and Fred said something to me about, you'll be okay, don't worry about it, you'll be all right. You know, just trying to help me, and I said, well, don't worry about my putting, I'm gonna make the putts before it's over.

Well, we finished thirty-six holes and finished together, and the other guys said, remember what you said back there? You were right. Their eyes just rolled up, I was making birdies everywhere. So, third round, I played really good, putted good again, and I was in the bunker at eighteen, and I was looking at the scoreboard, and I had to get up and down out of the bunker to keep a one-stroke lead.

There were two guys who were there all the time, I can't remember exactly who one was, it was either Beman or [Lee] Trevino. Those were the two who were there all day, and [Ray] Floyd was right behind them, and then Nicklaus and all those guys. I was playing with Trevino in those days. We played twosomes. And I thought to myself, I have to get up and down out of the bunker . . . and man, in those days I was working like crazy on my bunker play because I was a terrible bunker player when I came out.

And I looked up at that scoreboard, and I said, well, I need to get up and down to keep the lead. It became important later on, because I did, I got it up and down and kept the lead.

So it rained all day Sunday, we didn't play, it rained all day Monday, we didn't play. And you know, everybody's saying, when are we gonna get to play? It was supposed to rain all day Tuesday, and in those days we used to go up through Tuesday. So, again, I was staying at a Holiday Inn, and about three o'clock in the morning—I was asleep—I woke up, I guess it had quit raining.

I was on the second story of a Holiday Inn, which was

where we stayed back in those days, and I just opened my door and looked out, and there were stars out there, and it wasn't raining, and the wind was blowing like hell. It was just gonna dry everything out. I thought all day Sunday and Monday that we were gonna play. But finally, about Monday night, I thought, [if it had ended there I would've got] $15,000, which was what I was gonna get because they would give me three-quarters of the winner's purse. And it wasn't an official win either.

So I panicked there for a second, and I'm looking out, and I said, man, we're gonna play. And boy, did I get really nervous, I could remember saying to myself: Well, what would you do if it were your choice? Would you play for the $20K and the victory, or would you take the cash?

And, I don't know, being as honest as I can, and my nature . . . I said, aw, hell, I'd give 'em the money and play for the victory. And it calmed me down, that was a conscious decision, if I had it in my hand, I'd give it back and play. Which was a good attitude actually.

So it turned out, we get out there, and we're playing, and it's still really wet, so they're gonna play lift-clean-and-play. And I'm paired with Trevino, and that's the first time I've ever been in Lee's group at the end. And I always thought him to be the leader . . . it was a big honor teeing off last in the last group.

So I'm standing on the first tee thinking they're gonna call Lee Trevino's name, and then mine. I'd programmed myself for his introduction and all, all the stuff they're gonna say about him, and then they're gonna call me, and I'm just gonna go hit. But I was programmed wrong, because I had the lead, so they called me first. It kind of really blew my mind.

Well, I teed this thing up, and I hit straight up in the air, straight right. There was a bunch of trees down both sides— well, I cleared the trees on the right, hit it over on the tenth-hole fairway. So Trevino hit, and we go down there, and now we lift-clean-and-place everywhere. I mean, I had to hit it through these trees, I couldn't get over 'em—if I'd teed it up, I could have put it on the green.

But I didn't think [lift-clean-and-place] would improve my lie, and I hit the damnedest five-iron down around some trees. I sliced it, got it down around in front of the green, and I'm pretty sure I started with a par, because I think I either got it on the green or just off it. I think I had a gimme for a par. And the second-hole iron was maybe the hardest hole, like a two-iron, three par, and the green is really, really fast.

I got it on the front edge, and I putted it about three feet by. Now I've got this thing broken down, if you've got any guts at all you can make this—I mean, it's not a mystery. All you've gotta do is get it started straight and put it in. If you've got any control at all, you'll make it. Well, I made it.

Then I was gone. I was going along, I was playing fine, and nothing really unusual was happening, and I get to the seventeenth hole with a two-shot lead. And I pull it down the trees to the left, and I've got . . . I can hit a low shot and get it right up on the green or right in front of the green, or I can pitch it out and be seventy, eighty yards short of the green. I'm thinking pitch it on the green, make sure you make a bogey, I've got a two-shot lead.

But it was a shot I could hit. It was a low hook, you were taking a chance, because if you hit a tree it could go back in the woods, I mean, there was nothing but woods to the left. But I looked down, and I said, you know, I know how to do this . . . this is a shot I can do. So I hit this low hook five-iron and ran it right up on the front edge. To me it was the shot to play, you know, you don't necessarily give up strokes, if you don't have to.

So I played the shot, and there was a group of people behind me, not too many people, it was a Tuesday. But I'll never forget hearing the guy behind me, he said to his buddy:

and you said he couldn't afford to try it. I've never forgotten that. You know, I can hear it, it's just one of those memories that you have.

And I thought, you know, it did take some guts to try it, but it was the shot. You know, shots should be dictated by the lie, and not the situation. And I went into the last hole with a two-shot lead, which is a hell of a lot better than a one-shot lead.

I parred the last hole and won by two. I don't know whether Trevino and Beman tied, or whether one of 'em wound up being third, I'd have to look, I can't remember. But you know, there wasn't 150 people around, it was a Tuesday afternoon. It had been on national television, but I mean, they're long gone, everybody's long gone.

So I get the check and the trophy, but like I said, there's not a hundred people left. And then that's the first time I was ever the last guy in the locker room . . . I mean, there's nobody there. When you win tournaments, by the time you go to the locker room, I mean, there's only one guy there—that's the locker man, with both hands out. That's all that's left. And that was my first experience at that. Where the hell did everybody go? And I mean, it's always lonely in the locker room afterwards, because you're the only guy there, but on a Tuesday, I mean, you can imagine.

And then, 'cause I won later at Tuscon, the Joe Garagiola, I mean, I know I've got the record for Tuesday wins, I won twice. Both of 'em had been big tournaments on national TV, and hell, by the time Tuesday rolls around, everybody's gone, TV, everything. I had my own private tournament . . . twice.

It helped my being anonymous on the circuit. I beat Fuzzy Zoeller in a six-hole playoff. The only place it was carried was California. The show went off the air in the rest of the country. It gets lonely when that happens.

So there was a lot of stuff that happened there, obviously I can remember it, and that was the first win. Hell, I got in my car, I had to drive to, I think it was Jacksonville, I think that's where we were going. I can't remember, but I had to drive wherever it was, to the next Holiday Inn, to play the pro/am the next day somewhere.

But it's okay, because I never sleep the next night afterwards anyway. Usually, after I've been successful, I feel pretty good about it afterwards, and then about an hour or two later, as soon as I get off by myself somewhere, home or wherever I'm going, I mean, it's just like the weight of the world . . . I just fall asleep for about two hours, and then I'm awake for the rest of the night, and then I'm playing. I mean, that's just the way it's been for me every time. I do fall asleep like I'm exhausted, and man, I just go to sleep, whew, and then I wake up about two hours later, and now you think of all the stuff . . . like oh God, what if that didn't work?

The experience, you know, I could tell you on that tee shot, on that Sunday, playing the eleventh hole, I mean, the wind was blowing so hard, it's usually a seven-iron. And I hit a four-iron, knee high, and just chipped it up and put it about four feet from the hole. And Trevino says, hey, pal, you've got me if you can do that. I gave him some shots that he could appreciate in the wind, because he's a pretty good wind player.

I mean, here's a shot that's about 150 yards or so, and I hit a four-iron, I mean, those greens are only about as big as a nickel down there. So I just hit it low, about waist high, get it on the front, back towards the hole, it ended up about two feet. I remember him saying, hey, pal, you do that you've got me—you know, kind of a left-handed compliment. He didn't surrender, it was just, you keep doing that you're gonna win.

When you win, the number-one thing for me is the feeling of satisfaction. In that particular case, that puts you in the club, or the fraternity, or whatever you want to say. Players will take you more seriously. And if I was to rank wins, you know, in my mind, I'd put the second win as the biggest, there's a whole lot of guys that, for whatever reason, win one, but the numbers dwindle a lot when you get the second one. And then the second one, it's like, now when your name goes on that board they pay attention.

So I think the validation is . . . obviously you have to have the first win before you can have the second one, but in ranking a guy's career, you know, which wins are most important and everything else, the majors and what have you, the second one's the big deal. I didn't win my second one until Milwaukee in '72. I rank that very important, just the fact that you can do it again.

I was pretty successful, I finished third in the U.S. Open at Marriott in '71. Trevino shot 280, I shot 282, and I tied for third. You know, I had some good tournaments, was making a living facing the top fifty or sixty in those days, but hadn't won by then. Anytime you go that long you have doubts.

On the Senior Tour, the tournament that I wrote down, other than Pensacola, that I put a note down, would be my most emotional win, which was at Napa last year at Silverada, when it was the first time I won in almost two years because I had cancer surgery. And it was toward the end of the year, it was my first full year back.

With all the stuff that I'd done, I kind of started playing at number nine. I might have birdied eight, I birdied nine and ten, and I had about a five-foot birdie putt on eleven. It was really hard to get to where the pin was—I hit a nine-iron on the third [shot] of the par five to keep playing around the water. I had the chance, I figured I really had to make some birdies on the back nine.

To get the ball to the pin, you've gotta flirt with the back edge of the green, and I mean, it's just a little deck up there. You can't bounce it back there, you know, you have to carry it up there. If you hit it about four yards too far, you hit it on the back and you go over, and then you might make six, you ain't gonna make five. I got the ball back there about five feet from the hole.

In Napa my good friend John Fox, who was a Delta captain, had just retired from Delta, and caddied for me there. He plays there all the time, and he really knows that course. And in the shade and everything, I said to John, you know, it looks like this goes left here, but my instinct is telling me it's straight.

And he said, I promise you it's straight. And I made it, I got a birdie at eleven, I ended up birdying thirteen, fourteen, fifteen with pretty sizable putts. But while I was doing that I got to thinking, I was thinking of Arnold Palmer, you know, and Arnold was a great comeback player, and I was trying to make a charge. So in my mind I was kind of using that as a motivator, it was kind of like I was talking to Arnold, I was going to use that as an advantage to try and get this done.

Making those three pretty sizable putts on thirteen, fourteen, and fifteen, got me there, and then eighteen was kind of a birdie hole, but I didn't birdie it. The year before I'd birdied it, I either won or tied. John Bland made a thirty-foot putt to beat me from that hole, and now I come in the next year and I don't birdie the hole. I've got Littler and David Brunsman, both big hitters, par five, they need to birdie to tie, and both of them reached the green in two. Eagle's possible if you hit straight to the fairway, but it's a hard hole at the start, dogleg to the left. They don't hit straight, they both make fives, so I win the tournament.

It was very emotional, because of the cancer thing, and Arnold not being co-sponsor and not playing and me thinking about Arnold when I was going down the back nine—you can call it a motivator or a crutch, but I'm using his history and record to get me around. I felt like I was sharing—Arnold wouldn't feel it, but that's how I felt, he didn't know anything about it. I felt like I did it for both of us, in my mind that's what I was thinking and that's how I felt.

And that was very, very emotional, my most emotional win by far.

I did a quick interview on television, and I talked a little bit about Arnold like I did to you. It was one thing to have John Fox as my caddy, who's a pilot and knows the course, I could tell him that there's no way I could get nervous, he was nervous enough for both of us. I was trying to keep him under control, we were joking, he was pretty hyper. But it kind of kept things in perspective, as far as the golf.

It was meaningful—it had been almost two years since I'd won. So you get those thoughts—you know, am I over it, can I still play with these guys, there's always a thing on the circuit that people won't let you forget. I don't care who you are, if you don't win you're just thinking about it, if that's what you're out there for. You know, some guys are just happy making money or living the life, and that's fine, but I can't imagine that myself.

I know I was very emotional, my one feeling when I won was the feeling of satisfaction, that I'd beaten my peers. This one was . . . I'm gonna say, tears in my eyes, it was emotional, I felt it more in my heart. You know, I don't know how to describe it, it just seemed almost unimportant. I don't know—excitement doesn't describe it, I just felt more . . . I felt deeper. This was a lot deeper emotionally . . . it was more of a mental thing than to beat 'em with my golf, it was more of a mental thing. I'm having trouble finding the right words.

I don't think I went home, I think I went to Pebble Beach, because I think I went down there with a couple of friends to play golf for a couple of days. At that stage it was about the last thing I wanted to do. I can remember the moment, I can remember everything there, and I'm trying to think, where the hell did I go? A lot of times I go to Pebble Beach afterwards to play golf with my friends. Sometimes I go to L.A., sometimes I go home.

I can't remember what the next tournament was either, because Napa's not the last one, 'cause I usually just show up on Wednesday night and play Thursday in the pro/am, so I don't recall. I can't even remember—I'm thinking about going to the airport, whose plane was it, where did I fly to?

The first two that I mentioned, I would say that I was climbing the ladder. With this one, I felt like it kept me on the ladder, or towards the top of the ladder, if that makes any sense. The other two, you're still scratching and climbing, and Napa, it was more a proving that you still belonged on the ladder. So there might be more satisfaction in staying on the ladder, I don't know.

The first one's a big one, especially after you back it up and play for thirty-some years and prove that you belong. The first one, you've got to get that one first. I would say, regular tour to the Senior Tour, I've had a lot more success on the Senior Tour circuit than I had on the other one, although I was successful. I won eight tournaments. You know, the TV didn't break, and we'd finish on Tuesday.

The maturity, if I had it to do over again and I could switch 'em, the same amount of success and put it on either circuit? I believe in my mind I would just keep it on the senior circuit, because I was old enough to really enjoy it. I just was old enough to really appreciate what I'd been able to do on the senior circuit, where on the other circuit I was running hard, trying to make a living, trying to do all this . . . I don't know if it would have meant as much.

I know now, looking back on it, I probably could have done a little better, some things I could have done a little differently and produced a little better outcome in some situations. But I was too busy doing it to even be thinking about it. On the senior circuit, where there's a time frame, you really appreciate . . . I appreciate more what I did down there than when I was doing it.

I mean, I never won the Masters, which was the big thing, I always kind of wanted to. I finished third, fourth, fifth, whatever. But now, I kind of feel good about playing in ten of 'em, if that makes any sense. But when you're doing it, it doesn't feel like the privilege that it really is when you're there doing it. I mean, it's the same way with the U.S. Opens. I've never won, I've finished second, I've done all kinds of stuff . . . but looking back, just the privilege of playing in all of 'em is quite a kick.

And I went to the Ryder Cup in Spain, I was just getting over my illness there. I didn't know anybody, didn't introduce myself to anybody, never went inside the ropes—the only player I ever saw who recognized me was Mark O'Meara. A lot of the gallery stuff surprised me, hey, aren't you . . . ? I was stunned by the gallery bit, because I wasn't out there to be recognized, I just wanted to see it, just wanted to experience it from the other side.

And not being able to get past the guard to go on the practice tee . . . you know, I didn't try, but I said, you know, if I tried to get down there, I couldn't walk out there. You know, I could call one of the guys and get out there, it wasn't like I knew I couldn't. But I went as John Q. Spectator. Well, now when I go walk out on the practice tee for the first tee, I kind of think it's a privilege, because I've already intentionally put myself on the other side of the ropes.

So when you play the senior circuit, I appreciate what I'm doing more than when I was doing the other one. There are so many more things that you take for granted when you're younger. And I don't know if I'm saying this right, but it is a privilege to be in the league, no matter what your record is. The other side of that coin is that the real guts is to put yourself in that situation, to get there and put yourself in there in front of the world.

Sometimes you do good, and sometimes you fall on your face, but the real guts is being able to stick your nose in there and let 'em know that they're seeing the best you've got that day, even if it isn't good enough.

Those professional golfers out there, they all overwork

themselves. All professional athletes overwork themselves, and especially some of these guys that get paid so high in some of the other sports and come out and don't perform very well. Everybody's saying that guy's lazy, and it's just the opposite, that guy's feeling so much pressure, he's working his ass off, and he's lost his innate ability to just play, because who in the hell's worth $25 million? It puts too much pressure, trying to live up to the dollar signs, it's just the opposite of what people think. They overachieve, they're not underachievers, I mean, that goes for about 95 percent of 'em.

BRUCE CRAMPTON

For the last five decades Bruce Crampton's name has appeared regularly on the leader boards of both regular tour and Senior Tour events. For his greatest day, though, the Australian native chose the victory that launched his career when he won the Australian Open at the tender age of twenty.

Well, the greatest day in golf that I had came in the latter part of August of 1956, when I was twenty years of age, and it happened in Royal Sydney Golf Club in Sydney, Australia. It was the day that I won the Australian Open Championship at the age of twenty.

Let me just set the stage a little bit. . . . I had been taken overseas along with Frank Phillips, another young player, by Norman Von Nida, he was Australia's best player at that stage. I had turned pro in 1953, and I had to serve a two-year apprenticeship, during which time I couldn't play in any tournaments in Australia. And actually, we went overseas in 1956, Norman took two of us overseas, and the first tournament that I played as a full member of the PGA of Australia was the 1956 Australian Open.

It was a seventy-two-hole event, and we had to play thirty-six holes on a Saturday. After having shot 72–71 on the first two rounds, I shot 78 on Saturday morning and found myself several shots behind Kell Nagel. I've got a picture of the score-board from 1956 in Australia, it was sent to me recently, so I could tell you the actual number of the scores if I looked at it, and maybe I can call you again and fill that in for you.

Anyhow, I was several shots behind Kell Nagel after the morning round, and I can remember sitting on the patio over-looking the first hole, which was a hole that I could drive with a driver, some 250 or 260 yards. And I remember saying, if I can drive it on the green in the afternoon and make three . . . I had watched Kell, and he was ahead of me, I'd watched him make par on the first hole, and that would cut the deficit.

Well, as it turned out, I did drive it on the green and I did make birdie, and then I birdied the next hole, and by the ninth hole on the last round I had caught Kell. I remember there were two par fives, fifteen and sixteen, with the wind behind me, I could get up close to the green. I didn't birdie either one of those, I was a little frustrated going to the seventeenth hole, which was a long three-par, 220-some yards back into the wind—what we call a "southerly" in Australia, a south wind, which is a strong wind. The wind comes off the ocean.

And I hit a three-wood there, I just blistered it with a three-wood, and I put it on the back corner of the green—the green kind of sloped from front to back and the flag was kind of in the back left. So I was at least thirty-five or forty feet from the flag. I can still see that putt run, I hit that putt, and the caddy was holding the flag, and it just looked gorgeous running up there, and I made it.

So now I've got a one-shot lead going to the last hole, which I could hit with a three-wood, it's a dogleg left back to the clubhouse. I hit a beautiful three-wood, and then I hit a six-iron the second shot that never left the flag stick, I mean it was so straight and pure, it came up about four feet short of the flag. And I made that putt to win by two shots.

The reason that it's so memorable is that, first of all, every sportsman strives to be national champion of their own country, so that was that. But more importantly, as it turned out, that victory earned me an invitation to play in the 1957 Masters tournament in Augusta, and that's what brought me to the United States.

So the main reason I say it was the greatest moment in my career was because everything that has followed in my career, everything that's taken place since that time, [came] directly [out of] that victory, the Australian Open Championship in 1956.

I had a very bright career as a youngster—I'd actually represented Australia as the number-two player, the number-two amateur, in international matches against New Zealand. And I should have really been in the Eisenhower Cup in 1953 to go to St. Andrews, but because I was so young the Australian golf union felt like it would be bad for me to be around all the drinking and the socializing, that I wasn't old enough to participate in that, so they left me out of the team. I decided that if that's all there was to amateur golf, then I was gonna turn pro, and as I said, I had to serve a two-year apprenticeship.

Everything hinges on the Open—it wasn't like it is over here now, in fact, first prize is £250, which is the equivalent of $500. So golf has come a long way . . . but it's the title, the fact that you have won the Australian Open and been national champion of your own country.

The emotions . . . I don't know, I was obviously very nervous, but I was confident in my game, and as it turned out, I was able to do well under the pressure.

It's one of the better golf courses in Australia. It's since been redone from the way we played it. It's on a sand belt, it's not too far from the famous Bondai Beach in Sydney. It's got a sand base with what they call "couch" (pronounced *cooch*), which is really Bermuda grass, but it's referred to as couch grass in Australia . . . and big greens. It was one of the premium A-grade clubs, you know, it was a very snooty club, it was very difficult for professionals to get to play on Royal Sydney.

I don't remember anything except the last four holes, to be honest with you, the first hole in the afternoon and the second hole, but from there to the fifteenth and sixteenth greens I don't remember too much. But I do remember the two closing holes because they were so significant, it was just like I played them yesterday.

There was one other thing that happened that you might like to mention. Peter Thomson, you know, was at the height of his career, even though Norman [Von Nida] was the glamour guy and *the* player—Thomson had already won the British Open I don't know how many times by 1956. But Peter did not play in the Open championship that I won. So immediately after the tournament, of course, the press started asking the question, well, would Crampton have won had Thomson played in the Open?

Three weeks later—in fact, my birthday was on the twenty-eighth of September and the Friday of this tournament was the twenty-eighth—we had to play thirty-six holes on Saturday. The tournament was the Speedo tournament in Melbourne, on Peter's home golf course, the Victoria Golf Club in Melbourne. It was a five-round affair, and after three rounds on Friday night Peter and I were tied for the lead. I can remember I went out with Norman Von Nida, some of the pros, and friends. We had a birthday party celebration for me.

It was a par 73 golf course, and I remember going out in the morning, and I shot even par, 73, and Thomson shot 70. And you could hear the talk around the clubhouse, well, that's the end of that, you know, Thomson's gonna win.

Well, that afternoon it was one of those dream rounds, I made nine birdies, I broke the course record by four shots and won the tournament by four shots and shot 65. And that kind of took me from the middle rung of the ladder, if you will, right to the very top of the ladder as far as Australian golf was concerned.

I can tell you an interesting story about coming to play in the Masters in 1957, which is a true story. I elected to play seven tournaments, six or seven tournaments leading up to Augusta, the first of which was the Houston Open in February.

And at that stage we did not have television in Australia, we did not have jet aircraft, and I didn't know anybody in the United States. In fact, when I left I came with fifteen dozen golf balls under my arm, in fact, you saw that picture on ESPN when I won the Grand Masters in Kansas City, the Mastercard Grand Championship. They showed a clip off home movies which I'd given them a long time ago, of me leaving the airport in Sydney with this packet of fifteen dozen golf balls under my arm [going] to the United States, because I wasn't sure I could get golf balls over here.

Well, as I said, we didn't have television, and the only thing that I had seen about Texas was Wild West shoot-'em-up stories in the movies. So I was in the air for some thirty-two hours by the time I got to San Francisco—you know, two stops on the way, and it was something like an eight- or nine-hour trip down to Houston in a DC-6 or a DC-7, whatever American Airlines was flying back in those days.

And I got into Houston about eleven-thirty at night after being in the air for some forty hours, and the reservation had been made for me at the Rice Hotel, and I was arriving approximately a week ahead of the tournament. We flew into what is now the main airport, and I caught the regular limousine service to go downtown, and when we got to the immediate downtown area everybody that I saw was in western gear.

I saw covered wagons, I saw people on horseback, I saw pistols being fired in the air, and they were blank, and I said, this is Texas, this is what it's supposed to be. I went to bed that night, didn't think too much about it, I got up the next morning, went down to get breakfast, and found that the waitress couldn't understand what I wanted.

Now the wheels started spinning, and I started thinking back to those Wild West shoot-'em-up stories, and I realized that whenever a stranger got into town, nine times out of ten he'd end up getting lynched because he was the troublemaker. I figured if they found out I was from Australia, you know, Lord help me.

So I shut up for three days—I pointed at what I wanted, and I didn't talk to anybody much. In fact, I even went back up to the room, and I put a chair up under the door the way I saw them do it in the movies. . . . Remember how they used to do that?

Well, eventually I met a gentleman named Spinny Gould, who was in the insurance business, from St. Louis, and he explained to me that it was stock show week, and all the western people were in town. He introduced me to Jack Flick, who had won the Open and had a big yellow Cadillac that people in Davenport, Iowa, had given him, and Bob Gaiter and Marlon Marusic were the first friends that I made.

We went out and saw the rodeo, and Roy Rogers and Trigger, and had a great old time. But that was my first introduction to the United States, so you can understand that I was excited, but I was a scared young kid, heading over here where I didn't know anybody.

But I can tell you this too—I finished even par in that tournament, and I think I finished tied for fourteenth, and I won more prize money for that tournament than I won for winning the Australian Open. And that's when I said to myself, Bruce, son, this is where you need to play your golf. And I've played basically in the United States ever since.

There's no substitute for victory, and it doesn't happen often enough that you get used to it. But in all honesty, without putting down any of the tournaments over here, and they're always a great thrill to win, I always reflect back to the Australian Open as the most exciting and the best because of what it meant to me. And there's no telling what would have happened had I not won that Open. Everything in Bruce Crampton's career that has taken place since that time is a direct result of winning that national open championship.

LEE ELDER

Lee Elder won a total of twelve PGA tournaments during his groundbreaking career, eight on the regular tour and another four on the Senior Tour, and he was a member of the 1979 U.S. Ryder Cup team. To Elder, though, there was little doubt that his greatest victory was his first win, not only because it came after a winless stretch of seven years but also because it allowed him to become the first person of color to play in the Masters in 1975.

I have several of them that I'm pretty fond of . . . my first win to qualify for the Masters is certainly one. I think the second one is probably the Ryder Cup, and also the third one would probably be the match with Jack Nicklaus at the American Golf Classic in Akron, Ohio, in 1969, at Firestone. They are certainly three memorable events that occurred in my life that I was really happy about.

But I think that if I was gonna select one, it would probably be my qualifying for the Masters, getting my first tournament win after seven years on the tour, and really wanting to play at Augusta. Even though the highlight of representing your country at the Ryder Cup was certainly one, I feel that the most significant was certainly my first tournament win on the PGA tour.

The actual day, I started out, I think that I was a couple of shots in back of Peter Oosterhuis going into the last round. He was leading the tournament. I shot 67 the last day, he shot 69, and we went into a playoff. But probably the most significant thing was that I birdied the last two holes. I birdied seventeen, which was a par three, and birdied the eighteenth. Actually, my drive hooked slightly left into the trees, and I had to play kind of a low draw-out, and I put it in to make me about ten or fifteen feet from the hole, and I made the putt for a birdie to tie him.

But I was very fortunate in the fact that on the first extra hole we both bogied it. That was the most significant thing, the fact that we both bogied the first extra hole. His drive went to the right and so did mine, we both chipped up short of the green, and then we both missed the putt. But he missed the putt last, so that's why I say that I really felt fortunate to continue on.

Then we tied with pars at the second hole, and then at the third hole, the par four coming back, I holed about a twenty-foot putt for a birdie to beat him.

I think that it was so significant because of the fact that it was the week after the Masters. So that meant that I had to wait a whole year to play at Augusta, which really turned out to be an awful long year, it looked like it wasn't ever gonna come about.

It's certainly one that I'll never forget, because I probably was the most celebrated golfer, being a minority, and just qualifying for Augusta to play at the Masters—you know, everybody wanted to be recognized with me. I think I went on more speaking engagements and more banquets. . . .

As a matter of fact, I was weighing 175 pounds, and when I got to Augusta to play I probably weighed around . . . oh, probably a little over 200 because I had picked up so much weight, just wining and dining.

It was really a situation [with Oosterhuis] where, being a

couple of shots in back of a name player like that, I figured, well, I'm gonna have to really play well if I'm gonna beat him. As a matter of fact, I was watching, I was in front of him, it really gave me a chance to put the heat on him, and let him see some birdies and things that I was making.

It seemed like every time I made one, he made one. He was right there with me during the course of the round. On several occasions, I had missed a couple of short putts where I could have gotten a little bit closer to him, but I was not able to make 'em.

But I never gave up—I kept telling myself that there was always hope. And I think that the majority of the people really wanted to see me win, because they knew what it meant, knew what it meant to me—the majority of the gallery was in between both of us because we were so close together. I just had to keep telling myself not to get caught up and get hyped up and try too hard, to where I really made a mistake and blew myself out of the chance to win the tournament.

It looked like he pretty much had the tournament in hand because, like I said, I birdied the last two holes to tie him. I was very happy with that, to finish like that, but even when I birdied the last hole, he was still coming in, he still had a chance to make the birdie. I was fortunate enough that he did not, but that's what made the excitement really come about.

All that week I had been pretty much close to the lead, I really had played pretty well all of that whole week. I really had not had any terrible scores or anything, I was always pretty close, either in second or third place. As I recall, I was never any lower than third, I think. I think from the first round . . . I might have been about fourth after that first round, and then after that I kept steadily improving the next three rounds. I was just kind of hanging in there and letting them know that I was around.

But you know, I had been so close on several other occasions. I had finished second a couple of weeks before that at the Pensacola Open and the Western Open in Chicago. And I had kind of been around or near the top for several weeks, so my game was really beginning to gel, and I knew that it was just a matter of time before I really put it all together and became a winner. I really didn't have any idea at Pensacola, because I really did not like the Pensacola golf course. I had played there before and been kind of in the thick of things, and I think I shot a 75 or 76 in the last round a couple of times there, and I really did not give myself a chance to win.

I think what happened [when I won] was the fact that I was gabbing with some friends of mine that owned a restaurant there, a fellow by the name of John Trensetella and his daughter, who was a high school kid. They had really kind of took a liking to myself and the fellow I was playing and traveling with a fellow by the name of Jim Wickers, who was also another pro on the tour.

And she [Trensetella's daughter] made a sign, bless her heart, that she brought to the golf course on Sunday, and I got on the tee, and it said, "All things are possible for he that believeth." And I thought that was just really . . . it gave me the strength to really work hard at it.

I had promised her that I was gonna win this golf tournament. I think Rosey [Trensetella] was about twelve or thirteen at the time. And sure enough, the next day when I did win it, it was such a relief.

After the win, it really was a big sigh of relief and joy, and a big party. We celebrated all that evening with some friends that I knew there, and also the Trensetellas, who I was staying with. We just had a wonderful time.

As a matter of fact, he had a big party at his restaurant. A lot of the press, Tom Place, who was PGA media secretary, and several of the other writers were there, and quite a few of the national television networks, because it was a history-making aspect, and so quite a number of television people came in from all over the country.

So it was a big to do, everybody wanted to get a firsthand story, a lot of interviews. I think I was up till about three in the morning before I finally closed my eyes, but it was really a big sigh of relief. Because so much had been made of the fact that no black would ever play at Augusta, because of the things that Cliff Roberts said, statements he had made, so it was such a great relief.

He did call to congratulate me, but I did not talk to him, I was in a press conference with Tom Place. I was told that he had called, that he wanted to extend the invitation to Augusta. And the press wanted to know if I would accept. I told them that I would think about it, and that I would have an answer for them in a short period of time, maybe a week or so, but I wanted to kind of look at things and talk to some people.

At no time was I ever not going to accept it, but I just didn't want to come right up and say, hey, I accept it, you know? Because I feel that that would have been giving in. Really, I wanted to try to see what statements he would make now that a black had qualified for Augusta. Within the next week or so, [I wanted] to see how he was going to receive the news, and what kind of a press conference he was gonna have.

But it was all favorable, and I think that's probably the reason why I got on the phone. I thanked him for calling me, said I'm sorry that I was in a press conference, I did not have a chance to speak with him, but I would accept to play in the Masters as soon as I received the invitation.

It was really a different experience for me, because I received a lot of letters, pros and cons, several threatening letters, you know. But I think those things are gonna happen when you're the first to do something of that magnitude, to make history by being the first minority to accomplish what I did. I thought pretty heavily about it. I talked with some people I was very close to. One was Link Werten, who was the sports editor of the *New York Times* at the time. We were very close friends.

And I spoke with him about it, also a couple of people around the Washington, D.C., area that I had been doing some promotional advertising for. And so I had a chance to sit and chat with them and talk to 'em about it, because I wanted to try and do the right thing and not make any mistakes. I knew that it was going to reflect on a lot of the minorities that would qualify after me, if I went there and demanded so many things and did things that were not really conducive to the other players.

So I decided that I would just kind of lay back and relax, and really weigh the whole situation of how long it had taken me to qualify for it. I went on the tour in 1968, and here it was seven years later before I got my first win, although there were a lot of people that wrote letters to me that said that I should stick it in their face. . . . That was not gonna solve any problems.

It was something that I had wanted. I don't think that the people that had said those things had known how important it was, important enough that I was going to accept it and go there, and try to carry as many minorities as I could possibly carry there, which was certainly something that I accomplished in doing. I would like to have carried more, but I was able to get fifty-five tickets through the Augusta people and other people that relinquished theirs to me so that these things could come about. And I think that was the most important thing, the fact that I had so many people that wanted to come that I was able to get tickets so they could come.

It was an all-positive matter. . . . I'd heard so much talk about it, I had thought so much about it, I had dreamed so much about it. I'll tell you, the most rewarding and refreshing thing is the drive down Magnolia Lane. You know, you've heard so much about Magnolia Lane, the beauty of it, the azaleas, the dogwoods, and everything . . . because, I'll tell you, from the time I rode through that gate to the clubhouse, it was really everything that I expected.

I feel that it really helped the sport, because now, since my qualifying, we had two other blacks that have played there, Calvin Peete and Jim Falk. And they have constantly said to me that my participating in the Masters really gave them the incentive to go and work hard and try to qualify themselves. They wanted to play at Augusta, and they accomplished that.

I know that it helped my golf career, because I put so much pressure on myself by trying to qualify to go to Augusta. Now that that had happened, I was more relaxed. I was able to go ahead and play the type of game that I knew that I was capable of playing. I wasn't uptight about every time the press came and asked me a question about, would I ever be a black player at Augusta, and things of that nature.

So I felt that it certainly helped me prove to myself that I was capable of playing the type of golf that I was now beginning to play, and not to have to constantly work hard in trying to qualify just for that tournament. I mean, almost every year, when the first part of the year rolled around, that's all you could hear, was, you think that a black is gonna go, because we had our chances before, and we never could seem to accumulate enough points to qualify for it.

When they changed the qualifications, it certainly helped, it made it a lot easier, because I really felt that we were really [more] capable of winning than accumulating points from year to year. Because a lot of times you may go and you may have three or four tournaments, and then all of a sudden I'd go for four or five weeks and not play too good. So it's a consistent thing that you really have to do when you have a points system in golf.

I think that the one thing that really allowed me to do that was my dedication and hard work toward the game. I had been kind of lackadaisical before and really had not worked at the game, and really not tried to improve. I went to practice an awful lot more and worked a lot harder, and actually what I did was I went to several teachers around the country to have them look at my game, because I was . . . you know, I wanted to improve so badly that I knew that I probably needed some help.

And I think that is the one thing that I wanted to do. I wanted to maintain a consistency, which I certainly did, because I was constantly in the top sixty money winners. At that time they were taking the top sixty money winners that were exempt throughout the year, and I constantly stayed in that top sixty money winners. So that let me know that I had improved and that my approach to the game had changed, because I had consistently and constantly been in that top sixty.

I [got that help] because of the fluctuation of my score. In the past I'd go out, and one day I'd shoot 67 or 66, and the next day a 75 or a 74 would creep in there, and I said, well, something has to be wrong. If I can go out and play one day this way and then come back another day and do this, something has to be wrong, and I have to try and find some way to put my finger on it so this will not happen.

And this is one of the reasons why I think that I went and asked somebody, because you really cannot see the mistakes you're making yourself, you have to have someone else to kind of look at you and really know what you're doing. Jim [Wickers] and I used to look at each other quite a bit, because we played a lot of rounds together, we traveled together, and it was a situation where we knew pretty much each other's game.

We always tried to help each other out. He had such an awkward swing that I could never correct him, but he always pretty much knew my game. Even today we talk quite a bit. He lives in Napa Valley, California, and I get a chance to see him once a year, but we were very good friends. And I think that is what helped me so drastically.

Nobody wants to play good one day and lousy the next day, you'll never be a winner that way. And still today, I see so many guys that are really top-notch players, that are good players, that are just really not that consistent. One bad round seems to creep in there for 'em, and really I think that if they would have someone take a look at it and see that, I think that they would probably do the same thing.

I'm happy to say that I have seen over the years a lot of improvement in the integration of the game, with more minorities becoming involved in it, with more guys trying to get on the tour, to play, with more playing in the Nike tour, the Future tour, and things of that nature. That shows me that there have been a lot of improvements in the relationships.

Also, the big corporations are now beginning to more or less sponsor the minorities that are involved in the game . . . it used to be awful tough to get the manufacturer to go behind a black when he was trying to get involved in the game. Certainly the influx of Tiger [Woods] has helped. That helped a lot. I see it when I go around the country. I see more and more of the youth out, especially the black youth, hitting balls and playing out on the public facilities.

As a matter of fact, I do a lot of speaking around the country for different organizations, and I get a chance to see these youths. So I'm very happy, that by me being a diabetic I get the chance to do some speaking for Bristol-Myers, who I've become involved with through their products that I use. I get a chance to go around to the different cities and really try to explain the situation to them.

So I see a lot of the young black youth. As a matter of fact, I started a youth program in Indianapolis some three years ago, and already we're up to 250 kids in that program in that area. So it's really a great plus.

And I think that's due to Tiger being such a great role model, and the impact that he has had on the tour, on the media, and the impact that he's had on the game has certainly been so helpful. That is probably the reason why we see more and more of the minority kids that are out talking up the game today, and the fact that the PGA has a good program, and in their program they've gone around the country, trying to get kids involved in it. And then that First Tee program of Tiger's is certainly one that is gonna do an awful lot of good for the minorities.

I know that the young minority kids are not going to be able to play at no country clubs, simply because their parents are simply not in a position to have them play the country clubs. The country club itself is not gonna open up and just let them come on and play without someone in the family being a member, and I think that's gonna remain that way. I'm happy to know that the public facilities are certainly building and opening up more [courses] and making golf available to them, so I certainly see that influx as the reason why more and more of them are beginning to turn to the game of golf.

I mean, we might as well face it, unless you have a family member that is a member of a country club, you are not gonna be able to go to it. Yeah, there are some that will let minorities come on and play once on a Monday when they're closed or something of that nature. But just to open it up and say, come and play or practice anytime you want, no, they're not gonna do that, that's not gonna happen.

Golf, you have to participate on the golf course, and a lot of times the kids do not have the golf equipment to go to these courses and play, plus they do not have the money to pay the green fees. So it's a lot different. I'm hoping that there will be a dominant player that will come up like a Tiger Woods, or two or three or four, or whatever may be the case, to be out there with him, to give him some help.

But most of all, we are a dying breed as far as the females are concerned, we do not have one black female participating on the LPGA tour. We do not have one that is out there day to day, and that's where we need to turn our attention and

focus on, trying to get them more involved. I think that probably the reason why they are not involved is that the black
colleges that the young female athletes elected to go to do not
necessarily offer golf, and what they're gonna have to do is to
try to work harder to get scholarships to white colleges that
do offer golf.

BRUCE FLEISHER

Bruce Fleisher cut a swath through the Senior Tour in 1999, leading the money list en route to becoming the Player of the Year. One of his greatest days was his victory that season at Key Biscayne. But Fleisher's greatest day took him back to the beginning of his career, when he won the U.S. Amateur and got to play a round with a certain member of the Big Three who helped put golf on the map in the second half of the twentieth century.

Well, gosh . . . my greatest day in golf. I've had so many wonderful days, Bob, it's hard to really set down one. Probably I would have to say first round of the 1969 Masters, playing with Arnold Palmer as an amateur. Yeah, if I was to go back, even through all my wins, U.S. Amateur, Bank of Boston, certainly the Senior Tour this year . . . yeah, I would have to go with that. That day was very special.

You know, at the tender age of twenty, and playing with Arnie, who was still at that time a pretty dominant figure, certainly the favorite . . . that was a special day. I don't think I slept all night. When I teed that ball in the ground on the first day and was introduced, how I ever got that club back was beyond me. I think I played by him, but I hit the shit out of it—don't quote me on that—but I hit the hell out of it, about thirty yards past the King, you know? That was pretty impressive.

I wish I had really been smart enough to really keep a log of it all. I can always go back to my memory, but I would have to circle it and say that that was one of the biggest highlights of my life.

I think it was Tuesday afternoon. At that time I wasn't really familiar with [the procedure], certainly there were so many things going on that week, you know, I really wasn't familiar with the formalities, that the U.S. Amateur would be paired with the Masters winner—I think he must have won a major in 1968. Why I played with Arnie, I'm not quite sure, because usually the U.S. Amateur plays with the top dogs, you'd have to go back, I don't know if he won the Open or the Masters that year.

It was pretty nerve-wracking. Again, everything was centered around Arnie in those days, you know? And of course, coming off the U.S. Amateur and winning the World Cup, going to Augusta and fulfilling my dream of playing in the Masters, I mean, what can I say? It was an experience that, obviously, very few have the opportunity to experience.

I can remember Hubert Green and myself going out on Tuesday night, and you know, you're in awe of anything anyway that's going on. Amateurs at Augusta back then, I don't know how it is today, were treated—we seemed to be treated on a different level than the actual professional was. I just think because of Bobby Jones and because of the mystique and because of the tradition. You know, we stayed in, they call it the Crow's Nest, on top of the clubhouse. We were fed royally, at a very, very low price. I remember eating steak and eggs every morning, we had New York sirloin for something like twenty cents—they had to charge us something, maybe a buck. Because of our amateur standing they couldn't give it to us for free, I remember that distinctly.

You know, with the press and so forth and so on, and certainly being the amateur champion, I was kind of tagged as the next Joe Namath of golf. You know, the professional was just kind of there and played, but for some reason the amateur was kind of special, I don't think it's as strong today as it was back then. Because of the dollars they play for today, I mean, good God almighty.

Well, you know, I was never a real hard worker—I was always more one of these natural guys that, unfortunately, took it for granted. And certainly my play proved it. I don't really remember my preparation, except I was restless, obviously nervous as hell.

And you know, once I settled down, it was the greatest day of my life. I shot 69, he shot 73 that day, and of course, the whole thing . . . between the media and the hype of the spectators, I remember one of them calling me "Brucie Baby." The following day, of course, I was right there around the lead, I was playing with Billy Casper, who was another personality you've read about your whole life, you know?

And I remember walking up to the sixteenth green, where all the teenagers and the kids were screaming, "We love Brucie Baby," and he laughed for fifteen minutes. I ended up three-putting, but it was an incredible thrust that went through you, an incredible rush—fifteen thousand kids screaming, "We love Brucie Baby." That happened the second day.

The scoreboards were still pretty available [on the first day], but I made quite an impression shooting a 69 against the King. And then, you know how things get around, the media, news gets around, this nineteen-year-old kid who hit the ball 290 yards, and he beat the King, you know?

The one thing I do remember . . . he didn't say too much, he didn't like me beating him, and of course, I don't blame him. You know, I was knocking them by him, of course, I was 165 pounds, and I could really rip it, you know? Now I can't hit it out of my shadow. I remember walking down the ninth hole, and I put my arm around him, because, you know, I was a head taller. And I said, "Mr. Palmer, when do you ever stop being nervous?" Because I was still shaking.

He looked up to me, and he said, "Bruce, the day I stop being nervous is the day I quit golf"—which means, if you're not really uptight, you're not really focusing, and you're not concentrating. The adrenaline isn't flowing, that excitement isn't there, and that's what I really remember about that.

I think the gallery at Augusta is pretty well . . . it's not like today. Back then Augusta was really a different animal. They really watch what's happening under the ropes, and keep people far enough away, you don't really get intimidated. I remember afterwards, you know, you were mobbed, because they were grabbing my shirt and my glove and my hat, and ripping my clothes off, that I remember . . . my shoes, my socks . . .

Again, he was still the King, so a lot of emphasis was on this young kid beating Arnold Palmer, and again, that was many, many years ago, so I'm trying to grab back in my memory banks, it isn't all that clear. I do remember the press, it was a pretty restless week.

Well, actually, I think I shot 74 [the next day with Casper] and really shot very well, I just didn't putt very well. Then I came back, I think, with 71. So I was actually still in the hunt until the last day. And I played with Dale Douglass . . . and I gotta tell you something, I shot an 82, I can give you a very, very good excuse why.

Wendy [Fleisher's wife] had come up with my mother on Saturday, and she was there watching me Sunday, and so . . . I'm not gonna say any more, aside from the fact that, if I could have found a hole Sunday, I would have jumped in it. You want to talk about gagging—I gagged from the gold tees, boy.

And it was a lesson to be learned, I took a lot for granted, and it was kind of a day when I couldn't do anything right. I got every bad bounce and every bad break you can imagine.

But see, I've learned from that, I don't believe in good or bad anymore, I just believe it is what it is.

I was still low amateur, so winning low amateur in the Masters, and winning the U.S. Amateur Cup, and of course, getting up and saying a few words during the ceremony, I still felt like I won, because I beat Jack Lewis, and Vinny Giles, Steve Melnyk, Michael Menalik, John Bauman, and that was one hell of a bunch.

It was a great ten amateurs that played, you know? And really, believe it or not, I was playing the amateurs, I wasn't trying to win the golf tournament per se, that may or may never happen, you know? There are a few guys that come close, I know [Ken] Venturi did come close, he had his day, and Billy Joe Patton, and so forth and so on.

I, unfortunately, never got the upper hand on the other tour. You know, I won after being off for seven years, and between me and you, God only knows why that ever happened—you know, because it wasn't that it was so much a fluke, it was just incredible how that all came about. I think as you grow a little bit older in this game you start realizing . . . maybe things change.

And certainly your attitude as far as . . . you know, golf was never really life and death with me, but it was my living, and I probably put too much emphasis on outside things that affected me. Most people think of the negative anyway, as you well know. It's like your writing—I'm sure most people will say, you know, it's pretty good, but . . . you know what I'm saying? I'm trying to make an analogy.

I know that when I would have a good tournament, Bob, I would say . . . instead of saying, gee, nice week, I would say, gee, you three-putted seventeen. And really, after continually hearing that, you know, day in and day out, it plays on you, you know? Instead of saying, wow, what a nice week, you'd say, you finished tenth, or whatever.

And again, by not winning—and back then it was Monday qualifying—you were never thrown in with the winners. Because it's a different league. You know, it's like Payne [Stewart], people ask me about Payne. Payne was a very dear friend. Payne was in a league of his own. I never associated in the golf life with Payne. I associated in the social life with Payne—golf-wise, I played one time with him in all the years that I was on tour with him.

Or just like Jack Nicklaus—I think I played twice with him, or [Tom] Watson, I played once. So it's not like you really are on the same level, so to speak, at a playing level. Yeah, I think it helped, if you got out of the box like a Lanny [Wadkins] or Corey Pavin, who won right off, right out of the box, now you're thrown in.

It's just like the Senior Tour, Bob . . . when I won Key Biscayne, shit, I was thrown into the tournament winner. You know what? I learned by playing Trevino and Hale Irwin and these guys, instead of playing with the qualifiers. Like Howard Twitty was forced to play with some of these guys that weren't breaking 80, you know? It's a big difference.

Well, you know what, I'm a very sensitive person, and if you knew me you would know that, number one, I had to change. I enjoyed this year, the dollars were terrific, I found out what my tax bill was today, and I'm throwing up—but to be quite honest with you, there are so many tragedies that happen at this stage of our lives. I don't know how old you are, but, you know, my father's very sick, my mother's not well, Payne certainly is a tragic thing that I'll never forget and will never be forgotten. I lost some very close friends that lifted me when I turned fifty that have passed that I wish could be here today for this.

In all the glory, all the happiness, and all the dollars, I gotta tell you something: It's wonderful to wrap up 1999 as mine, as leader of the money list, and this award and that award, but in reality, you know, playing at fifty isn't so bad, number one. I certainly went out there trying to make my life as comfortable as I can, number two.

And the winning's nice, but further, the Senior Tour, honestly, isn't really all about winning, except when you win, you do collect. The Senior Tour is about what's happened, I guess, time, the evolution of time, this will heal . . . you know, the Arnold Palmers and the Gary Players and the Lee Trevinos will someday put the clubs up. And that's gonna be a sad time, because of being a baby boomer and growing up with these names.

What's happened today, the young don't know who Bruce Fleisher is, they know who Tiger Woods is. So, you know, as time goes on, Watson's coming, [Tom] Kite, and pretty soon [Nick] Faldo, and I can go on and on. I think the Senior Tour is alive and still kicking, but the Senior Tour is really more about the spectator really being able to get closer to heroes.

Certainly for the baby boomers . . . not the young people, because it really doesn't draw many young . . . the Senior Tour isn't so much about winning. Unfortunately, the dollars are getting bigger, and it's certainly a great thing that you can go out there and make a lot of money, but still, you have to realize that the Senior Tour is not the junior tour, the junior tour is really what it's all about.

It's just an extension, and a great place for a bunch of old farts to let their hair down. And a lot of 'em still aren't having fun, which is sad. It needs to loosen up—I really don't have the answers for you.

Well, I've won a lot this year, and God knows how I did it, I really don't know. I let my guard down a few times and let a few get away, but I was fine with that, it didn't bother me. I won't go into the tournaments and talk about it, but I would have to say the most rewarding was Key Biscayne, because, number one, it was my first tournament. Number two, it was at home in south Florida. I had a lot of friends behind me.

And I had an angel on my shoulder by the name of Nelson

Gross that, even to this day, I get emotional thinking about it, because Nelson lived for me, like a lot of other people live through me. I'm fifty, he was a little bit older. I think Nelson was in his sixties. He was brutally murdered a couple of years ago. I just cringe and I get mad thinking about it today, because we had so much fun and we had such a friendship. My best friend today is seventy-three years old, a guy by the name of Sol Ostroff, who also lives his life through me, and is with me every day and watches every swing.

But I would say the last nine holes of Key Biscayne, thinking of Nelson and praying that he's with me, is probably the most emotion that I was able to let go. I cried at the end, and I really felt he was on my shoulder the whole back nine.

I leaned on him very hard . . . and you know, every player's a little bit different, Bob. I had a monkey on my back that people expected so much, or at least I thought they expected so much. To win that first week was big, I felt.

The shot that stood out is the last shot that I came off and I knocked it in the bushes, with a one-shot lead, and Sayo, doing the exact same thing when I opened the door for him. So I would say those two drives were big, and my lie, I was able to pitch it out sideways, and he ended up trying to hit it, and he whiffed it, so those were two outstanding days that I remember very well. They really changed my life.

Again, I broke down—I thought of nothing but Nelson. I only wish he could have seen me in person, so that was big. And of course, having my family and all my friends there, about forty or fifty of them. We celebrated afterwards, it was a . . . there's nothing like winning. What a high, you know? Even if it's at a Senior Tour level, certainly the tour today, to win those kind of dollars, is scary, you know, when you're talking about $3 million or $4 million, and you're talking about picking up $500K, $550K, it's scary.

Winning certainly breeds winning and confidence. That's really what it's all about. I didn't even feel like I hit the ball particularly well, maybe my thought pattern was good, my work ethics were good, I had a very good caddy that I leaned on, that I thought was a big help, Dennis Turning. He had been in the winner's circle quite a few times, and that's why I wanted him to caddy for me. I think he played a very big part.

But certainly, winning, having him giving me the confidence, he never let me back down, he was very aggressive, and I just kept pushing, you know? I kept pushing. Because the Senior Tour, again . . . I certainly don't want to belittle it in any way, but the Senior Tour, you know, is made up of fifty and over, and if you broke it down you would see that even this year no one over fifty-five won a golf tournament.

So if you took, how many guys between fifty and fifty-five, there's probably what, forty? Maybe thirty-five or forty? And of course, once you hit sixty and over you have eighteen or twenty-five guys, so it really becomes a numbers game. One of the reasons I think guys like Irwin can dominate is he's just a little bit head above shoulders, and feels that way, and can really dominate.

And you know, Watson could do the same thing next year, there's no doubt in my mind. He's that good. I think once he tastes the winner's circle, he's gonna be tough. He's gonna like it, you know? He's gonna like that feeling of adulation at the end, people making a fuss, you know? And you don't have thirty guys, you may have one or two—and that's big.

Well, the Bank of Boston [win] was incredible, because I'd not really played competitively, big-time. I played in a section, you know, I dominated south Florida for years. But that was a very mystical week, because for the first time in seven years I played in a major tournament, a major, I'm talking about a PGA cosponsored event.

To go there my first week out and win, it was just a fluke. I mean, I got in because Bobby Cole, I think he broke an ankle or a wrist or something, and I was an alternate, and my wife kind of pushed me out the door. I didn't want to play, because I had a very . . . see, what had happened was, I was working at Williams Island, and I decided that I'd had enough and I was ready to go play. I wanted to go back to the school. So at that time, I think it was April or May, I was gonna play the Hogan Tour to get ready for the fall school.

I had a guy backing me, and I went out and finished third two weeks in a row. It was the Maine Open and New Haven Open. And the following week was a week off, Hogan-wise, and I was gonna go play in Colorado. Well, Forrest Fezler, who I was rooming with, told me to go commit to the Bank of Boston, because I was in a category from the old tour days. It was a possibility that if [the field] was still short, I could get in. But I knew that once I went home that week, to get ready for Denver, that I wasn't gonna come back, even if I did get in.

But I did go home . . . the phone rings at two o'clock. I think it was Wade Cables, he said, Bobby Coles still pulled out, do you want his spot, and Wendy pushes me out the door and says, you're going.

And I went, and I shoot 64 and 67 the first two days. I've got a four-shot lead, and I get up Saturday morning, and man, I'm trembling. I say, honey, I don't like this feeling, I can't believe I put myself in this position. Because I know the world's watching. It's one of those things, unfortunately, you have to deal with.

And I went out and I shot 72, which was one over, which really wasn't a bad day, but the whole . . . you know, the tour passed me by. I was four shots behind going into Sunday, which really relaxed me. Now, was it me, it being so unexpected, so much pressure for me? I went out figuring, shit, I'm gonna get a nice payday, all I've gotta do is keep it in the top ten, and shit, I shoot 64 again.

I end up in a seven-hole playoff with Ian Baker-Finch, and

the rest is history. I won with that long putt. But that was an incredible, incredible high.

Well, listen, the playoff was destined. There was no doubt in my mind, the last hole I made a fifty-footer. I'd kind of skanked the ball around. I had a chance to close him out on seventeen, which was like the fourth playoff hole, and I let him get away there. He opened the door big. But I was getting it up and down.

I think the miracle shot was the sixth playoff hole. I pulled my second shot, and I had an impossible pitch. I hit to pitch it under a limb and over a trap, and had about twelve feet of green to work with. And he knocked a four-iron up there to about ten feet. At that time I said to my caddy, you know, Jack Key, I said, Jack, the best I can do is about twenty feet, God knows what's gonna happen from there.

I hit this shot, I don't even know how I hit it, but it came out real soft. I carried the bunker and kept it under this limb. It landed between the bunker and the green, which you had about a yard of long grass. It took one bounce to about three feet, he misses, I make, I go to the next hole, and of course, I make that fifty-foot putt. So it was in the stars that I won . . . no doubt.

Oh, that was the greatest feeling in the world. Again, I cried, the emotion. I played from '71 to '83, I got off for seven years, to come back to win my first event, it was $180,000 later . . . I'd never seen so much money in my life, you know?

The U.S. Amateur—God, you're taking me way back. I qualified, I won a spot. I qualified in a place called Lantana, down here [in Florida]. I remember winning a spot in a three-hole playoff, and I was really . . . I was a wonderful college player. I dominated junior college golf in Miami, but I was kind of a dark horse. No one had ever really heard of me, because, you know, I didn't have the dollars. I was on my own. I was parking cars at the time, believe it or not.

I went up there with a lot of confidence, but again, like I said, I was unheralded. I was long, I remember. God, I could really golf my ball back then. But I remember, I went out and played four solid rounds of golf. I remember playing with Hubert Green . . . Bob Barbarosa I think I played with the last day.

But to be honest with you, it's the only time I ever felt, they call it alpha, which is a zone . . . the last three holes I don't remember swinging the club, even to this day. I had hit I think it was a nine-iron out of the rough on sixteen, a three-iron to seventeen, which is a par four, and a driver three-iron to eighteen. I don't ever remember swinging the club, I was in some sort of mystical, three feet off the ground, and I won by beating Eddie Giles.

So that was a very, very incredible week there, because at that age I was the third-youngest ever to win it. And that held up for a long time, until Tiger came along.

Well, I remember . . . actually, on the eighteenth tee, someone had hollered from the gallery, if you make five, you win it. I remember when I got up to the green, I hit the three-iron to about twelve feet. I went up there, I saw the scoreboard, and the scoreboards back then were very shaky, and I think Eddie had shot 65 the last day, if I make five we tied and go to a playoff. So that I did remember.

But as far as winning, I know that the guy I had worked with, Charlie DeLuca, had flown up there with another guy by the name of Frank Purpedge, who's a wonderful player in his own right, and Wayne Van Bibber, they're no longer with us. They flew up from Miami on Saturday to surprise me Sunday, although I never saw them in the gallery on the last hole.

And you know, like I said, to win the U.S. Amateur is big, was big. And of course, that got you in the Walker Cup, the World Cup, and the Masters, I mean, it just did so many things.

Well, I just think I grew up honoring Arnold Palmer . . . Arnold Palmer was the guy, he was the King. I think all golfers owe everything they have, even today, to Arnold Palmer. He put golf on the map, he developed television, he was the man, with his charisma, with his talent, with his vigor for life, and with his patience.

You know, again, I've done many things in my life, I've had many ups and downs, believe me, and I would really have to say, I wish I could go back . . . I guess we all wish we could go back in time to feel that wonderful, exciting, nervousness feeling. That was something special.

RAY FLOYD

Ray Floyd won a total of thirty-five tournaments in his PGA career, twenty-two on the regular tour and another thirteen on the senior circuit, and he came within a single event of winning the Grand Slam. For his greatest days, Floyd chose a pair of remarkable rounds at the PGA and the U.S. Open, respectively. In the first, he left the field in the dust on the first day of play, while the second proved that Floyd still had the skills and the mettle to win a major championship at the age of forty-four.

Well, [picking a greatest day] might sound simple to you . . . you know, I've been pretty fortunate in my career, I've had some nice things happen, so to kind of pick out one, one day or one round, in some cases even a tournament's pretty difficult.

Well, I guess probably I'd have to go with the 63 I shot in the opening round at Southern Hills in the PGA Championship. And I won the tournament.

You might have to research, I'm the worst person—you'll have to do a little work on your own there. I apologize, but I'm fifty-seven, and this stuff starts running into each other—I might tell you it's the '82 PGA, it could have been any one. You know, one of these things, people laugh at me, but it's something that was never . . . I'm not good at recalling dates and how I was doing at the time, you know, it just seems to get all lost up. You know, I've been playing thirty-eight years on the tour, so you can understand where I'm coming from.

I wish I could be more specific and helpful, but anytime somebody knows me when they do an interview, I say, you better check me, because I'll give you a wrong year, or a wrong month or something sometimes. And even the number—I know it was the 63, and the reason I know it was that I had nine threes in a row in the round.

But you know, as far as how I was playing coming in, I don't even have a clue. You'd have to look at the records and see how I did in the tournaments that were in front of it. But in '82, you know, I won three events, I think I'd won Doral that year, see, I wouldn't bet on that, whether I won it in '81 or '82. I know I was right in the top of my prime right through there. But please check, because you make us both look bad if you don't . . . I want you to know what you're dealing with.

I remember in the big picture of things . . . a major championship at a marvelous golf course. Southern Hills is a very good, hard, and difficult golf course. It's hosted U.S. Opens and PGA Championships. So the quality's there. The PGA Championship is played in August, so I never will forget, on the cover of *Sports Illustrated*, it said, "Hotter Than the Hills," after I'd won the event, on that cover.

So, "Hotter Than the Hills," and it was, it was over a hundred degrees each day. And the humidity was way up, way up—I can't tell you what the humidity was, but it seemed as close to a hundred as it could get without raining, if you know where I'm coming from. It was really hot and muggy, and we had a lot of people that were dropping from dehydration and from heat prostration and stuff.

So it was an endurance week in some sense, because of the weather. I know that I took great care, what I ate for the week and what I drank, and I drank water every hole, and I kept a cool towel around my neck. Instead of walking down the fairways, I walked down the side that was shady. So when I look back and I reflect, and people say, well, tell me some things about that PGA Championship, the thing that comes to mind first is the heat, the humidity, and the conditions we had to play under.

Well, we don't have a lot of history at a golf course like that, because I have played the U.S. Open prior, I'm pretty sure—I think Hubert Green won a U.S. Open there. I think that was before '82. I had played the course, but I didn't have a great knowledge of the golf course. But I did have the benefit of staying in the home of a good friend of mine who was also a member of Southern Hills, and a single-digit low handicapper. I had the benefit of his knowledge. He told me about greens that broke different than they looked, and how a lot of the greens were a bit tricky, so I had the knowledge of a friend there staying at his home. I had that benefit—usually things like that backfire, but when you're playing with a guy that's a scratch or a one-handicapper, you know that you can listen and he knows what he's talking about.

It was the first round, and I was paired with Hale Irwin and I think Gary Player. I'm positive of Hale Irwin, because he was keeping my scorecard, and I'm pretty sure about Gary Player, but I think you'd best check that, too.

And it was a round that started I would say the week before, certainly no more than two weeks before. I was fairly confident because I had felt that I was playing pretty well, and I was looking forward to the tournament. I know that in the practice rounds I played well, and I started out pretty matter-of-fact. I parred one through six, and then the seventh hole I made a birdie, which was the first three of nine in a row. I made nine straight threes starting at the seventh hole.

The eighth hole was a good, long par three. I made three. Then I birdied nine, which was a four. I birdied ten, which was a four. I parred eleven, which was a three par. I birdied twelve, which is the hardest hole on the golf course, made a three. Thirteen I made a three, fourteen and fifteen I made threes. So I made a run of nine threes in a row through there, and then it ended up I parred two or three holes there. Then I birdied eighteen for a 63 on a par 70, which is a pretty incredible run in a major championship.

To this day, when people ask me what is the best round of golf I've ever shot, that was not my lowest round by far, but I think circumstantially, that 63 opening, or either the finishing 66 at Shinnicock to win the U.S. Open. I'd be hard-pressed to say, you know, which round of golf . . . you know, now, and when I say that again I don't know how I separate.

Maybe the 66 the last round at Shinnicock was my defining moment in golf, too, or the greatest day. Because to win the U.S. Open at age forty-four—at that time I was the oldest guy there to ever win it—could have been the greatest round, too, so you see where I'm coming from.

I think you get kind of into a zone where you're focused in on your playing, the task at hand, and each shot at a time. I know it's a cliché, in every sport you hear guys say these same things when they do well, and everybody tries to interview around that, but that's it when you're very success-ful, when you're capable of lifting the bar, if you would, and doing your best.

I think when your focus is good, your concentration, your comfort zone, and you're playing well, you know it, things are going well, the surroundings aren't—you're comfortable. Even though it was terribly hot and the humidity was there and you were wet from head to toe with sweat, it wasn't adverse. You're taking the situation and you're in control of it.

I think my all-around game at that time was at its best. I was driving long and straight. I had good iron play, because Southern Hills is long and you need good iron play. I was hitting greens, because in the major championships with deep rough, if you miss greens you're not gonna be successful.

My putting was good—I don't think that you win a major championship if you don't . . . I would say that, yes, it's happened, but it's certainly an exception more than the norm when a player does. Sure, you can have one of these incredible putting weeks or a short-game week where you missed lots and lots of greens and you chip in a few times and you make a lot of long putts and all the short ones. But I think that in a major that is not likely.

I think people that win major championships tend to have their house in order . . . things are pretty well rounded to be capable of doing that.

Well, it was pretty incredible. It was the course record. I don't know if it's been broken since, but certainly the competitive course record. It's just one of those rounds that, under the circumstances, is so impressive to shoot that kind of score. You know, they were talking about just a few under par maybe winning the golf tournament in those conditions, and here I go out and shoot seven under on the first round.

I think it built my confidence, knowing that I had opened up and had a nice lead. And I carried that lead through the tournament. I ended up winning the tournament by three shots. That was a quarter of the way home. You can't get overly excited about having a great round, but it certainly set me up for the win.

And I went on and played very good golf for the next three days to win that title.

The thing that I can recall vividly is walking up the eighteenth hole after driving perfectly. And the eighteenth hole's a fairly difficult hole. I hit my second shot in the sand trap or the sand bunker that's right under the right side of the green— a very easy bunker shot, at worst you get it out of there to two-putt. And I'm thinking about how I've won the tournament, in fact, I had a five-shot lead at that time walking up that fairway.

And I put it in the bunker . . . now I'm thinking how I've won the golf tournament, and I lost my concentration. I started thinking about what I was gonna say at the trophy presentation. Well, I go in and I leave the ball in the trap. Then I blow it out and two-putt for a double-bogey.

So there was a lesson to be learned. You have to get your job done and sign the scorecard correctly—the tournament's not over till it's over. I lost my concentration there with a big lead, but I think it's something I will always remember.

I think I took it from there forward. That's something that you can't neglect. It doesn't matter if you have a nine-shot lead or you're one behind, you gotta keep playing and you can't let up. You can't let your mind wander.

I'm not one of these guys that goes around and does anything a hell of a lot differently [when I win], if you know where I'm coming from. I know that I had to get on a plane that night and go to California for a corporate day that I had on Monday.

So that, unfortunately, is pretty much the glamour of winning or losing golf events. You're traveling. Your next day is already scheduled, now especially, a year out in front. There's nothing . . . you'd think, wow, we went out and dined and drank champagne and had a fabulous celebration at dinner, and my friends and family and stuff . . . well, no, I couldn't. I had to get on an airplane and go to California.

But it was very special, and to win a major championship, that was my third major at that time, made it very special.

Well, I was, as I say, it was my third . . . I guess your first major is of the utmost importance, and then I go back again and maybe I should be talking about Shinnicock, my last major, that I won at age forty-four.

The significance there was, people don't win major championships much after forty. And the U.S. Open, I'd always had a lot of trouble playing U.S. Open golf courses. I was always in conflict with the way they were set up. I don't want to be specific, but in conflict with the way the USGA sets golf courses up . . . anybody that knows golf will understand what I mean. I don't want to get into a contest here with the USGA.

You know, they play great golf courses, but they literally take certain aspects of players' games away from them because of their setup, I can say that. So I have never performed very well in U.S. Opens, and to come to Shinnicock and be able to finish there with a 66 in the final round against, really, a star-studded field—there were nine players or ten players within one shot of the hole with nine holes to go—was very special.

Well, the last round was bogey-free, I made four birdies and no bogies. And I birdied the sixteenth hole, which basically won me the golf tournament. To be able to do that is the thing that I remember most about that round, along with everybody being so tightly bunched coming there. I was the only person to break par. I would say that Shinnicock, without doubt, is in the world's top five. And to win on that caliber golf course was very, very, very special.

I was not concerned about anybody else—and that, again, goes back, I look back and I see the quality of the field, but if you're worried about players, a guy that may not have ever won that you take lightly can come in and have the greatest of rounds, or vice versa. Your quality players you expect to. You can't play individual players when you're playing medal-play events, you have to play the golf course.

I did stay in town that night, because I did one of the morning shows—they came out to Shinnicock and did it on the porch. So that is . . . I did get to stay in town, but when you win a major championship, your time with the media is very lengthy. You'd like to think, let's go celebrate the victory, but you never really have time. You just don't have these great elaborate dinners and drink champagne like you think. There's such a demand from the media from all over the world, and everybody seems to think they can draw that one little thing that you didn't tell everybody else. It's just not gonna happen, but you have to . . . you're very consumed after the event with that attention.

Well, at that time it meant a great deal to say, here I was, forty-four years old . . . and a lot of players are not competitive anymore, and have won the U.S. Open Championship. To do it as the oldest man to ever win, at a time when people are kind of writing you off, your career, [saying], he's finished, he's forty-four.

Now, to go back and say that I am now a member at Shinnicock. I have a home in South Hampton, and it's really very special to go out there and play the golf course. It's an area and a place that we love as a family. And I specifically love the golf course, so it's really meant a lot to me and my family. It's a special thing when I look back on it, most definitely.

I think the key probably was the week previous at the Westchester, when I was leading after three rounds. And I shot 77, I think, and blew the tournament on a Sunday. To have that experience, and driving from Westchester out over to Long Island on a Sunday night—Maria, my wife, kept saying, what are you gonna do? You know, I said, it's no big deal, it happens, but she kept saying, well, what if you have the lead the next week? Are you gonna shoot 77? You've gotta think about it, you've gotta address it.

And we had a kind of a shouting match in the car, if you would, I wanted to drop it. I'm pretty laid back about things, you know I tend to let it go, and she said, no, you need to address it, this could happen next week. And looking back, how fortunate was that, because you have to say, what was the reason, why did you? Was it your concentration, was it lack of it, did you get nervous—you know, why did you shoot 77? There was no reason, you've been in contention before, you've been there.

I think the experience of going through that, addressing it, and facing the fact that I blew it, and if it happens again I'm gonna be a little bit better in control, and I'm gonna pace myself and do the things that have made me a champion in the past. And that's the thing that I drew.

So I would say the week previous, the Westchester experience, was a great factor or a reason why I was capable of coming back on a Sunday under all the pressure, with eight or nine world-class players within a stroke with nine holes to go and be able to jump out of there and win it.

And that's what separates you. That's when you're winning, when your mind's good. We're all physically capable of winning, or we wouldn't be there. It's just the guy that has the best week with the mind is what separates you.

The Senior Tour to me is—if there were three rings, you know, one of the two on the side. It's not the big show, and it's not what it's all about. It's a nice embellishment to a career, it's great for golf, and the demographic fits marvelously. The Senior Tour has really been terrific for golf, for the older demographic who are our fans. And it allows us to keep performing.

But we are . . . you know, you're not in the same environment or arena as the regular tour. Guys that couldn't compete, that were away from golf ten or twelve years who weren't competitive, have come to the Senior Tour and been world-beaters. But that's not what it's all about . . . the other one's where the records are.

GIBBY GILBERT

Gibby Gilbert took a diverse approach to the concept of his greatest day. He started with an account of his first win on the tour in Houston, in 1970, and moved from there to his greatest round, when an intriguing visitor from above kept him from breaking Ben Hogan's course record at Pinehurst by a single stroke. Gilbert's greatest week led to his his first victory on the Senior Tour, where he parlayed a series of superb rounds into a victory at Kansas City in 1992.

Well, of course, your greatest day in golf has to be your first win, the final day of your first win. My greatest round in golf is a completely different day.

My first win, when I won Houston in 1970, and I suppose Sunday . . . I'd never been in a situation to win a golf tournament. I had no clue whether my game would hold up under any kind of pressure or not. Fortunately, I held up and birdied the last hole to get in a playoff with Bruce Crampton and won in a playoff. But I suppose your first win and Sunday would be your greatest day.

I just know that I had started on the tour in the spring of 1968. I hadn't won much money in '68 and very little in '69. And really, I don't remember how much, but I remember that Houston was an invitational tournament. They took the top one hundred players on the current money list, and I was ninety-ninth, to get in the tournament. So I had not won much money to that point.

And I won the tournament, and I just remember being very nervous all day long. I really surprised myself on a few shots.

To tell you the truth, I remember very little about the first few rounds. It was Houston Champions, in Houston, Texas, a very tough golf course, and I was just trying to survive out there, trying to make the cut. I think I only shot two or three under par to win the tournament.

And I just remember it was a struggle trying to make the cut, you know, just trying to stay in some kind of position to make a good check. Fortunately, I was in the last group on Sunday, paired with Bruce Crampton, and I don't even remember who else. Crampton was leading the tournament, and, I mean, this was when Bruce was probably top three or four or five in the world. And if he'd have said boo at any time that day, I would have jumped right out of my skin. But he was a perfect gentleman and gave me every opportunity to win.

Fortunately, he bogied eighteen and I birdied it, for me to catch him. And then I beat him on the third [playoff] hole . . . I remember I had a caddie named Ray Rodriguez. He was a postman and had never caddied before. And the last hole, I knocked the ball up on the green, probably six feet from the hole. And in those years they didn't have all the gallery ropes, when you hit your shot, everyone hit their shot on the last green, the crowds surrounded the green.

I didn't even see my ball land. And then when we made our way through the gallery, we got up there, and I see my ball about six feet from the hole—big applause, but I still couldn't tell. We walked on the green, and Ray says, geez, I hope you make this putt. And I said, so do I.

But then we're riding out [to the playoff hole] in a station wagon that had Crampton and his caddie and me and my caddie and a driver. I'm sitting in the back, and Crampton's sitting in the front. And I was so nervous, I was afraid to look at Crampton. And somehow I built up enough nerve to look up there, and I look up, and I could tell that he was nervous also. And that really gave me a lot of confidence, knowing that I wasn't the only one that felt that way. He was as white as a sheet—probably just like me.

I beat him on the third hole . . . I parred the third hole and beat him.

On Sunday, on eighteen, Crampton hit first. I bogied seventeen to go two shots behind. And Crampton hit first, and sort of popped his tee shot up—it was a long hole, he sort of popped it up to where he was gonna have to hit a wood. I hit a real good drive, and he pulled his second shot left of the green, probably twenty yards left of the green, with a three-wood.

I hit a three-iron, I can't remember exactly how far, probably about two hundred yards or so. And the pin was in the left rear, about six feet left of the hole. And Bruce didn't even get his chip shot on the green, so he had to really get it up and down for a bogey. And then he chipped his fourth shot very close, and went ahead and tapped in for a bogey, and I had a six-footer for a birdie to tie.

And I honestly don't even remember hitting the putt. I lined the putt up, got over it, and first thing I looked up and it was in the hole.

I really remember not too much going through my mind, because I'd never been there before. I didn't know exactly what to do—I didn't know if I was choking, I didn't know what was going on, because I'd never been there. You know, this was a new experience, and I just knew to give it my best.

It was just a long golf course in those days. The golf course was extremely long, we were hitting long irons, and all day long I just kind of kept myself in position to make a lot of pars. It was the type of golf course you were not gonna make a bunch of birdies on. I just kind of kept myself in position not to make bogies, just to make as many pars, and if I did make a birdie, okay. And I made a lot of pars all day long, I made very few bogies and very few birdies . . . sort of hung around.

Bruce teed off with a . . . I can't remember, but it seemed like it was a three- or four- or five-shot lead. He didn't play well Sunday. I don't remember what he shot. I don't even remember what I shot on Sunday. But he didn't play very well, he put several of us back in the hunt, I think Bert Green, Gary Player, and I were right there with two or three holes to go.

The first hole, we teed off on fifteen, and I don't even remember what I hit off the tee, it was either a driver or a three-wood, but I can't remember. It was a short par four, I didn't hit a very good shot—I hit it real low, but I hit it straight down the middle. And still, it left a short iron to the green. And I think I left the iron shot quite a ways short of the hole, maybe thirty feet short of the hole, and made a good two-putt just to stay in the hunt, maybe had it twenty feet from the hole.

And then the next hole, sixteen's a little six-iron par three, and the pin was over on the right side. I really had not made too many good swings on that tee all week long. I kept missing the green right-left, right-left. I hit a pretty good six-iron in there, a little to the left and behind the hole. You know, both of us had a pretty basic two-putt there for a par.

And then seventeen's a long par four, and Crampton gets up on the tee. I never will forget . . . used to have the TV tape of the thing, Crampton gets up on the tee and hooks it into the water off the tee. Well, if you hold the club a little tighter in the left hand, you have a tendency not to hook it, you know, you have a tendency not to let the club turn over. Well, I can remember squeezing the glue right out of the club grip to keep it from hooking, because that's my tendency anyway.

And I drove it down the middle, and the announcer says, that's low and long. And I drove it right down the middle, pretty long. Normally they put the crosswalks just out of the driving area, you know, where we can't reach the crosswalks? Well, I drove it to the crosswalks.

And of course, we're in Texas, and Bruce Crampton is from Texas. I remember this, and they let the gallery go ahead and cross. Well, someone stepped on my ball in the crosswalk, which is okay, because I got a drop anyway, I dropped it back. But then Crampton dropped out of the water and hit a good third shot up in front of the green, I can't remember how far, ten yards in front of the green or something like that. And the pin was in the left rear, and left of the green there's water, a little canal back there.

Well, on the seventy-first hole of the tournament, I shot at the pin, knocked it left of the green, and it went back in the water. I made a good bogey. My caddie asked me, when we were standing on the fairway, he says, where you gonna hit this shot? And I say, thirty feet to the right of the hole, hole high.

If you'd have taken a tape measure . . . I put it thirty feet to the right of the hole. And I just sort of eased that first putt up there about a foot from the hole, and tapped it in for a win.

I was very confident—I felt like I could two-putt, which is exactly what I had to do. You know, I don't remember what was going through my mind, but I just remember that when I put it on the green, I'd felt like I'd won the tournament.

The only thing I remember was Crampton's caddie was Walter Mongtomery, who died last year, a black guy—Walter Montgomery was the first one to come over and shake my hand. And then Crampton was right behind me, and again, you know, like I said, he was a perfect gentleman. Bruce congratulated me and told me how well I played, and that's all I remember. I don't remember in detail, I just remember that he did come over and he was very nice about it.

It made me feel good that he came over, because he blew the tournament. I won it, but he blew it.

I don't remember if the ceremony was on the eighteenth green, I just remember that I went blank at that time.

I had a good year the rest of the year. The whole key back in those days was to make the top 60, and I qualified for the tour in 1967, and if you don't make the top 60 or the top 125 now, you have to go back to school. I've never been back to school—I stayed exempt the rest of my career.

The greatest round has to be Pinehurst number two. I think it was 1975, the first round of the World Open—it was the only eight-round tournament that we have. And I shoot 62 at Pinehurst number two, and broke Ben Hogan's course record by two shots.

I remember we teed off, I'm paired with Sam Snead and Hubert Green, and we teed off on the back nine. You know, on the first day half the field tees off one, and half tees off ten, you have morning and afternoon. And I played in the afternoon, and I teed off on ten. Gosh, I don't even remember the first couple of holes I birdied, but I eagled sixteen and parred seventeen and eighteen to shoot four under on the back nine.

Then I missed a very makable eight- or ten-footer at one for birdie, and then I birdied two, three, four, five, six, to go nine under par. And I've heard people say that they didn't know how they stand . . . when I'm on the golf course, I know if I'm even par, one over, one under, two under, whatever. But this is honestly the one time, the only round in my life, I didn't know how many under par I was. And I really honestly didn't.

We were walking to the sixth green, and I asked Hubert, I said, Hubert, how many under am I? And he said, hell, I don't know, but you're birdying every one of 'em. And then I birdied the sixth hole, and went nine under. And then the seventh hole is a par four, dogleg right, and I hit a good three-wood off the tee.

The pin was in the left rear, and Billy Casper was sitting in a chair behind the green, watching guys come up. Well, the pin was so close to the edge of the green, people were putting it in the middle of the green, and putting off the end of the green, and all kinds of funny stuff. You know, there was a little slope, maybe four feet left of the hole, and they were putting off the green. And he was just sort of sitting back there, amused, you know, at where the pin was, he thought it was an unfair pin placement.

Well, I hit my second shot into the green, just left of the hole. And I mean, I'd just birdied five in a row, and I hit it in there, it looked like, three or four feet left of the hole. And I walked halfway to the green, and the ball's right there.

I get to the green, and my ball's gone. You know, it stood there for a second, and then rolled off the green. Well, I bogied the seventh hole, because it went down the slope of this hill. The eighth hole was a par five that we played par four, I hit three-iron about ten feet from the hole. And then nine's a par three, and I lipped it out for one, knocked it two inches from the hole and made a two for 62.

Come to find out, on the seventh hole, what had happened, this is what we heard . . . the PGA officials go out the night before and spray a little dot on the green, and this is where the greenskeeper sets the cups for the next day. And this was the first week they had done that.

Well, the greenskeeper came to the green from the left side of the green, saw the first little white spot, and set the cup there. Obviously a bird had flown over the green, or whatever, and made a little white spot—that day, the pin was supposed to have been in the right rear. And it was a missed placement on the greenskeeper's part.

Of course, the bird made a spot, and the greenskeeper made a spot.

But I mean, I shot 62, and if the ball had stayed four feet from the hole like it should have, it could have been a 60.

The reaction? You know, I have several course records, but

I had a five-shot lead in the tournament. That was the biggest thing. After one round I had a five-shot lead, and I was excited about that. But when I walked off the eighteenth green going to the scoring tent, one of the guys back there told me, he says, you just broke Ben Hogan's course record by three shots.

And you know, I was excited, but still, you've got seven more rounds to go. I had the lead after four rounds. I had a three-shot lead after four rounds, but then the second four rounds I didn't play very well, so I don't even remember how I finished. But not good.

I had a greatest week on the Senior Tour—my first win was in Kansas City, and I shot 62–65–66 and won by nine shots. You know, that was the greatest week. I've had a few low rounds, but nothing really outstanding, or whatever.

Everything that week was right—the driver was good, the irons were good, the putter was good. I just had all the confidence in the world. I had a six-shot lead going into the last round, and [Jim] Colbert started off with a couple of quick birdies, and I made a bogey to start off with, so he pulled within three shots. After that I started making birdies. I made six birdies from there on in, and won by nine.

But I just had all the confidence in the world, I mean, everything was going my way, obviously.

The first victory on the regular tour's no contest—much better. The Senior Tour, I mean, it makes you feel good to be able to win at age fifty. But on the regular tour, I mean, that was my first win ever, of any kind. I mean, the regular tour, that started the rest of my career. It gave me a lot of confidence to let me know that I could do it.

The Senior Tour, when I went on the Senior Tour, I thought I could still win. When I was on the regular tour, I had no clue if I could win. But when I went on the Senior Tour, I thought I could win, but I knew I was gonna have to put it together.

I started playing golf when I was thirteen years old. And from day one, all I ever wanted to do was play professional golf, to play on the tour. I've never had a backup, you know, for any other job, I never thought of doing anything else—all I've ever thought about was playing golf.

Golf is my life . . . I still, to this day, love golf. And I guess, you know, winning on the PGA tour, something that I've watched all my life, and dreamed about all my life, and finally on that day in 1970, it came true. It matched up with my childhood dream . . . every bit of it.

There just wasn't enough of it. I only had three wins on the regular tour, but I mean, the thing is, it's so hard to win. There was a lot of good players back in those days, and there's more now. It's so hard to win—the guy that plays the best, most of the time, does not win. The guy that gets the luckiest wins.

But, I mean, it was just an unbelievable feeling, and you know, it took forever for it to sink in. It took forever. I just remember, it was not too long after that, I finished second at Westchester. I had a chance to win there, and it just gave me unbelievable confidence.

HALE IRWIN

Very few great golfers have a background in college football. Hale Irwin used the same "never say die" attitude he had as a defensive back at the University of Colorado to become a success on the links. Irwin's attitude and approach produced an array of greatest days, starting with his first victory on the tour, which in turn led to his first U.S. Open victory and his subsequent great victories in major tournaments on the Senior Tour.

My greatest day in golf . . . fictional or otherwise?

Well, probably the three U.S. Opens always come to most people's mind, including my own. But I think the first victory I had as a professional had to rank in there at least with the others, simply because it was at a time, young in your career, when you're, at least for myself, I was struggling a bit to establish myself, and really not having any notoriety other than as a University of Colorado football player.

It was a pretty exciting time, particularly around Harbortown—the Heritage Classic back in Sea Pines, that was a pretty exciting time. Our daughter was just gonna be born a month later, so between being close to starting a family and the first win, it was a pretty exciting time.

The fact that it was only two and a half years into my career,

I was still learning how to play the game, in the sense that all of us go through the qualifying, for some reason or other, get on the tour, we think we've got a pretty good handle on how to play, and then you get out there, and you start playing every day, every week. And back in those days you had the Monday qualifying lurking over you. If you were a qualifier and missed the cut, then you had to go to Monday qualifying.

So there was always that specter of the Monday qualifying, and could I make it—there's just a lot of obstacles thrown up for the young person. And I don't want to say that they're not now, but just referring only to my early days, there were a lot of obstacles for me, because I don't think I was as talented as some of the other players that were coming out.

I think my talents were yet to be honed—I think raw talent, in terms of being able to play the game, I was equal, but I had not learned how to use those talents. I had not learned the variety of golf shots, the little chips, some of the bunker play, the fading and hooking with regularity, playing shots, being able to accommodate successfully the situational golf as it comes about—when to be aggressive, when not to, how to play with a lead, how to try to catch up. All of those things, I had not really learned those.

Being successful in Colorado at the state level was not enough to really give me that confidence. I didn't get to play a lot in the summer anyway, between working and trying to get ready for football practice—you know, my season was very short indeed. I just didn't have those skills.

So I was still sort of in a learning curve when I finally broke through. I had lost in a playoff to Billy Casper in 1970, and that really showed to me, hey, maybe I can succeed out here. Although I threw away a two-shot lead and I lost to him in a playoff, you know, that was still a plus.

And Harbortown was an extremely difficult golf course in those days. The thing I had over some of the other players, I think, was the discipline, and the "they'll never beat me" kind of attitude that you had to have playing football. That really carried the day, more so than my great golfing skills. It was more of an attitude than anything else.

I think it was just . . . when you get out there and maybe you're not hitting the ball real well, and you just might get up and slap at a shot, just in frustration. I tried not to let the frustration boil over into a negative situation. It was pretty much the same about every play in football, when you're my size, playing against others that are at least your size and most likely much larger and much faster. I had to out-try them, I had to out-think them. And that was what I tried to do playing golf.

We're talking about going back some twenty-eight years—it was the week of Thanksgiving, so I'm not going to recall exactly, other than I know that my wife wasn't there and it was relatively chilly. My MO in cold weather is not particularly good, but I do recall going out onto the practice tee. Because of those conditions and because Harbortown was such a difficult course, I was working on just trying to keep my swing rhythm as slow and as methodical as I could make it, and just hit the ball solidly.

In other words, not to try to do anything fancy, because the course . . . it wasn't of great length, but it really required straight shot making, and not so much left-to-right or right-to-left, but just hit the darn ball straight. So I thought more than anything else of just trying to keep my tempo, which has always been a problem for me in that I oftentimes get a little quick, so even when I was younger I had more of a problem. So I really tried to concentrate on my tempo and just hit the ball solidly. Not worrying if it went slightly left-to-right or right-to-left, but just hitting it solidly.

I can't remember who I played with in those early rounds—I can certainly remember that I was having some respectable rounds. I can't recall the scoring, other than maybe it was 70–71–69, something in that area. I might even have a 73 in there if I recall. I think the record can certainly tell you, but those scores at that time were pretty good golf scores.

We first played there in 1969, and it was you, the alligators, and the golf course. There wasn't development around it, there was no out-of-bounds when we first played there, and now when you see it, you've got condos and homes and out-of-bounds on every hole. So it was pretty much a pretty raw golf course, and very difficult.

So in '71 it had not changed appreciably, but it was coming into its own in terms of conditioning. What we were seeing in the November time frame was a course where the Bermuda had gone dormant, the overseed was not particularly prevalent at that time, so we were playing pretty raw conditions. The course was very difficult, and the scoring, consequently, reflected a higher [number] than what you would compare to today.

Still, fairly good golf scores—I do believe my final round might have even been 74 or 73. And people say, boy, that's pretty high . . . well, they didn't know what Harbortown was like back in those days.

But the thing I do remember is playing the last nine holes. I was either tied for the lead or in the lead, and I hit a bad drive on the twelfth hole over to the right-hand trees, from where I had to pitch out. And then I hit a sand wedge from about eighty yards, I believe it was, to within fifteen feet of the hole, making that for a par. And I can recall that to this day, how excited I was, how nervous I felt—I believe that kept me in the lead.

So as we go around the rest of the golf course, I was hitting some pretty good golf shots, but when I got to the last hole, it's a wide-open fairway, and sometimes those wide-open fairways are the hardest ones to hit. I hit a very good drive, and Mac McClendon, with whom I was playing, made the comment, get down, because he thought I'd hit it too far into the marsh on the other side. I didn't, but when he said that, I can remember getting a real nervous start—oh, what was that all about?—and thinking maybe I had miscalculated.

But it was in good shape, and from that point on I had a five-iron to the green. If you can conjure up the golf course now versus then, the marsh came right up to the edge of the green. It was not quite an island green, but very nearly so. Today they've allowed the grass . . . it's all built up, and you can hit it left of the green now and still be in playing shape. But then, if you were left of the green, you were in the marsh.

So I had a pretty tough shot. I hit it on the green, and I was probably thirty feet from the hole, and putted it up within a foot of the hole. And when I tapped in that putt, it's almost like I had chewing gum on my putter blade, it felt like the ball stuck to the putter. I could not believe the feeling.

But when it went in, I had achieved the success that we all hope for as young players coming on the tour. And I can remember going to the airport that evening, not really needing an airplane—I was flying. I just felt so good and so proud, you know, the comments, congratulations, I'd never received that before. So it was really something quite special.

The award ceremony was very, very nice, because they bring out the Scottish band, they've got the drummers, and the cannons shooting, with all the plaids. And the players that had won before me, Arnold Palmer had been a winner, Bob Goalby had been a winner—the field then was always good, with Jack Nicklaus, and Gary Player, they were always good players.

I don't remember who finished second, I can't really tell you, but it was one of the better tournaments, simply because it was a harder golf course, and back then, players weren't quite as selective in their schedule as they are now. So you did in fact have players playing a good bit of the time, and all the good players played that. So I felt this was not a smaller event, it was an event of some stature, and I felt very good about that.

And I think that's why I went on to win that same event in

'73, and then that really led up to the '74 Open, which was probably my next greatest thrill, if not the equivalent of that. But those two wins, Harbortown, I think, helped me get through Wingfoot.

I think I tied for second the week before [Wingfoot] in Philadelphia. And during the practice rounds, I had been playing a couple of practice rounds—Leonard Thompson had given me a ride up to Philadelphia, to Wingfoot, prior to that event, so we played a couple of rounds together in the practice rounds.

And it was just unbelievably difficult. You know, I had played in a couple of Opens prior to that, and Wingfoot was a golf course that was just unmerciful—it was unrelenting. Driving was very difficult because the rough was anywhere from six inches to over a foot. You could pick the grass up and lay it down, and it was just a gnarly, tangled mess. So any ball into the rough was history.

The greens were probably as fast as you might see at Augusta National now, and very firm. I just remember going in there thinking, boy, if I could just make a lot of pars. I'm not even gonna think about making birdies, because I just can't see any big head on this course, and just try to keep the thing in play.

What I tried to establish in the practice rounds . . . and everybody was grumbling how hard the golf course was, putting was just almost impossible. So with all that grumbling, I thought, well, good, I've got everybody, 90 percent of the field is gonna give up. If I can just apply myself, and you know, the old formula of out-trying 'em and hang in there, who knows what could happen? And that's really what I tried to do.

So through the first couple of rounds I was in good shape, and the last round I played with Tom Watson, and he had the lead. Arnold Palmer was close by, maybe Bert Yancey might have been close by. So there were a number of probably five or six players within a stroke or two, and I being one of them.

And I just felt like, okay, if you tick off the players that you have to look out for, certainly Watson at that time was maybe even a rookie, because he had not been on the tour. He's what, four years younger than I, so he may have been on a couple of years. So I thought, well, he's got a lot of potential, I don't know if he's gonna hang in there. Palmer certainly has the experience, but he's sort of on the other side now of that great career he had had in the sixties.

So I just sort of thought, well, I've got just as good a chance here as anybody. And I went into that last round and just tried simply, as I had before, to keep the ball in the fairway and under the hole. In other words, try to get every putt uphill . . . downhill putts were just impossible.

And I made about a thirty-five-foot putt on the ninth hole, which normally for membership play was a par five, they had converted it to a four. And I had hit a four-wood to the green, some thirty-five feet from the hole, and I made a putt that probably broke three feet over a couple of rises, sort of a washboard, to take the lead.

So then it was going into the back nine. Tom was having some problems, and a player out of the pack by the name of Forrest Fezler was having a reasonable round and had emerged as one of the front runners. It still was anybody's game, and I just played the back nine fairly solid, like everybody else you're definitely making some bogies, which I did, but I wasn't losing ground by making some bogies.

And at the seventeenth hole I do recall hitting the drive just off the left fairway, and literally taking a wedge and just chopping back to the fairway. And I had another wedge, probably, oh, a hundred yards from the hole, and I hit that one to within twelve feet and made a very difficult left-to-right curling putt for a par.

In those days you didn't have a scoreboard on every hole. And I didn't know what I was doing, I didn't know my position in the field, other than I knew I was close. Well, on the walk to the eighteenth green somebody said, you have a two-shot lead, which shocked me. I remember thinking, my gosh, here I'm thinking at best I'll have a one-shot lead and more likely tied, and this person's telling me I've got a two-shot lead.

Well, I just said, that can't be right. So I just concentrated very hard on putting the ball on the fairway . . . again, going back to the elements that make a sound golf swing, as much as you can under that kind of pressure, just putting it in the fairway.

The last hole was playing just as hard as any hole in the golf course, and if you hit it off the fairway, a double-bogey was very easy to make. So it was important to put the drive on the fairway, which I did, and from there I had 194 yards to the hole, and that shot was slightly uphill, and we had a bit of a breeze blowing left to right.

I chose a two-iron, because if you're short and right of that green, it was . . . again, the mess down there in terms of rough was very difficult. The green was hard to putt if you didn't have it in the right spot. So I just said, okay, here we go— two-iron, aim it left, go through the swing thoughts.

And boy, I don't know if I've ever hit a better two-iron. It went left of the flag a little bit, and the wind blew it right over the top of the hole. It was behind the hole about twenty-five feet, and I got it on down there and got a two-shot win.

But I could not breathe. I'll be the first one to tell you that I couldn't breathe, I couldn't muster up saliva if somebody put a gun to my head.

And then afterwards, of course, the presentation, I was very proud of the moment and all that stuff. And I went back to the hotel, had room service with Dale Douglass and his wife Joyce, they were good friends, and still are to this day. We had room service, and they were very kind and helped me celebrate my first major victory.

Visions of sugar plums . . . having just never done that before. If you've done it, and you do it again, then you have an idea of what's coming. But after the first time, you really don't know, it's like a kid in a candy store—what do I want, what's gonna happen? Do I get all of this, do I get some of it?

You really don't know. All I knew was that I had my name on that trophy, and the U.S. Open was the tournament that I'd always held in the highest [regard] of any of the other tournaments. I had climbed as high as I could climb in professional golf by winning that tournament.

Throughout my entire career I've wanted to hopefully maintain the same personality, be the same person I was as a kid in Baxter Springs, Kansas. I always tried to remind myself where I came from, and through all the fortunate things that have happened to me, and the money that has come my way, all the opportunities I've had, I still like to remind myself of square one.

So I did not try to let it change my life, other than the fact that it started providing some opportunities that I had not had before. Simply that now I had a ten-year exemption, which, when you're talking about making the top sixty at that time, that was very big. Now you could start really kind of laying out your next ten years, at least, in some sort of fashion that did not have an asterisk next to it saying, well, this is only gonna happen if you qualify. So I had the opportunity now of having some comfort in laying out a game plan, if you wish.

It also now meant automatic invitations to British Opens, and other events if I so chose. And money then is still not nearly what it is now, but at that time it was significant money. I remember being invited to a couple of tournaments in Europe where there was a $5,000 guarantee, and to me, I thought, this is financial nirvana. It just was unbelievable. I'd never had something like that before. I was more accustomed to playing in a pro/am or an outing, and maybe getting $800 or $1,200, and feeling like that was the cat's meow.

So this to me was the financial bonanza that, in retrospect, I didn't accept every one of those invitations. I just felt like . . .

and I had no experience at this, but I just felt like, you can chase yourself down too much. Chasing the dollar, you're gonna wear yourself out. And I just came upon that formula maybe accidentally, but I think it's one of the reasons it extended my career as long as it did, that I have just not chased down that dollar everywhere in the world and beat myself up doing it.

Well, the Senior Tour event would probably have to be the U.S. Senior Open at Riviera. You know . . . after the first day, where I had just shot 77, it looked like I had pretty much blown myself out of the tub. To come back over the final three days from a fairly large deficit and get myself into a position where I had a chance to win. Playing in the last group, I'd worked myself from nowhere to somewhere, and going out and being able to play as I did, come back over the final three holes as I did, birdying the last hole as I did.

As we all know, that last hole at Riviera is not the simplest hole in the world, that would probably have to be . . . and that was a tournament that I had set as a senior, figuring for whatever value or good that there is that I wanted to win both the U.S. Open and the U.S. Senior Open. That was a goal I had, that's why that first round was so disappointing, just to sort of say, okay, and sweep it behind you, don't talk about it, don't think about it, you've got a long ways to go, it's a course you've won on before, it's a course you like, let's just go out and play it.

And so that would have to be the most exciting time I have had [on the Senior Tour].

It's a great satisfaction, you know, a great pride in having come back from that awful start. Now, bear in mind that it's been a couple of years that have gone under the bridge since I've been in that position back in 1974 to 1998. But it's still the same sort of welcome nervousness. To me that is why I still love this game—there's no other feeling quite like that rush you get from being challenged and coming through. You don't do it every time, certainly, and that's why the ones that are successful mean so much.

And I think that's why that tournament meant so much, because (a) it was a goal, (b) I'd started out so poorly, (c) I'd come back, used my "never give up" attitude, I guess, just play it out to the end, and just rely upon what I know I can do and not try the impossible. I can't win it on Friday, I can't come back from a 77 and win on Friday, so use the next fifty-four holes to position yourself to have a chance. And that's exactly what happened.

You know, for our discussion, we can call it the football mentality, I'm not certain it was that mentality—the football mentality is pretty basic, you clobber me and I'll clobber you. Mine was not necessarily a survival instinct, but there was a touch of that, because I was always the smaller guy on the field. Not always, but pretty much, and I was never the fastest player on the field.

So I approached it more from the standpoint of, I've got to read my keys. I've got to know what the other players are going to do before they know what they're going to do. You know, I have to be able to sense and read and anticipate to get in the right position. Particularly being a defensive back, not blessed with blinding speed, I had to be quick, and my decisions had to be accurate, and I had to be resourceful in what I did.

And so that is the mentality that I'm talking about, rather than say, the linebacker or the lineman who is in there beating heads all the time, and they don't have an opportunity to really think through the finest aspects. They're in there just slugging away, there's a more raw, basic mayhem.

I think we have almost such a dichotomy between today's player and the player of my day, and even slightly before me. The advent of television, and money coming to the seniors, not only the Senior Tour but the regular tour, has presented a whole new dimension on how some of these kids view golf. Or for that matter, maybe life. It's not just sport, it's a big part of our lives, but I think in the long run it's basically, how they view life. It would be very difficult, because the basis from which these kids are coming is so different.

You know, when I started, the predecessors of mine were really just establishing the game . . . forgetting money. Now, when you talk to players, it's money. Before it was sort of the game, and the integrity, and the character of the game. Now, it's the money—and oh, by the way, there are these other things that I've read about. And I think that's unfortunate.

Golf, in and of itself, is a great character builder. It teaches you an awful lot about yourself. And money can't buy that. But therein lies the problem, I think, it's that many of the young kids come out anticipating these great riches and forget that they have to understand themselves first, and the game will help them understand themselves. So it would be very difficult.

It's almost like asking that same question . . . how would you describe Willie Anderson? You know, I have no idea, because I've never played with those gutter percha, I've never played with a coat and tie on, you know, I played only on good golf courses. It's hard to understand that. But I think I have a better understanding of it than some of the kids do today.

I think I've always . . . and I don't preach this, but I would hope that the way I've played the game, and my approach to it, by putting golf first, would be the carrying argument or the carrying topic. Simply because I think golf is bigger than any of us. And there are some people today that think they're bigger than the game, and I think that's unfortunate because they just are not.

And by being an integral part of the game, a part of the learning curve of being a human being, I think golf is a great vehicle to get there. I know it's helped me, I know it's helped my son, I know it's helped my daughter—you know, it's helped my family understand themselves. And I don't think you can be a contributor in our society until you understand yourself first. And I don't think some of these kids coming out today understand that concept.

I think there's a basic difference between confidence and arrogance, and I never, ever want to put somebody's confidence down. But when arrogance creeps in . . . and having that infallible feeling is fine, if you feel that way inwardly, I think that's terrific. But when it becomes an outward expression, then I think you've got some problems. I think the knee-jerk reaction now is to be flippant and arrogant, and you start putting others down and not being respectful to your opponent.

That's why in match play—people say, oh, you should beat him, and I say, oh really? You know, I've always tried to give my opponents 100 percent respect for what they've done. That keeps it in balance.

It's a topic that another gentleman and I were talking about yesterday . . . how do you turn the basic belief of our society around? We didn't used to have road rage. How about cell phones? The whole thing has become, what can you do for me? And I think we've put "me" in front of everything else. We've become so materialistic, and the rush . . . for what?

I'm rushing too, don't get me wrong. But I think the older people understand, they've come out of the Depression, they've come out of World War II, the Korean War—they've understood need, sacrifice. My generation went through Vietnam, but that was such a horrible time . . . the people after that really have not. They have not suffered, they don't know what it's like to be a part of a team or a part of society. It's okay, if it's not that, then it must be me.

And you know, that sounds pretty grandiose, and I don't mean to get on the stump, but I think it goes deeper than just what you tell some kid about golf. I was out . . . we opened a course here in Phoenix the other day, and they had some juniors out there, and that's the message I tried to get through to them—stay in school, stay off of drugs, keep golf fun, and respect the guy next to you. And those are the points I made, and that's where I come down on it.

LEE JANZEN

When it comes to greatest days, Lee Janzen sure knows how to pick winning tournaments that presented formidable competition. The first was his victory at the Phoenix Open in January 1993, when he inadvertently kept thousands of fans from seeing the kickoff to the Super Bowl between the Dallas Cowboys and the Buffalo Bills. Janzen's second greatest day pitted him against Payne Stewart in the U.S. Open, a victory that became even more meaningful in the context of Stewart's memorable history at the Open and the tragic plane crash that took his life in 1999.

I guess some of my thought is that if I had a day that I picked out as my most exciting day, that I probably won't have a day that surpasses it. But I guess I could pick a day up until now.

So I would say, I'm thinking about all my wins, I just started right there. I thought about the Ryder Cup, the first team I played on, but I lost both my matches, so I wasn't really that excited. And I could have been more excited the second time, because I won a couple of matches even though we lost. And we made such a great comeback, but then there was still the defeat.

So I'd have to pick the '93 U.S. Open . . . or, you know what, the '93 Phoenix Open is probably the most exciting day I've had in golf. Now that I think about it, that has been the most exciting day. I guess they'd both be pretty close.

Well, the Phoenix Open was my second win. I won Tuscon the year before, and I was sort of stunned when I won, I didn't know what to do. And we'd planned a vacation the next week, so I was really just kind of in a state of shock for the next week, so I didn't really celebrate like I could have.

And then, just about a year later, and I knew—you know, when you win a tournament, they're so rare, and it's such an accomplishment that you should enjoy it. So we happened to be going over to a friend's house, who we actually stayed with that week, and they had rented a big TV that week, and we were gonna go over and watch the Super Bowl.

I was a big Cowboy fan, and they were playing the Bills. I won the tournament, birdying four holes on the back nine, made about a twenty-footer on eighteen to seal it, and then went on back to the house to watch the Cowboys just pummel the Bills. We had about forty or fifty people over there, and you know, I was on the phone just off and on, it was just like a big party and a big celebration, and the whole day was a riot.

I played fair the first day, and then the second day I think I shot like a 65. And it all came in the last five or six holes . . . I birdied thirteen, I holed a four-iron on the fourteenth hole for two. And then I think I birdied fifteen and then maybe birdied seventeen and eighteen or something. I was six under for the day, and I think it was all in the last six holes. That got me near the lead.

The weather was somewhat challenging on Saturday. I think I shot like a 73, which you can't usually do at Phoenix. I was maybe in fifth place going into the last round, and it was fairly windy, and then when we made the turn, a front or something came through, the wind started blowing through, and it turned all the way around, from blowing straight out of the east to straight out of the west.

As it went all the way around we were playing the eleventh hole, and on the twelfth green it hailed—I had my umbrella out because it hurt. And the group behind us was a couple of groups behind, and they ended up getting the worst of the wind, because they played eight and nine into the wind. And ten was a dogleg, that hole the wind switched, so they ended up playing eight, nine, ten, eleven, and twelve all into the wind.

And they go out in that direction, so they could have easily, you know, if they were playing faster they wouldn't have had to play all those holes into the wind. And actually, they all made a double-bogey in that stretch, and that got me back into the tournament.

For the most part I hit the ball really well all week. I was playing well, and the wind really started to pick up, I would say, on twelve and thirteen. I got up and down out of the bunker on twelve, and I guess my sand play is really what did it for me in the end, my bunker play. I got up and down on twelve out of the bunker for par, I birdied the thirteenth hole, then I got up and down again out of the bunker on fourteen.

Then I birdied fifteen, and then on sixteen I hit into one of those pot bunkers to the left, and I didn't even have a shot. But I left it in the bunker—I don't know if you've ever seen that bunker at sixteen at Scottsdale, but once you get in there you might not ever get out. But anyway, I hit the next one about a foot away.

And at that point I think that kept a one-shot lead, even with the bogey. And then I birdied seventeen and birdied eighteen, but that bunker shot pretty much did it, I ended up winning by two.

All I remember is David Frost, Andrew Magee, and Robert

Wren were in the group behind us. I thought it was Andrew Magee. I'm pretty sure it was. And it came to eighteen, and I had a one-shot lead, and I anticipated Robert Wren would birdie seventeen, it was playing straight downwind. So I thought I'd have to birdie eighteen just to make sure I won, or at least to avoid a playoff, which I did.

And then he went for the pin, hit it in the bunker, made a bogey, and Andrew Magee made birdie and leapfrogged him to finish second, two shots back.

Well, certainly the weather was making it play tougher. And the course that year was about the thickest I've ever seen the rough there, so the conditions were tough. Which I thought was great, I was just trying . . . it changed the game kind of, because normally there the weather's great, it's warm, there's not much wind, and you just try to make as many birdies as you can, and sometimes twenty under par wins.

But the last day you were just trying to make pars and keep the ball in play, and keep the ball on the right side of the green so you didn't make bogey. I was fortunate, I made some birdies, that was the difference, I made birdies when nobody else could.

I know I was really pumped up after winning, we had a lot of friends there from Arizona that we'd met. But I also knew that the Super Bowl was about to start, and everybody was leaving anyway. We were probably about fifteen minutes away, and I can't tell you how many friends I've had call and say they were at a bar, and the whole bar was against them because they made 'em leave the TV on the golf to see the end.

So I don't know if I got any friends that day from people I didn't know or not, they might have disliked me because I was on TV and they wanted to watch the Super Bowl.

The ceremony was pretty short, because I was really interested in getting back and watching the game, too. I think I pretty much said that, too, to the fans, I said, thanks for being here, but I know everybody wants to go home and watch the Super Bowl, so let's go.

Later that year, playing at Baltusrol, that was the first time I was exempt. And I played extremely well all year, the win there, and I had some other top tens . . . I had seven top tens going into the U.S. Open that year. So I was playing about as well as I'd ever played in my career, as far as finishes go.

I went in there with very low expectations—I had never made the cut in the U.S. Open at that point. And all I said was, I was gonna try and hit the first fairway and make a par on the first hole, because I'd never done that. And I birdied the hole, and that just seemed to relax me, and I played the whole tournament that way.

Well, that was my fourth year on the tour, and I had to qualify that year, which a lot of guys had to do every year, because there were fewer exempts. And I had qualified for the tournament, but I just never made the cut. So I played in '91 and '92, and I played in '85 when I was in college, I qualified as an amateur.

But you know, the U.S. Open was always . . . that was the biggest tournament in the world for me. Then I made the cut, and I was there near the lead, and I think because of all the good tournaments I'd had, I had that experience behind me, and I knew I could play well, in the lead or near the lead.

I didn't really think that I was going to win, or that I wasn't going to win, I was just playing golf and trying to do the best I could. And then when I got down to the end, I just ran out of holes before I could do anything wrong.

The practice rounds, I looked at the course, I think I prepared myself about as well as I ever did for a tournament. I looked at every hole. I walked the course on both sides of each fairway to figure out where the best place was to come into every green.

The rough was fairly manageable, because it was quite hot,

and the grass just wasn't growing. It was actually staying out of the rough. So I knew there was a chance of getting on the green out of the rough occasionally.

So I looked at every hole, at where I wanted to be, and fortunately all week, if I did miss it, I always missed it where I wanted to be. Maybe only a couple times did I miss in the wrong spot, maybe a handful of times. So I spent most of the week not in very much trouble—I don't think I made higher than a bogey on that course, which is usually pretty good when you can go a whole week on a U.S. Open course and not make above a bogey.

And I made a lot of birdies that week. I think that just came from my confidence of playing so well leading up to the tournament. I think I made more birdies than anybody in the field that week, and I always seemed to make a birdie right after a bogey, so I always overcame my mistakes right away.

[I shot a] 67 the first day, and I think I was in fourth. Three guys shot 66, I was one shot out with three guys ahead of me, and then I think all three of those guys played poorly the second day, and I shot another 67.

And back in those days they televised in the morning, they had like a two-hour time frame where they weren't on, and then they came back on. And then during that time I birdied three holes in a row, and it wasn't on TV. So when I went off the air, I don't think I was any better than maybe on the bottom of the leader board, and when they came back on I think I was up by two with two par fives to go.

So I was thinking, make two more birdies . . . but I was so nervous, I just couldn't do it. Even though I had won two tournaments in the year and a half before that, I'd been near the lead, that was the most nervous I'd ever been on a golf course, because now I was leading the U.S. Open.

But I managed to par the last five holes, even though I was that nervous, and I think that really . . . that may have been the biggest turning point for me in the whole tournament, that I was able to par those five holes to take the lead. And then I had to sleep on the lead, but I just knew that if I could be that nervous and par those five holes, then maybe I could keep that up the next two days.

I was six under, and Watson, I played with him on Saturday, and I believe I had a two-shot lead after two rounds. So he must have been four under . . . I can't remember if anybody else was four under, but Payne Stewart and Nick Price were in the group in front of us, and I do remember Paul Azinger was up there too.

At that time I never looked at it as though they were chasing me. I think I was more concerned with, you know, this is the U.S. Open, I'm a relative unknown, the world is gonna look to see whether I can do it or not. I really feel like I had nothing to lose.

But the one thing that drove me was the fear—you know, so often you see a Cinderella story at the top of the U.S. Open, and then they fall apart at the end. So that fear of doing that, remembering what Gil Morgan did the year before in the U.S. Open in Pebble Beach, because I think he got to ten under and shot, what, twelve over or fifteen over on the weekend. I think, what, three under won [the tournament]? [*Editor's note:* See Tom Kite interview.] You'd have to look that up. I think he was ten, he got to ten, maybe even eleven under, and three under won. So it was really his tournament to win, and he just let it slip away.

That was on my mind, that even though I got ahead, I could not let up for even one second.

I was really fired up [the next day] starting out, and I birdied the first two holes. I had a four-shot lead at that point. I kept reminding myself that no matter how far ahead I was, I could not let up. And sure enough, I three-putted like the fifth hole. I might have even bogied another hole before that—I made a silly bogey because I hit about a twenty-footer uphill and gunned it by the hole, and then missed it coming back. It was just a good reminder that I had to play each shot smartly and not be a hero.

And so I just played pretty well the rest of the day and finished with a one under par and kept my lead. I was up by one at that point, after three rounds, and I was paired with Payne Stewart the last round.

Like I said, that was about the most nervous I'd been on Friday afternoon with the lead. That's about how I felt teeing off on the first hole. It was a long morning anticipating teeing off, I think we teed off well after two, and I tried to stay up late enough to sleep in to take care of some of the morning, but I woke up fairly early, at like seven-thirty. So I had about seven hours to burn before I teed off. You get pretty bored sitting around the house.

I went to the course and putted a little while, hung out in the locker room, and just kind of walked around and ate some lunch. When I finally went to the range forty-five minutes before I teed up, Payne was already walking off the range, and I could see that he was walking swiftly. So I knew he was all pumped up, too, and you know, his nerves were there.

And so he was already leaving the range that early, so I knew that he was eager to get out there too, and if he's too eager, if he's already leaving the range and there's forty-five minutes to go—most guys don't ever leave the range that early. So actually, that was comfort, that he was feeling like I was feeling.

The first hole I hit a good drive—the wind had switched a little bit, that hole had been playing downwind, and there really wasn't much wind, and it was very hot. It was a little bit cooler that day, maybe it was in the low nineties instead of the hundreds, and it had rained the night before a little bit, so it softened the course a hair. I hit a good drive down the first fairway, I had a four-wood to the green, because it was playing long. Hit that into the bunker on the front right and got up and down.

That may have been the best thing that happened all day, too, to be able to par that first hole, especially to be able to get up and down out of the bunker.

I did manage to bogey the next hole—I had a very easy chip shot from just in front of the green, and just didn't hit a good chip shot, and missed the putt. But I came back with a birdie on the third hole, which was what I'd been doing all week. Every time I bogied a hole I seemed to come back with a birdie.

Neither of us really did much [after that]. He did not do anything to really get the crowd to yell or scream loud at all in his favor, we were pretty much playing the same. I think he bogied one, he may have parred one, I can't really remember for sure now, but he hit a drive under three on seven. I hit in the bunker—I ended up making a good putt for a bogey, and I think he made a bogey, too. And we both parred eight.

And then he made a long par off the fringe on nine, and I made a good par-saving putt—I think I was still one up at that point. And we parred the next couple of holes, and then at twelve I missed a short putt for par, and we were tied then. So I think he was just safely making a bunch of pars.

And then we got to thirteen, we both parred, and then fourteen, he was in the south bunker, hit a good bunker shot, I think he almost holed it. And I had about an eighteen-footer from behind the hole, and I was thinking, I'd hit some practice putts to that pin earlier in the week, so I was very confident, I knew exactly the line. I rolled it in.

Nothing had happened up until then, so I was feeling . . . the whole week was starting to get to me, as far as fatigue. And I really felt like I got a shot of adrenaline when that putt went in, for the last few holes—and I needed it.

I hit a good drive and a good second shot the next hole—it was a tough pin, so it was hard to birdie. We both parred. On sixteen, I hit first and hit a five-iron, I hit it really good, if it had carried about two or three more steps, it would have hopped up onto the green. I had a fairly close birdie putt, it kicked a little left, it was in the rough just short of the green. And he hit it on the back of the green after I did.

And then I had a great lie—and he was actually away, but I ended up going first, just out of courtesy, a lot of times players go first when they're off the green, and I chipped in. And if I could go back and change anything I'd like to let him putt and then I chipped it in and still made it, 'cause that would have been the proper thing to do.

The seventeenth, for the most part, I was just playing for par, just to make sure I didn't give him any shots. I hit it below the green on seventeen, probably twenty-five feet, and rolled it up for an easy par. He had a tough putt from above the hole that he nearly made, and on eighteen he bombed his drive after I hit in the right rough. There was trouble left, so there was no way I was going left. He bombed his drive, so I laid up after thinking about trying to knock it over the water, then thought better of it. I chipped out, had a four-iron to the green.

And he hit—I don't know if he caught it clean or not, but he hit an iron that looked like it was gonna roll onto the green, which would have given him an eagle putt, which means I'd have had to birdie to win. He ended up in the bunker, I hit a four-wood onto the green about eighteen feet from the hole, so he had to hole his bunker shot and I had to miss my putt.

He hit it out to about six feet, and he putted first, and all I had to do was two-putt. And the way I was probably feeling then, I didn't know if I was actually going to be able to two-putt from eight feet, because I was so . . . I realized what was about to happen.

Well, when he won the U.S. Open in '91, he was behind Scott Simpson until late in the round. And you know, Scott made a mistake on sixteen, I think he made a double-bogey, and Payne also made a long putt—he made a charge at the end. So I was thinking the whole time that he was gonna draw on that experience, he was the one trying to chase me, so he wasn't the one playing protecting. He was gonna be aggressive, so I was ready for him to make birdies and play well.

So I knew that I had to keep going. I knew I couldn't give anything back, and I was the one . . . I ended up making birdies at the end.

I hit my putt, and it went in, so it was somewhat of a relief, but it was just really utter amazement that I'd won the tournament . . . only my fourth year on tour, my third win, I was just getting used to what it took to win a tournament on the tour. I don't think I really quite understood—you know, I knew it was the U.S. Open, and it was my dream to win the U.S. Open, but I don't really think I knew how big the U.S. Open was in everybody else's eyes.

Just the attention I'd got afterward—you know, I'd won two tournaments up till then, and I was pretty proud of that. But I didn't get any attention in comparison to what I was about to get for the U.S. Open. And that was the big difference—I mean, I still have people coming up to me, even in 1998, five years later, congratulating me on the U.S. Open in Baltusrol, saying, you know, I was there, or, I saw you on TV. It seemed like everybody in the world watched, where the audience for the regular tour is much smaller.

I had a hard time containing myself, because my wife was the first person I saw—I saw her in the scoring trailer. I saw my roommate from college, his dad was on the USGA committee, I saw him coming off eighteen, there were tears in his eyes. Then I saw Rocco, who was on my college golf team, Rocco Mediate, there were tears in his eyes. We hugged, it was just amazing.

And then I signed my card, and I was just really trying to hold myself together, because I knew I was actually gonna have to go out and speak now. And then my wife came in, and she just lost it, and so I did, too.

And then we were on the eighteenth green, you know, I

didn't know what any of that stuff was gonna be like, with all the people still out there on the eighteenth. And all the photography, and then the press conference afterwards, how long I'd be in there.

And then the club sets aside a room for the winner and fully stocks it, and I had some friends who qualified for the tournament, Pete Jordan was one of 'em, and he stayed afterwards. So we went in this room, and I had some friends who flew in for the last round, too, so I had quite a few people there.

We had a great time there, and when it came time to leave, we went to the hotel and spent the night there. I was supposed to go to Cleveland and play in a pro/am there the next day, but I just delayed it until the next day. And Chris Berman joined us—we had about fifteen people, so it was a good celebration.

That was a lot of fun—those two [tournaments] were comparable, it was just how much fun I had after the tournament. Because, you know, the last couple holes are somewhat nerve-wracking . . . it's hard to say they're exciting.

I would say it took . . . for the first one, I don't know if it put more pressure to win on me or not. But after winning three times in '95, I really felt the pressure was off, that I didn't *have* to win, that I just wanted to win. And I didn't have to win anymore to prove that I could win. I just think the U.S. Open, the first time, put me on the scene. I really wasn't on the scene yet, and I got looked at more, I felt, somewhat, the pressure, and then to come through and win tournaments after that . . . I really felt like the pressure was off.

And then the last three years I've been on tour is probably the most relaxed I've ever been on the course. I used to get pretty much nervous every round.

My wife and I were just talking about [playing against Payne]. Before his accident, he and I were gonna be linked together through golf history, forever, because of our two duels. You know, I played golf with him in a number of other tournaments, too, that I played extremely well in, and he also had some good rounds, too. So it wasn't just those two tournaments that are gonna be remembered.

It's gonna be a big void, knowing how often I got paired with him, and how I performed and how he performed. I'm gonna really miss that.

The U.S. Open in Baltusrol was the first time we played together—I saw what a competitor he was, that it doesn't matter what kind of shot he hit before, the next one, the next one is the only one that mattered. And he just got after it.

He happened to be one of my favorite players when I was in college, so I'd already known what he could do before I played with him, because I'd watched him so many times. And then we became friends after the first one, you know, playing on the Ryder Cup team together. I played with him the last round of the Players Championship, we seemed to get paired together quite a bit. And then, of course, living in the same town, occasionally we'd get together.

And the other thing, too, the first thing I realized at Baltusrol when he came up to me after I'd won . . . his graciousness, and he was so genuine, that I had won, and he was really happy for me. And I think that was probably because he knew what it felt like to win the U.S. Open, and how great it was.

He knew, just as well as I did, that they give the trophy to the guy who has the lowest score after seventy-two holes, and that's what it takes. And I've played on the tour ten years, I've played over 250 tournaments, and I've only won eight. So that's not a lot. My conversion rate is not great, but that's the way it is on tour. You don't win much, but when you do win, it's an accomplishment.

So we've all had our tournaments that we could have won, should have won—majors just seem to be the ones that are more heartbreaking when you don't win. I was just fortunate to do the right thing those two times.

I've seen the excitement on [the faces] of young players that are in their first five, six years on tour. And they seem to have that new excitement. That's the most important thing you've gotta carry through your whole career on the tour. It's so easy for guys that have been out there for like seven to fifteen, eighteen years . . . they just go through the motions. You know, sure, when they have a great week they know what to do, but for some other weeks they could maybe kick it into gear if they were in their third year on tour and not their twelfth year on tour.

I think part of it's scheduling. I played a lot more my first years on tour, but I think that was because it was new to me, and I loved playing all those weeks, and I didn't care if I played thirty weeks or thirty-two, I just wanted to play. I'm learning now that I can't schedule like that, I've gotta play fewer than that, and try to get breaks in between so I get my mind on the next tournament. You know, when you play five in a row, when you're playing that first one, you don't have your mind on the third one or the fourth one or the fifth one. Sometimes I've noticed that by the fifth one I'm flat.

TOM KITE

When Gil Morgan ran away from the field in the first round of the 1992 U.S. Open, the rest of the weekend looked like a wash for the competition. But the golf gods had other ideas when it came to the weather that weekend at Pebble Beach: when the wind began wreaking havoc with the golf scores, Morgan's day at the beach suddenly became a horse race between several fine players. The best of the best that day was Tom Kite, who persevered to earn a hard-fought victory that became his greatest day.

I guess it would be the last round of the U.S. Open, 1992, Pebble Beach.

I had been playing very, very well. I had already won once earlier in the year at Atlanta and was very, very pleased with the way my game had progressed and what I was doing. Obviously, playing Pebble Beach was pretty exciting, because I love that golf course so much. I had won out there before and had the course record—and have the course record.

And so I went to one of my favorite golf courses playing some of the best golf that I've ever played, and I felt very good about everything.

Pebble is a pretty easy track to prepare for when you're playing a major championship out there because we've played it so many times during the old Bing Crosby and during the AT&T tournaments. So it's not quite like some of those other golf courses that we haven't seen for ten or fifteen years, if at all it—Pebble is a very easy golf course to prepare for when they have an Open there.

So the practice rounds were very relaxed and easygoing. As far as I was concerned, there wasn't nearly the urgency to learn an awful lot in a very short time frame, because I knew those greens, and I knew the distances, and I had played it under different conditions, so the comfort level was quite high.

The concerns that I had during the week were basically maintaining what I had going. I had been playing, as I said, quite well leading up to the tournament—just trying to maintain that. And then, of course, there's always the concern as to what is the USGA gonna do to the golf course, are they gonna change it dramatically from the practice rounds on Tuesday and Wednesday until the second and third and fourth round of the tournament, because they have the ability coming in there with total control to be able to keep the greens rock hard and dry the golf course out and get them very, very fast.

Of course, out there you always know that there's a chance the weather's gonna change and make it even more difficult. I had played very well, but Gil Morgan had played unbelievably well. I was hanging around par, one or two under, as a matter of fact, throughout the entire week. I never had any nine holes that were. . . . I had right at par on every one of those nine holes. I went three under par for the entire tournament—let me see, I think it was three 35s, and the rest 36s, so I played very consistently.

But Gil was seemingly running away with the golf tournament, he was playing so well. He got it to twelve under par at one time, and it became apparent that for anybody to win the golf tournament under Gil, he was gonna have to do something to kind of help them out. And certainly what he got started on Saturday and then followed up with on Sunday was not to be expected, because he's such a good, solid player, but you know, he started backing up a little bit on Saturday, and then the weather conditions made everybody back up on Sunday—or just about everybody.

Well, because you don't really have any control over anybody like that, the concerns are not great. It's almost like you're a spectator watching, because you really can't control what the other guy's doing. The main thing is to keep playing as well as possible. And of course, seeing somebody shoot that low gives you a feeling of confidence that maybe you can start making some birdies, as he was, and get it well under par.

The golf course, throughout the first part of the week, was fantastic. Everybody, even those players that later criticized the USGA pretty harshly, were raving about the golf course early in the week. Raymond [Floyd] was one that just blitzed the USGA after the final round, but you look at his quotes early in the week, and he was saying it was the best set-up U.S. Open he had ever seen: the golf course was fair but difficult, the rough was high, the greens were firm but not out of control. And so early on in the week you were left with a situation where the golf course was very well accepted by all the players.

Unfortunately, what that usually means is that somebody's gonna shoot a low score. When the players universally accept it as much as they did at Pebble Beach, there's always the possibility that somebody's gonna go very low, and Gil was doing that. Not related to the weather, he started backing up on Saturday, as happens a lot of times in the U.S. Open, and of course then Sunday, because the scores had been so low on Thursday, Friday, and Saturday, the USGA was pushing the golf course to the limit. They were taking it right to the edge of the envelope and trying to make it as difficult as possible.

And then, of course, the weather conditions changed dramatically, and to be honest, they were caught with their pants down. They ended up looking very foolish in their golf course setup, and you know, part of it is because they were pushing it as much as they could, and part of it's because of the change in the weather. They weren't watering the greens, and all of a sudden when you start getting those greens that are that small and you start getting 'em that firm with the wind blowing the way it was, it just made it almost impossible for anybody to get the ball on the green, much less close to the pin.

And so it became a scrambling nightmare for everybody—everybody was missing fairways, everybody was missing greens, and getting it up and down was very difficult for everybody.

Well, I was kind of like everybody was—when Gil started backing up, he let a lot of people back into the tournament. So everybody's interest level perked up significantly after he started backing up a little bit on Saturday. And all those guys that were in the hunt really got excited about what was going on.

Then he started off Sunday morning, and you know, the conditions were not too difficult early on in the day, and so when you were warming up, there was really no anticipation as to how difficult the day was gonna become. And of course, you hadn't been out on the golf course at the time, so you didn't know how dried out the greens were, and certainly how dried out they would become as the day went on.

So it was just anticipation of, well, I've got myself in the hunt, now let's go out and really shoot a good score. Little did we realize that a good score was gonna be three or four or five over par.

I wasn't playing with Gil, so I really don't know too much about his round. I ended up getting paired with Mark Brooks, and so I really can't comment too much on Gil. But it became very apparent very quickly that the golf course was gonna be brutal. Certainly by the time we teed off the conditions were significant, in that they were causing everybody headache, and you could look at the leader board and see that there were very few good scores being posted.

As we started off, I ended up starting off very quickly, I made about an eighteen- or twenty-foot putt on the first hole for a birdie, and I said, oh boy, this is gonna be. . . .

And then I almost made birdie at two, I hit it just off the green, and almost got it up and down, and didn't hit a great chip shot, almost made the putt. And then three, I hit it in probably about ten feet above the hole. The thing that happened on three is that I was playing with Mark Brooks, he had parred one and birdied number two, and he hit it about fifteen feet from the hole at number three.

And he proceeded to four-putt from fifteen feet, he had a downwind, downhill putt that really didn't look like he hit it too hard, and all of a sudden he was playing pinball wizard all over the green. From fifteen feet he turned what looked like a possible birdie, sure par, into a double-bogey. And I was fortunate enough to two-putt there, and I came off that green just shaking my head.

Fourth hole, I caught a flyer on my second shot out of the center rough and put it in the back bunker. I had an impossible bunker shot, knocked it all the way down to the front of the green. The pin was toward the back, and three-putted from there, so I made double-bogey.

And I walked off that green and saw my wife and some good friends standing there, and told them, golly, the USGA has really done it to us today—because at that point that early in the round, of course we had late tee times, but the greens were already down to nothing. I mean, we were basically putting on roots. You look at all the old photographs from that day, and the greens are not green, they are brown, and really very, very difficult.

Fortunately, from that point on, I played a wonderful round of golf, a good, controlled round of golf, and made putts, and really controlled myself well, emotionally and mentally, throughout the round, and was able to do some pretty neat things.

Well, it's one of those days that you just have to dig deep into your memory bank and kind of . . . it's a lot of guesswork in determining what clubs you're gonna hit. You know, lay up on the eighth hole to the ditch, which is 280 yards, it's a normal layup with a three-wood or something like that, make sure you don't go over the ditch, and I laid up with a four-iron. And then probably hit a 200-yard eight-iron on my second shot there.

The hole before, number seven, which is about 115 yards, I hit a six-iron . . . just trying to punch it down, keep it down out of the wind. So there were no normal shots, the conditions didn't allow you to play any normal shots, everything was some sort of manufactured shot that was requiring a tremendous amount of guesswork to choose the right club. And even if you guessed right, you had to get a little bit lucky.

It was: What can we do to survive? Where can we put it where we've got the best chance? And you know, obviously in a situation like that, chipping and putting becomes paramount.

Well, things really started happening. I kind of hung in there in pretty good shape through the front nine, and then things started happening on the back nine. I made a good save on ten, and almost made birdie at eleven. Then twelve was playing incredibly difficult with a strong, strong left-to-right wind. And the green, as you know, is very shallow from front to back, and I hit a shot in there, probably thirty feet right of the pin.

And when I hit it on the green, the gallery went absolutely crazy, I mean, it was a much louder yell than you would ever anticipate for a shot that ended up thirty feet right of the pin. It was just an indication that nobody hit, or very few people had hit, that green in regulation prior to that time.

And then I made that thirty-footer coming across the green— it's an interesting putt. I've made a lot of long putts on that twelfth green through the years, and I had a good feeling on that one. For some reason it's a green that I read very, very well, and it's a green that I have a lot of confidence on.

So I made that putt, and that gave me a little bit of a cushion to play with. You know, a good solid par on thirteen, no problems, and then fourteen, I knocked it right up in front of the green in two, just short of the bunker on the left, and was able to play a flop shot with my sixty-degree wedge up there to about three feet. And when I made that for birdie, I had a nice little cushion just to hang in there.

Of course, you know, trying to protect a lead playing those last few holes was not exactly something you want to do. Those are not the easiest holes. But I had a good, relatively easy, par at fifteen, you know, in front of the green in two putts. Then on sixteen I drove it just in the right rough and hit a good shot, but it ran through the green, and I was not able to get that up and down, so . . . bogey. And all of a sudden, I had a lead, it was three shots at that time, but certainly nothing that couldn't be thrown away on those last couple of holes, as hard as the wind was blowing.

Seventeen: I knew that from that championship tee, with the wind blowing the way it was, that I needed a driver to get to the green. But it's just kind of one of those things, you know, you just won't allow yourself to pull out a driver on that shot. And you're hoping beyond hope that somehow a three-wood's gonna be enough club. You know you've just got to hit it perfect, but it's just hard to imagine, with the distance that we had, that you would have to hit a driver to reach the green. And of course, what happens if you catch a little lull in the wind, you know, you hit a driver over the green, and . . .

So I ended up pulling out a three-wood, which was a little bit of a bail-out, I guess, and put it in the front bunker. And I was actually not too dissatisfied with that at all, because I felt like, well, the worst-case scenario was, I'm gonna make a four and probably will make three the way I'm getting everything up and down.

And I got up there, and all of the sudden I've got a bunker shot where I'm having to stand out of the bunker, and the ball is down below my feet, and I'm playing into this thirty-five- or forty-mile-an-hour wind. And I've got a lot of sand to go over, not much green to make it stop, and certainly if I played the shot I knock it over on the eighteenth tee, or the ocean, or whatever. You know, a lot of negative thoughts can creep into your mind if you allow them.

So I made up my mind what I wanted to do and went in there and did it relatively quickly, just to make sure I didn't hesitate. Knocked it up there, you know, about eight feet, I missed the putt, but at least I avoided disaster by making a bogey there.

Hit a good drive on eighteen. Decided to go ahead and hit a driver off that tee as opposed to playing safe off the tee shot, because I felt like that would give me an easier second and an easier third into the green. And at that time I had a two-shot lead, all I needed to do was dodge disaster. And so I hit a good drive there right down the middle of the fairway, and it rolled down over to the right side of the fairway, stayed in the fairway, just close to the right edge, but left of the trees.

Under different circumstances I probably could have knocked it on the eighteenth green in two, I hit it so far there, but certainly with that lead I didn't need to. And I played a little six-iron up the fairway to lay up, sand wedge on the green, two putts, and that was it.

Well, when we made the turn, the last leader board that I saw was at eight green/nine tee. And at that time my caddy and I commented that it looked like over par might win the golf tournament, or certainly even par might win. And then there weren't any scoreboards while I was playing nine, ten, eleven, and twelve. And all of a sudden I walked up on the twelfth green and saw that [Colin] Montgomerie had gotten in. Now let me see—he had gotten in at even par, [Jeff] Sluman was one under, and I was three under.

And we kind of joked as we walked on the green, well, even par is not gonna win the golf tournament, or over par is not gonna win it, obviously—the even is already there. And everybody else was backing up like crazy. So once I got to that point, Montgomerie was the guy that I was concerned with, mainly because he was already in the house, he had already posted a score. Granted, it was very, very early, but he had already posted a score, so you had to be concerned with him. And of course, Jeff Sluman was playing very, very well at the time and ended up finishing second also.

The last putt was a kick-in—all I had was about a fifteen–eighteen footer coming down the hill on eighteen. And I knew that all I had to do was just not have a heart attack and I was gonna win the tournament. So after I got the third shot on the green, I knew that the tournament was mine, there was no way I was gonna lose the tournament from that point on.

So really, the excitement and the show of emotion that I felt was out there on the eighteenth fairway after I knocked that ball on the green. I knew I had it won at that point. From that point on, for the next hour, it was just an incredible rush and an incredible high—you know, standing out there, on the eighteenth green there at Pebble Beach, receiving the trophy. And having some fans up there in the stands that were from Texas, singing "The Eyes of Texas," was pretty cool.

You know, being given the trophy, and all week long I'd kind of had a little running commentary with Chris Berman, because on Tuesday or Wednesday of that week Chris had informed me that I was his pick, that he thought I would win the golf tournament. So Boomer was pretty pumped up at that time, and that interview with him was pretty special, and a lot of fun, because we were both kind of yukking it up a little bit. And that was pretty neat.

Well, my family was out there, so we had a wonderful evening that night . . . and golly, I don't even really remember having dinner. I know there were a couple of cocktail parties that we went to, and one that the USGA had, and one that Del Monte Properties had.

And we went by those with the trophy, and that was pretty neat, and ran into the superintendent at Pebble Beach when we went to the USGA function. And he said, is there anything I can get for you, and I said, oh, yeah, I'd really like to get the flag from the seventh hole where I chipped in. So while we were there at the cocktail party, he got in his truck and ran off and got that flag for me off of the green. It was still out there flapping in the breeze on the seventh green.

So that was pretty special . . . got it hanging on the wall here right behind me. So you know, they sell a lot of the eighteenth flags, but I've got the one that really counts in my book, the one that I chipped in on.

Other than being able to get the media off my back a little bit for not having won a major championship, it really didn't change my life that much. As a matter of fact, I really made a conscious effort to not let it change it. Well, I was pleased with the way my life was, I was very happy with my relationship with my family, and with my lifestyle, so I really was not looking for a change, and not wanting a change.

You know, I made a real conscious effort to—you know, I knew that a lot of guys had had letdowns after winning the U.S. Open, and I made a real conscious effort and spoke about it with my teacher, Chuck Cook, and also Bob Rotello, the sports psychologist, about how we addressed this issue of not letting there be a letdown. You know, we want to make the rest of '92 and '93 and on be really good years—which they were. And so we really worked hard to keep pushing, to not get lackadaisical and lazy. We really tried to keep doing the same things that we had been doing before.

There were just a number of opportunities where you just sit there and say, okay, there's a lot of money, but . . . do I really want to do this? And if I do this, am I gonna be able to start off the next year in a good frame of mind, ready and relaxed and refreshed? And you know, I came out strong the first part of '93 and won the Bob Hope, and we shot 35 under, and we won the L.A. Open two weeks later, doing some really nice things.

So I felt like, certainly, with twenty-twenty hindsight, that was definitely the right call, to not chase down the almighty buck and just continue to . . . now, that doesn't mean I didn't do things, but I just felt the reins a little bit.

Obviously you don't win a tournament there without getting a big boost in the confidence, that was huge. So that helped an awful lot, and you know, I felt like I could go from that point on and win in any tournament that I was playing in.

I had proven myself as a pretty good player, but all of a sudden it was kind of like, well, once I get in this position I know I can win now, because I've done it. I've won a U.S. Open, I've done a lot of things. So I always felt like I could win tournaments, but now it was just a little bit more confidence, a little bit more of a cocky feeling when I was coming down the last few holes. When I got there, I felt like, why should I be worried about what's going on, I know I can handle this.

I guess to a certain extent I'm surprised and a little bit disappointed that I wasn't able to win major championships before the '92 U.S. Open. I certainly had some opportunities, and on some of those I failed miserably, and on others some players really came out and did some great things. So for whatever reason, I was not able to follow that up with some major championship wins.

Again, I was determined that I was gonna continue to play well after winning the Open, which I did. Unfortunately, though, in March of '93 I started developing some back problems, and that limited me a little bit.

So I wasn't able to build upon that in terms of major championships, I almost had to withdraw from . . . well, I should have withdrawn from the Masters in '93. I played that tournament without ever hitting a practice round, just kind of spending my time in the fitness trailer, trying to get treatment the whole week of the Masters. And I did not do well at the Players' Championship, didn't have a great run at Baltusrol as defending champion because of that, and I lost a little bit of confidence there.

So I guess I'm a little bit disappointed that I wasn't able to follow up major championships with other major championships.

But you know, I've got the one, and I guess if you can only win one major championship, it would be the U.S. Open. And if you had to pick a golf course to win it, Pebble Beach is not a bad place to have it. So I'm still pleased with that.

I've been very blessed in that I've had a lot of good things: being named captain of the Ryder Cup team, winning the Bobby Jones Award, you know, all my wins, playing seven Ryder Cup matches, Vardon trophies, and things like that. Those are nice to have and really good things. But that's my only major championship, so I've gotta go with that.

TOM LEHMAN

In 1996, Tom Lehman had a career year, winning the British Open and the Tour Championship and leading the money list at almost $2 million while taking the Player of the Year Award. But as with his teammate, Hal Sutton, Lehman's greatest day was defined by his 1999 Ryder Cup experience—in the U.S. victory that was one of the greatest comebacks of the sports century.

That's a no-brainer for me—it was the Ryder Cup this year on Sunday.

I guess, you know, I felt like we were definitely favorites, although I think we all felt that the European team was a lot better than they were given credit for. And the first few days of play we were just getting killed, and basically they were making every putt they had to, and we were missing them all. But on Sunday night, I think we all felt like we were still gonna win.

And on Sunday it was just one of those days that I'll never forget—the crowd was so incredibly juiced, our play was outstanding, and things just started steamrolling. First match out we won, second match out we won, before you know it we had won six matches, and the crowd was just going bananas. The excitement, the electricity, it was a beautiful day, there wasn't a cloud in the sky, I don't think . . . everything was just perfect.

I played one match the first day. I played with Tiger Woods, and we got beat, and we really didn't play that great. We didn't play poorly, we just didn't make any putts. The second day I sat out in the afternoon, and then the next day I played with Phil Mickelson in the afternoon. And we played very well, we beat [Lee] Westwood and [Darren] Clarke. We beat 'em two and one, and we really should have beat 'em worse—we both played very well that day.

The team, though, was struggling—I don't know, it was just one of those things where the harder you try, the worse you do. And Sunday night we had a great . . . we had team dinners every night there together, we just kind of had a great time hanging out. We watched a couple of videos, everybody had a few things they wanted to say, it was a real bonding experience. I thought the team was close before then, but after Sunday night it was just like brothers.

And you know, on Sunday everybody was just pulling for each other—we all expected to win. I think to a person we all expected to go out and beat 'em. Even though it was immensely exciting and thrilling, I wasn't surprised.

I really was struggling with my short game coming into the tournament—which, you know, in a Ryder Cup is not where you want to be, you want to be putting great. And you know, the first match with Tiger, I hit off his shot, and I drove it just like a champ. I drove it in every fairway, but I just could not get a putt to drop. And the good putts that didn't go in and the bad putts that didn't go in, I didn't make anything, and we lost.

So then I played with Phil on the next match, and again, I hit the ball just fantastic. I made a couple of putts, then I missed a couple, I think I missed about a . . . I'd say no more than a four-footer on the thirteenth hole that would have put us, I think, four up with five to play. Basically, the match would have been over, but I missed it, and we lost the hole. Before you know it, we were going down to seventeen, and they had a chance to even win that hole. So I was hitting it A-plus, but my putting was F-minus. I spent the whole week trying to get it figured out.

And then the next day, the singles, I played a really, really good round. You know, first match out I was taking a lot of heat, knowing we couldn't afford to lose anything, especially the first one. But I hit . . . I mean, I hit every green, and I think I missed one fairway, and that was by about five inches in the first cut of rough, and I shot, I think, four under. I made some good putts and really didn't miss too many, but that match was really a textbook round of golf.

I just hit it in the fairway, and I hit on the green anywhere from five feet to twenty feet, and actually missed a couple of putts. I missed about a four-footer for a birdie on nine, I missed a six-footer for birdie on fourteen, you know, I was leading at the time by two going into nine, I think I was four up going into fourteen, and those putts really could have stuck the nail in the coffin, but as it was I went three and two.

But there really wasn't any one putt or one shot that turned the tide, it was just really steady play—I never gave 'em a chance to get back in the match.

As the day went on [the crowd] got more excited. I started walking down the eighteenth hole, and some big guy yelled out, Tom, you're a corker. And I said to Kenny, what the heck is a corker? I think it's a compliment, but I don't know for certain, even today. I think it's an Irish term.

It was the first match out, and down four points . . . I was out first, and Hal Sutton was up second, and they had three guys that hadn't played at all the whole week, their third, fourth, and fifth. And you know, we all felt very confident that the guys who were playing them were gonna take care of 'em pretty easily, which they did.

And so we kind of all felt that the first two matches were

critical, and being the first guy out, I felt like my match was essential. We couldn't afford to lose the first match. And you know, playing against Lee Westwood, who was ranked fourth in the world, it was a big job.

I was very nervous. I remember I got on the first tee, and the European fans were chanting this European song they always sing, this *Olé, Olé, Olé, Olé* song that drives everybody crazy. So the Americans decided they were gonna counter that by singing "The Star-Spangled Banner," and they started singing that to try and drown out the Europeans, so it was kind of like leading the choir—first you'd hear "The Star-Spangled Banner," it was kind of like I was conductor. Which . . . I was talking later to Mark James, it was one thing that really ticked him off. And I told him, sorry, live with it.

I looked down the [Sunday] matches, and I just didn't see one match where the Europeans were favored. And you know, even though on paper maybe they should have been—you know, like I was underdog to Lee Westwood. Certainly I think that Hal Sutton wouldn't lose to Darren Clarke—those guys are both very good players, I just think that we were every bit as good.

Even the matches that they were supposed to favor—[Jim] Furyk versus Sergio [Garcia]—you know, I liked Furyk, because he's proven he's tough. And to overlook him is a big mistake. And you know, Monty [Colin Montgomerie] against Payne. Payne was really jacked up to play Monty, I liked that match a lot, too. So I really didn't see any weak links in our lineup.

So I really felt like, you know, somebody's gonna lose, there's no way to get around that, so it's up to me to make sure I do my part. I was nervous the whole day, I had butterflies, but it was also one of those very determined, focused days. I mean, every shot I was right there with it.

So I got off to a start when I birdied four, five, and six to go one up, then two up. And I looked behind me, and sure enough, Hal goes one up, David had gone up two, Phil's up three, and Duval starts going crazy, up one, up two, four up, five up—he was six up at one time. It was like a feeding frenzy, and I think everybody who was playing kind of fed off that.

After I was done, my wife, Melissa, and I, we just decided we were gonna go find the other players and cheer 'em on. And a lot of the matches were nearly finished—by the time I finished, I was the first match out, but I wasn't the first match finished. I think Davis Love [III] beat somebody six to five or five to four. He finished first. So when I finished, there were basically six matches that were done or nearly done.

So we kind of went backwards, and we found a couple of guys. We watched a little bit of [Mark] O'Meara's match, and then we started just kind of following Justin Leonard. He was four down, and we decided to stick with him, so we kind of walked alongside of the fairway watching him, and then dropping back to watch Payne. So we kind of went back and forth between Justin and Payne, and then jumped ahead to O'Meara when he was going to the seventeenth and eighteenth holes.

It became obvious at that point that all we needed was one match. Furyk was smoking Sergio, so one of those guys, either O'Meara or Justin or Payne, had to win their match. So we kind of bounced between those three, and when O'Meara lost on eighteen, we ran back to catch up with Justin and came down seventeen, and obviously we all know what happened there. The whole team was kind of in that same mode, it was, okay, we've gotta get one of these guys. So there were guys following Mark, there were guys following Justin, there were guys back with Payne.

That's the thing about the Ryder Cup that was so great, because when do you ever see other players out there cheering for you?

I'm not really sure if Justin would remember, Davis was walking with me the whole way. I just remember telling him at some time, remember, you're the British Open champion—we all know you can do it, or something to that effect. And just giving him a smack on the butt, to let him know that we had faith in him.

He was pretty focused at that time. Actually we kind of caught him on the twelfth hole. They were putting for par there, and he won the hole to go three down. And then he won the next hole and birdied the next, and then we kind of followed him when he made that bomb on fifteen to tie the match. The crowd just went berserk. So that was . . . all the guys were walking along, though, just really together, the wives, the co-captains and their wives. It was just a real . . . everybody really pulled together.

Well, I think that Payne . . . conceding the match to Montgomerie was really very sportsmanlike, and the right thing to do. It was crazy, there was bedlam on the eighteenth green and the last match there. The Cup was already won, and you know, it was just crazy, and I think what Payne did by not making everybody putt, just conceding and shaking hands—it was perfect, a fitting finish to the tournament.

You know, but the celebration afterward was special. It wasn't just the players . . . the crowd didn't want to leave, I mean, the crowd, they hung out there by the eighteenth green and the clubhouse like for hours, screaming and yelling and waving flags. Everybody was spraying champagne, and you know, it was just great. There was unbridled enthusiasm.

When we all got together in our team room there at the golf course before the closing ceremonies, it was more just a lot of back-slapping, high-fiving, hugging, and just feeling good together. There was so many in there, you know, I don't know who all the people were and where they came from, but it was a typical aftermath of a big tournament or a big championship.

And you know, just the closing ceremonies, and this, that, and the other thing, and we finally got home to the hotel, and then we had a team party that night. And we were up until two or three in the morning at least, and that was just fun. Everybody was in a great mood, and dancing, and having something to eat, and hanging out, and enjoying each other's company. Just kind of basking in the glow of realizing we'd accomplished something that was incredible.

We left the next morning, and we came home, and I think, really, it was probably that, everywhere I went when I got back to Scottsdale here, to the supermarket or the gas station or the mall, people were just stopping me and my wife and shaking our hands and saying, hey, you made us proud to be an American. And it wasn't like after a win with congratulations, it was, you made us proud to be an American. No one's ever said that to me before because of a golf tournament.

These people, it made them proud to be part of the Stars and Stripes, and it made them proud to know that Americans had, you know, what I consider to be a fighting spirit. That's a special compliment . . . I really appreciated that.

The earlier Ryder Cups, we were big favorites and we lost. And it just seemed like there was a lot of urgency to win this one, we couldn't really . . . even though we were getting beat so badly, there was never really any here-we-go-again-type feeling. It was like, okay, we're down, you know, but we can still win. And I think if we would have lost, it would have been a really deep blow. Especially to me, I definitely wanted to be part of a winning team.

And to win it in that fashion, the biggest comeback in history, by far, you know, it adds something that I'll never, ever, ever, ever forget. I'll always be able to tell people, yeah, I was a part of that team. I think that's the lasting thing, in terms of the impact on me, is knowing that I was part of a group of fellow people, great players, great people, who pulled together and had one of the great head-to-head . . . the greatest comeback in golf probably—at least in team golf.

I guess in the rearview mirror, obviously I guess it was something [the celebration] on the seventeenth hole. I mean, because of the emotion of the day, it was almost unavoidable. But I wish it wouldn't have happened, I wish we could have a do-over, take a mulligan, and not allow that to happen, that we wouldn't have gotten in José Maria's [Olazabal] way.

You know, but then, also in the rearview mirror, I take . . . I timed it on the video, from the time that Justin made his putt until the time the green was clear again—it took forty-five seconds. Which is forty-five seconds too much, but still, it wasn't like it was ten minutes. [Padraig] Harrington had taken almost ten minutes to hit his second shot on seventeenth against O'Meara—he walked up to the green, then back to his ball, and dilly-dallied, and by the time he hit it it was nearly ten minutes.

So my thinking is that rather than both sides throwing arrows at each other, why don't we get together and figure out what would be best for golf. And toning down the celebration probably is a good thing, and speeding up play is another good thing.

I think that [the financial controversy before the tournament] was way blown out of proportion. The press got a hold of something—the press basically stoked that fire, so they have their share of blame in that. But the end result is that PGA America did a great thing, they gave each player $200,000 to give to charities that they chose to give them to. And I think that's what most of the guys wanted, they said, look, there's a lot of money that's being donated to charity, but it's not our charities, it's not something that's close to our hearts. All we'd like is that, let us have some kind of input on doing something that means something to us.

And then they did that, and I think it was really unfortunate that it got carried out beforehand in the press the way it did.

It was great being able to be on that team with Payne. Again, looking back, and having him not being here anymore, we were able to share in that last big hurrah. I feel very fortunate in being able to do that. I know it brought us a lot closer. When you go through such an emotional experience, the bond you form is so close that no matter what happens from here on forward, the guys are gonna be special. I got to see a side of everybody that I'd never seen before, I got a lot closer to all those guys, and Payne is no different.

I got to know him and his wife a lot better and really appreciate them a lot more, and know them more as people rather than as a golfer and a golfer's wife. To be able to share that with him, to have a chance to share that with him, becomes more special even now. We sit and watch the video of the Ryder Cup and see him swinging that club and hitting shots, and at the same time it's joyful and sad, to know that he's gone. It's joyful to know that we were able to share that with him.

I've never had somebody say that to me, hey, I'm proud to be an American, from winning a golf tournament. From what everybody's told me, it was much like the Americans beating the Russians in 1980 at Lake Placid, a similar-type feeling. And I remember watching that game, and how jacked I was. I was in college at the time, and a lot of the guys on that team were schoolmates of mine. The pride that I felt because we beat the Russians was almost uncontainable.

And it was similar with this. Winning a major was just great. . . . if I had to pick a second, it would be that one. But this one was impossible to beat—you can't top it.

WAYNE LEVI

Wayne Levi was the PGA Player of the Year in 1990, and between 1979 and 1990 he won a dozen tournaments. But the first time was the best for Levi, whose greatest day was the Houston Open in 1979, when he turned a bunker visit into a momentum-generating series of shots that would take him to victory.

When I won my first individual tournament . . . the first tournament I won was the Disney team event. When I won my first individual tournament, that's probably the greatest individual moment of my entire golf career.

I was playing at Houston, and the year before—this is '79 in Houston—Bob Mann and I won the Walt Disney team event [the Walt Disney World National Team Championship]. But now it's an individual event, and we're out there playing in Houston, and we're off to a good start. I think I'd become exempt at that point because of the team event, but you know, I hadn't won a regular tournament, an individual tournament.

I was playing okay, but the year wasn't going along too great. I think this was in May, that was probably when we played there. My game was pretty decent, and we got going, and the tournament started, and I shot a pretty good round to start the tournament.

And then we had a rain delay—that's what I remember. It rained real bad, so now they had to switch the tournament to a double round. I think it was the third round maybe, it rained real bad, and they had to switch the thing to a double round on Sunday. I'd never been in any of these, so I didn't know if this was good or bad.

So anyway, the third round started early in the morning, and I shot a real low round, a heck of a round, taking the lead. So I was in the lead going into the last round of the event, on Sunday, and I remember to this day where this tournament turned.

It was pretty close, and we got to the tenth hole, and I drove into the fairway bunker. I think I was tied for the lead at this point, and I drove into the fairway trap, and I had no shot. I had to chip it out. This is a long par four, a 450-yard par four.

We didn't play the course we're playing now, and the tenth hole was the hardest hole on the course. So I drove into the trap, I had no shot, I chip out . . . now I've still got 210 yards to the hole. And the guy I'm playing against, he's hit his second shot on the green, in two. I'm two, but I'm 210 yards away.

So I said, this is a crucial shot right here, I don't want to go a couple shots down. I hit this two-iron, and I put it about three feet from the hole. And the other guy three-putted, and I made my putt, and I beat him by a shot on that hole. That turned . . . I mean, it looked like I might go down by two, and I end up going up by one on that hole. And it turned the whole thing around, and I don't think he recovered from that, and I went on to win the tournament.

I don't even know who I was playing against—you'd probably have to go back and look, I forgot. But he finished second, I think.

That was the turning point of the tournament right there for me. And I remember going down the last hole, and I had a two-stroke lead on the last hole, and I had this water on the right-hand side. So I hit my drive to the left, just to the edge of the left rough, so I kept it away from the water. Hit my second shot, looked like it was gonna go right in the hole, and it ends up short in a bunker, exactly where I didn't want to go.

So I'm in this trap, and I'm sitting there . . . you know, you're about to win for the first time ever by yourself in an individual tournament. I'm sitting in this trap, and I'm just thinking about a hundred things that can go wrong in this trap. I said, whatever you do, you don't want to skull this thing over the green and back in the bleachers, back up near the clubhouse someplace. So I'm trying to think positive, but I'm thinking of all these negative things.

So I get up there, and finally I hit this thing, and I hit it a little heavy, and it just gets out of the trap onto the fringe. So I've got about a twenty-footer, and I make it. Really, I had two putts to get down in to win this thing, but I canned it, and I won my first individual tournament.

My wife and I had only been married a year or so, and she comes running out, and we were hugging and everything, and it was the first time I'd won. And she was pregnant, too, at the time . . . it was just a great feeling, just a tremendous feeling.

I had a two-shot lead going to the last hole, and it was just . . . he hung in there, and I gained another stroke from that tenth hole, so I was two up going to that last hole. And I said, just make a par here, somehow, you know, don't do anything nutty.

That was it, that's the only thing that kind of . . . there's not a lot going through your head, you're kind of focused in one direction, there's not a whole lot of other things you're thinking about. The money, I wasn't thinking about that really— just winning.

The course was in great condition, it was at the Woodlands

in Houston. You just had to be careful, the course was playing long, too, like I said, because it was real wet, you didn't get much roll. You just had your total focus on kind of getting this last hole played and getting it done and over with. And bingo, you're the winner.

You double things . . . you knew it was gonna be a long day and you were gonna be tired, so you didn't practice a lot the night before, which I usually do, because I like to practice. I'd never done it before, I was kind of new on the tour. I knew it was gonna be a long day, and it was hot, almost ninety. It was gonna be a long day, and you just kind of had to pace and gear yourself for a long, long day. It's not like there's one round, and tomorrow will be another round, so you kind of refocus yourself, it's all gonna happen today.

And luckily, it's probably in my favor, because I came out playing great. So I figured I'm gonna play good in the second round, too, you don't play good in the morning and terrible in the afternoon. I played real well in the morning to take the lead, I think I shot 64 or 65, I don't remember, but I think it was that type of score. And then the last round was another real good solid round.

It was different from the Disney win because it was an individual win. But winning my first tournament in the team event was tremendous too, because I played probably my best golf that I ever played when we won the the Walt Disney team event. Geez, I made, I think, twenty-five birdies and an eagle, and we shot 34 under or something like that as a team. I got twenty-five birdies and an eagle, so . . .

It was probably the best golf I ever played.

I'd already won a tournament . . . it wasn't an individual one, but I'd won a tournament and knew I could do it, knew I could play, knew I could shoot consistent low scores. And that certainly helps.

I don't remember all of exactly what we did after . . . but we just kind of looked at each other and said, we made it, we won a tournament. It's something you strive for all your life. You really don't ever . . . before you win one, you don't ever know if you're gonna win. And we did it. So it was just tremendous. I think that night we went out and had a nice dinner, you know, we were just elated about it.

They brought us up there, and they interviewed you, and you talked about your round and how you did and stuff. It was exciting.

I don't exactly remember who all the characters were in this thing. You know, it was 1979, that was a long time ago. But it was a heck of a field, there was a lot of good players playing in this thing. When you go back and look at the record and the final results, you'll be able to see who was there and who was up there and stuff. It was exciting.

Oh, it was terrific. Winning a tournament . . . at the time you had to qualify on Monday all the time, do the Monday qualifying. Now I'd won a tournament, I was exempt for the rest of the year—for the next two years, in fact, which was terrific. When you're a young player, that's the big plus—it's not the money, it's the fact that you're gonna be out there for a couple more years at least, to get your game going.

I worked on my game all the time anyway—that's what made me the player that I am. I worked as hard as anybody out there, so if there was some aspect of my game where I wasn't doing well, I just worked hard enough on it until it did get better. You're just able to pick and choose the tournaments now, plus you're able to play in all the good events, the invitational and stuff like that, which was a lot better, a lot nicer. It was a lot more fun at that time. It increases the excitement of playing out there.

It's your first win . . . the doubt that you'll ever win at all is something that kind of sticks with you as a young player. You're new at this, you get out there, you've got all these big names out there that you're playing against, and you know, these guys kind of intimidate you a little bit. You're trying to fit in, you're trying to be a part of this thing—and let's face it, winning's why you go out there. If you've got any drive in you, you want to win, you don't just want to be a participant. And that's what you're worried about.

Once you get that close, you don't want to give that up. You probably know you're not gonna get a whole lot of chances, so you've gotta take advantage of the ones you do get. And the thought process is, once you get this win, you'll be the type of guy that will be accepted, you're in there, and people will pay a little more respect to you and stuff. It's important when you first get out there.

It takes a while for it to really sink in. Down the road you start getting invitations to this tournament and that tournament, you're a tournament winner now. And that happens even now, when you're a tournament winner, you get a lot of different perks than when you're just a good solid player and making money. I got to play in the Masters that year and the next year and everything . . . it was important.

BOBBY NICHOLS

Bobby Nichols has had a career filled with some remarkable days, from his comeback after a high school car wreck that left him paralyzed from the waist down after being unconscious for thirteen days to surviving a lightning strike that also almost took out Lee Trevino and Jerry Heard at the Western Open in 1975. But Nichols's greatest day took place in 1964, when he held off Nicklaus and Palmer to win the PGA Championship on Nicklaus's home golf course in Ohio, leading for all four rounds and setting a tournament record that survived until Nick Price broke it at Southern Hills in 1994.

I guess probably the finest day would have to be the final round of the PGA Championship in 1964. Leading up to it, I had led all four rounds, or really, all three rounds, and the pressure was building up, and up till that time I hadn't won a major. So it was added pressure in a lot of ways.

And then the last round, Jack and Arnold . . . let's see, they were about six shots behind. They both played right in front of me, and I played with Ben Hogan. I believe I had a three-shot lead going into the last round, so I was playing in the last group with Hogan and Tom Neoporte. Right in front of me was Arnold and Jack and Mason Rudolph.

I was playing very well coming into Columbus Country Club

for the PGA that week. I was really kind of searching, you might say, for different things—I had Jackie Burke looking at me and Gardner Dickinson was helping me. I remember a couple of occasions, I was just kind of searching, asking here and there. Back in those days, guys had a little bit more time to spend and kind of gave you a little bit more personal help, you could say. I was just trying to get something that would work.

It was funny how things fall into place, because on the first round, I remember on the way to the golf course, the courtesy car driver who was supposed to pick us up had a flat tire. And that was kind of a nerve-wracking thing, because here we are standing on the side of the road with a flat tire as I was gonna go play. But anyway, we got there on time, but it was a little hectic.

As I say, I really didn't feel like I was playing that well [during the week]. I got off to a great start, shot 64 the first round, and that kind of set the tone for the week, it kind of gave me a lot of confidence. I got better—the better I putted, the better I started hitting the ball, it seemed like. One goes with the other, one in front of the other, whichever you want to say. That's the way it is in golf, something works for you in your game and the first thing you know you're doing things that you didn't think you were capable of doing that well. But like I say, things started clicking.

I putted well that week. I had a few free putts, but I still putted well. I had a 64, and then a 74, still led the first 135, and then 69 the third round, I still led after three rounds. And then a 67 the last round.

The weather was pretty darn good. It was relatively hot, but it was probably picture-perfect as far as playing golf. Not too windy, it was hot, the greens were good, hard like they normally are.

Obviously, I liked it pretty much . . . you know, back in those days, they take those 72-hole golf courses and make a par 70 out of it. Generally what they do for major championships is they try to cut the par down from 72 to 70 if they can, and make it more difficult and that sort of thing.

I didn't get much rest that week, I was just pretty excited and pretty nervous. I started off with . . . I was playing with Ben Hogan. I think actually he kind of helped me, you know, he's so reserved with his mannerisms, it helps someone to calm down, it wasn't like screaming and hollering and hooting and hollering, like you might find with someone else. With Hogan it was more of a respectful type of gallery, they were applauding, but it was a controlled applauding, you know, you could tell the difference between applause and yelling.

So it started out the day, and I started out with a good tee shot and that sort of thing, but then I wound up three-putting the first hole, that kind of unnerved me a little bit, I gave a stroke away. I kept playing along, I remember birdying the third hole and the sixth hole, and it seemed like as the round went on I felt more at ease, because I felt like I was more in control, and the things I was doing were relatively working to my advantage. Things were happening in my favor, I should say.

After the three-putt on the first hole, I three-putted another green, but I made a couple of putts that kept me going. It seemed like in a round there's always crucial putts you have to make, two or three that you're faced with. And if they go in, it just kind of helps you.

I don't know if I was doing anything differently, it's hard to put your finger on it, why a ball goes in the hole when you do things good. That's what's so frustrating about golf—you go along, and you work your fanny off, and nothing really happens, in fact, sometimes it gets worse, you might say, the harder you work. And then all of a sudden things start clicking, and you just say, God, when things are working for you, you wish you could keep it, but it kind of comes and goes—some people, obviously, more so than others.

I was behind [Arnold Palmer and Jack Nicklaus], they were in front of me, and of course they were on fire, they were making a lot of putts, making a lot of noise, making a lot of runs. And they both wound up shooting 64s that last round, so that was quite unnerving, because I knew that they were playing well by the reaction of the crowd. We had a little hollering ourselves, but not necessarily that loud.

Of course, when you're young, you can handle nervousness a lot better than when you get older. It was quite nerve-wracking for four days, leading a tournament—it's hard to keep going, get some rest, and hopefully everything kind of kicks in, keeps your momentum going.

I really wasn't settled, I had only a two-shot lead going into sixteen. I made about a ten-footer for a par, I remember that, which maintained a two-shot lead. On seventeen it's an extremely difficult par three, and I remember putting it on the green, and I made a long putt for a two, and that jumped me to a four-shot cushion. I knew then that if I could just hold on to the club I had a pretty good shot at winning.

But I never felt comfortable, because the eighteenth hole had an out-of-bounds to the left. And I certainly felt like I had to hit a good drive, because even with a four-shot lead I didn't want to hit it out of bounds. And I managed to hit a drive right down the middle of the fairway, and that was . . . what a gratifying and good feeling, to walk down the fairway with a four-shot lead and know your ball's in the middle of the fairway. All you've gotta do is play it safe for a par, or even a bogey or a double-bogey, I don't guess you're gonna lose four shots in one swing.

They both birdied the last hole, Arnold and Jack, but I still had a three-shot lead after they finished.

It happened so fast, that last hole I can't remember exactly, but I was excited. I really didn't think . . . I was just so happy to feel like I'd gotten a major under my belt, and that was fun. Something I'll remember for a long time. And then, of course,

Hogan shook my hand, congratulated me, I have a picture of that here at my house. It was quite gratifying—he seemed very happy that I had won. And of course, I was ecstatic.

Well, after the awards ceremony I was more concerned about my wife, she was pregnant with our second son. And that was in August, the baby came in October, but she spent the whole week in the hot sun, I was kind of concerned about her. We went back to the hotel and relaxed after that, it was just a wonderful feeling to have won a major championship. We had a few drinks and sat around the hotel, just kind of talked and that sort of thing. It was fun.

When you do something like that, the confidence just stays with you for quite some time. And of course, it's something that, you know, back in our days the PGA Championship was by far the best, because of the lifetime exemption, which was unbelievable back in those days. Even today I can play the regular tour anytime I want. Of course, I play the Senior Tour, but the lifetime exemption still exists today, so I have the lifetime option.

What I'm trying to get at is that way back then that's why that tournament was so important, you had that extra incentive with the lifetime exemption. Of course, in those days it's just like it is today, you can be here today and gone tomorrow. So it also motivated a lot of things, it kind of set me up. I knew then that I could play when I wanted to, and didn't have to play when I didn't want to. With the lifetime exemption I had no status that I had to maintain.

A little later on I was offered the job at Firestone, that was in '68, four years later. I was winning some, but not a whole lot. Firestone was a great opportunity, and I took the job and stayed there until '80. But without that situation with having the lifetime exemption, I probably never would have taken the job, because I would have had to try to maintain the status every year.

That PGA Championship did all those things, and that was

probably one of my greatest decisions, to take the job at Firestone, because everything worked out real well.

It's obviously one of the majors, but I think they took a lot away from it when they took away the lifetime exemption. That's why I think . . . that's what set it apart from any other championship, the lifetime exemption. There's no telling what that's worth. Now it's good, it's ten years now, but it's not lifetime—for kids in their twenties it would be nice if they had a lifetime, rather than just ten years.

You're still rewarded, even today. Like I said, the pro/ams you're asked to play in, and of course, by winning a major it kind of sticks with you throughout your life. It's rewarded me a lot of ways, a lot of them financial, but in other ways recognition and what have you, being invited here and there. But it's funny, you can win a lot of other golf tournaments, but if you can just win a major, people remember those.

I think the magnitude of a championship . . . when you do win your first tournament, that's a tremendous day. But I think through all the other elements, the prestige, and all the other things, I still think that's my best day ever.

A lot of people would say their first tournament, and that was one of the greatest days I ever had—I can remember winning $2,800 and thinking I had all the money in the world. But like I said, that tournament had such prestige, and being a major, and all the other things that go with it, leading all four rounds, and then winning it is probably the most satisfaction I ever had.

Well, that's just it, doing it against Arnold and Jack added a lot to it, because actually that's Jack's hometown, so it was his house, so obviously a lot of people were pulling for him and Arnold when they were going at it pretty regularly against each other, being paired together. So it was really quite a spectacular show, with the whistling and hollering and what have you.

They were kidding me after, they said, well, you must have

made everything. I said, I don't know if I made everything, but you guys made your share. We talked back and forth a little like that, them telling me I'm saying I didn't make anything but shot 64. We were kidding each other back and forth, but it was all in laughter and fun.

MARK McCUMBER

For Mark McCumber, it was the connection to family that defined his greatest days. The first took place on his hometown course in the Jacksonville city championship that helped launch his career, while the second was yet another victory in Jacksonville during a remarkable career year in the late 1980s. Another memorable celebration with family and friends marked his victory at the Olympic Club in San Francisco, where he holed a long putt to beat Fuzzy Zoeller in a playoff.

That could be a lot of things for me, personally . . . I mean, there's no one thing. There's two tournaments—and then you get into what's more exciting, your first win, then the most important win as far as who-you-beat-type thing, you know, so there's a bunch of them that rush into my mind. And then even one goes back to when I was fourteen years old, so I don't know how to categorize it.

One day I could live over . . . there's a lot I feel that way about, but I'll tell you the two that come to mind the most would be the Players Championship in '88 in my hometown, and then a more romantic setting at a different time of my career, in an incredible venue, would be the Olympic Club against Fuzzy [Zoeller] for the Tour Championship in 1994.

Those two are side by side, but as I verbalize maybe I'll come to an answer myself.

At the time, and even looking back, the more meaningful win would have been the Players Championship, because, I mean, the Tour Championship is exceptionally prestigious, but it's thirty players—anytime you don't beat a full field, to me, it doesn't carry the same weight. But the venue was special, it was the end of a great year anyway. Now, most satisfying and rewarding would be the Players Championship . . . I'm answering my own question as I think through it.

And it was a long day. It was thirty-two holes of golf, too, so that would be the day.

Let me give you two scenarios, and they're quite different, really. The Players Championship in 1988, a lot of factors make it special—my hometown, where I was born and raised and went to public school, and my family's been from, my dad's family, since the twenties. So that made it special, my whole family was literally there, that made it special.

It was the Players Championship, and I think that was the year that forty-nine of the top fifty—it was the strongest field of the year, including any major. So you beat everybody, which is always rewarding when you play golf, and you rarely, even as a good player, get to beat everybody. When you think that you play four hundred tournaments in a career, five hundred tournaments, and if you win twenty times you're in the Hall of Fame—that's not a lot of wins.

So to beat everybody, in my hometown, with my family there, my grandmother, who I think was eighty-four at the time, was there, down to my children and my nieces and all. To set a tournament record made it special, to win by four shots made it special.

And there were signs of it coming in the fact that in 1988 I'd played five or six tournaments leading up to that, three or four on the West Coast and two in Florida, Doral and

Honda. And not until the Honda, when the wind was blowing forty miles an hour, had I shot one round over par, and that was 73, in the first six tournaments. And at Doral I finished second to [Ben] Crenshaw. I had the lowest stroke average of the year and hit more greens than anybody else for the year. I was leading in three or four statistical categories.

And so the table was set at a place I'd really struggled in, Jacksonville—I played my first Players in '79, so I played nine of 'em, and I actually struggled, I think because I always put too much pressure on myself to play at home and play well. So '87 was a breakthrough, because I finished tenth or eleventh and played really well for four days here.

And so I came into here brimming with confidence—it was a quiet confidence, I knew deep down I was playing as physically good as I've ever played in my life. And that last day was set up with a rain delay on Saturday. We had played four holes on Saturday and the heavens broke loose. So we had to come back at dawn on Sunday, and I had to tee off on the fifth tee at the Players Club.

I proceeded to play a very good round of golf and did not make a bogey. And then I went home for lunch. I got to go to my own house, I remember Paddy [McCumber's wife] made me a sandwich and a Waldorf salad, I watched *Ferris Bueller's Day Off* with the kids, hanging out, you know? And I went back to my . . . did the premier afternoon time, the two o'clock tee time in the last group, and proceeded to hit every green until I got to the last hole, where I almost intentionally played for five. I was playing away from the water, I did not make a bogey—I did not make a bogey in the tournament from Friday on the sixteenth hole until Sunday the last hole.

So mechanically, Sunday was just special. I hit fairways and greens, fairways and greens, it was an easy 67 or 68, whatever it was. And that allowed me the luxury of playing like I knew it was my tournament with about six holes to play, but still being cautious. And once I hit it on the green on seventeen, I knew nothing could side-rail it. So I had the last fifteen, twenty minutes to walk to seventeen, the playing of the entire hole of eighteen, to absolutely—you don't get this chance often in competition—I had already done my job so well and been fortunate enough so that I could absolutely reminisce and do all the things you're not supposed to do. I could think of all the emotions, they could all come out.

And then the kicker was that as I'm walking to the eighteenth green, and this is my hometown where I literally knew thousands of people personally, I glanced over across the lake and someone had made a banner, "Jacksonville's Winner." And it was the most emotionally charged I've ever been, it was hard to keep my eyes clear. But it was a happy time, because I reflected on all the things growing up in that town, and all the people that had been helpful to me, and first of all family and friends, and then to share that with them . . . it was incredible.

And then all the things—it's a ten-year exemption, it's the Players Championship, it's a tournament record score, and leading money winner through the spring of the season—all those different things. That was really, really, really gratifying, emotionally charged, all those things that you think about.

I knew it going into the tournament, I knew it in every practice round—if you go back and look at the tapes, and I remember it very clearly. Wednesday afternoon, I was gonna play—I really prepared perfectly. I didn't overprepare, I think I played maybe eighteen holes Tuesday, I didn't play Wednesday, I was gonna sneak out Wednesday and play nine holes. And Bob Goalby and Lee Trevino were gonna play nine, and they were working for NBC at the time, just to kind of look at the course.

And I knew a lot of the players of that generation—of course, Trevino I played a lot with, and Goalby through Dan Sikes, who grew up in Jacksonville. And so they were friends, and they said, Mark, can we play with you, and I asked them could I go out and play with them, so we went out and played together. And I think I shot 31 or 32 and really played flawless. I remember Trevino going, wow, you're playing good, and I said, yeah, I feel great, Lee, but I have to stay out of my own way, you know?

And then the first day I went out, and I played with Crenshaw, and I shot 65, and I holed it from over a hundred yards on the last hole for an eagle. I mean, it was like, if you ever thought that you're on, and I made two bogies that day and shot 65. So, I mean, everything I thought on Tuesday and Wednesday, from the get-go, I started on Thursday, and I never turned around.

I never was in jeopardy, I played my afternoon out—I played early Thursday, so I played late Friday, and that was when it was windy and all. So you go that hard round done with the greens hard and the wind blowing, even par, and then I shot eight under on the weekend. And the weekend was kind of odd, because I played four holes Saturday and then thirty-two holes on Sunday.

So I knew right from the get-go that nine holes was like a reaffirmation, that, man, you really are playing good.

I've always been able to isolate when I've won through the years, to be honest with you. When I look at an old scrapbook or who was there that week and I see where . . . I played with Payne and David Frost the last thirty-two holes, so, I mean, I knew them. Matter of fact, the only contest came head-on with David. I know I birdied eleven and twelve on Sunday to go from a one-shot lead to a four-shot lead, and from then on I kind of always kept it at four or five shots.

But looking back, when you see that Greg Norman was in the top ten that week, and I can't see another name, but I wasn't even aware of it when I was playing, who I was fighting off. But I've always been that way, I've never been one to look over my shoulder and worry and have any concern what anybody else is doing, I always figured that it took enough of my energy to do what I was gonna do. I couldn't do anything about that anyway.

The celebration was really neat. First of all, to be able to have my family sit in on the press conference, which is a rarity unless they happen to be out with you, and I'm talking Mom and Dad and all. It was cute, because my brother walked in, and he ordered champagne for the press room, and that's not something you would do normally, but again, it was my hometown.

And that night, we had just moved from across town, where I had grown up, to the beach, that winter of '87. And so by the end of the evening there were fifty to a hundred people at my home, and it was reminiscing, talking over stories when we were kids, it was a lot of old friends, family, and that went on till the wee hours of the morning. It was fun to sit in my study with my dad and talk about it, my brothers would come in—I have three brothers—and we'd talk about what it meant. And there was a lot of reflection that night.

You know, when I first thought about great days, you know, winning Doral in '79 as a rookie was just a fairy tale. But I don't think you're old enough—one win is wonderful, and it's special, but it didn't have the . . . and this is also my, at the time, sixth win. I've won ten times, officially, but it was the sixth win, one more kind of a punctuation that, you know, this guy can play a little bit. You know, all those different factors.

That [Tour Championship] was also special, that I knew I was really playing well. I had had a run that . . . Tom Boswell wrote an article, and he does more baseball [writing], but I respect him. And many years ago at Doral he was down there, I guess it was a way to get out of Washington in the winter.

He wrote an article that someone sent me, it was out of the *Washington Post*, where he went over my year, and he made comparisons . . . like, Shoemaker won the Kentucky Derby at forty-six, and then Nicklaus won the Masters at forty-six, those are specific events—and he talked about my year. Unbeknownst to me, he said this may be one of the career years in sports—and I'm forty-three years old.

Because when you go back, I was third or fourth in scoring, I was third or fourth on the money list—other than Nick Price, I mean, I won three times, Mike Springer won twice, and no one else even won twice. There were just a lot of factors that were bigger than I even realize, but when I look back, starting with the Anheuser-Busch, then I won Hardee's in September, then I was tied for the lead and played the last round with Nick Price, I think I was third or fourth at Canada. And then I won, it was like I won three of six tournaments and finished fourth in another, eighth in another, and eleventh in another.

So the only reason I'm giving you that information is that coming into the Tour Championship I was relaxed, I knew I was playing well again. I've been very fortunate in my career to have strings almost every year where I'd play a six- or seven-week string where I just felt like I could do almost anything I wanted. That was my feeling, obviously it wasn't true, but I felt very confident, and you get a physical and an emotional roll where everything is positive.

We had spent the week before Anheuser-Busch—Paddy and I had just gotten certified scuba diving—with some other friends and couples, I went down to the Bahamas, took the children and all. And we went diving, we dove for four or five days, had a great time. And I had worn some blisters so bad with my fins, I didn't realize it, because you're wearing sandals, you're not putting on tie shoes. And we flew home, and I put on docksiders, and my feet are a little uncomfortable.

And I get on a plane, this is like, we fly on Saturday, we were going to play in San Francisco on Monday, I had not touched a club for over a week, was mentally fresh—I always viewed the Tour Championship as kind of a bonus week. We knew we'd have fun in San Francisco, we took our youngest little boy, we went to *Phantom of the Opera* and ate at the greatest restaurants. There's an older couple who are best friends of my parents who I'd known since I was a kid, and we had dinner with them several times, they watched me play during the week.

It was just a fun week, and again, I got to the course, I love Olympic Club anyway, I played at the Open there in '87. And it was one of those weeks where everything was great, but I went to put my shoes on on Wednesday, and I could not put my golf shoes on. They hurt so bad—I cut the toes out of 'em and played that way in the practice round on Wednesday. And by Thursday I could tape 'em up and play, and that wasn't a factor anymore, but it got ironic that I couldn't even . . . I said, I may not even be able to walk with these things on.

I played the first round there with Phil Mickelson, and I remember—I was told, I don't remember this—I was talking to my brother or somebody that was walking in my group, and they were saying, boy, look how relaxed Mark is. Well, you know, Phil was still young, he was real new then, but it was like, Phil needs to work on being real relaxed . . . it was just two people talking. And they made a lot about my whistling and all, and that wasn't a sports psychologist's tip to be relaxed, that's just how relaxed I was—I mean, I really was. I was having a wonderful time playing the Olympic Club, and I was playing well.

And the real true measure of that was when I got to eighteen, and I had a one-shot lead at the time, and I hit a perfect tee shot—this is the last day, the fondest day, Sunday. I played the round basically flawlessly, I had not made a bogey, I went through a stretch where I birdied six, seven, eight, nine—the longest putt I had was four feet. I was in control of my game again, and I drove it down the middle. It was a two-iron tee shot, I had like 152 or 153 yards to the hole.

I've always thought I was strong on managing myself. I said, I want the shot out to the right of the pin, play to the middle of the green, don't try to get it all the way back there, because if you knock it over you're dead. Hit the perfect shot I wanted to hit, and the ball lands right where I want, and the gallery starts to applaud, and there's a weird sound in the gallery, like, ooh. I look and said to myself, now what in the world would that be about? But . . . no clue. So I said, well, maybe it's something all the way back to the front or something. I get up there, and the ball skipped, when I saw the replay, it got one inch into the back fringe and hung up, which is hard that it could have done that.

But then it left me with an impossible play on that green. I would have to play twenty feet of break from twenty feet. I hit a great putt that just touched the edge and runs about fifteen feet below the hole that I missed. So I make bogey due to no mechanical or mental fault, and I remember not even being upset. I remember thinking that I'd lost the tournament, but, hey, I did what I could do, and if that's what it is, fine.

And Fuzzy birdies seventeen to tie me, he'd already birdied seventeen, he pars eighteen, we go back to the playoff. And this playoff was one of those things why this day is exceptionally special. Here you are playing in front of I don't know how many people were really there, maybe fifteen thousand on the last hole? But if you've been there, the amphitheater effect at the Olympic Club at eighteen might be the most dramatic finish we have, as far as people. And it's so vertical, the hill—it's like Riviera, but bigger, they're on top of you.

And Fuzzy has been a counterpart of mine, he started the tour a year or two ahead of me, and we won our first tournaments within weeks of each other—he won at San Diego in '79, a few weeks later I win Doral. And he's an easy guy to play with, and to root for.

So we go back out in the playoff, and we're both whistling and laughing and talking, and he wins the toss and goes first. And we both hit it down the fairway, and we're walking down and talking, and I remember thinking, isn't this fun? This is, as a kid, what you dream about doing, the scenario where you get down there and everybody's right on top of you watching this playoff.

And we both hit conservative shots to the right front of the green—I really made a point to do that, because of what happened in regulation. And all of a sudden I got there, and I was very calm and all these nice feelings, and he's about a foot or two outside me on the same line. I remember thinking—and this is fifty feet away—I remember thinking, well, he's gonna dictate what I need to do. If he hits a putt, very easily he could putt his ball to six or seven feet and not be in the hole in four, and I might win the tournament with a two-putt, and I'll get to see the line.

As things have it, Fuzzy hits a great putt to about two feet or eighteen inches. He taps in, and I thought the pressure reverts to . . . I have no luxury here. But then I turn that right into, yeah, but I know exactly the line, let me just hit a good putt.

And this was one of those times in sports where what probably took six seconds, or four or five seconds seemed like a minute. I got over the putt, and I remember thinking, just hit the putt solidly. You know the line, get it started, hit the ball solidly—it was so uphill and so long that if you mis-hit the ball a little bit, that's when you could have that seven- or eight-footer left.

So the second I hit it, which seemed like it took about ten seconds, the instant feedback of the sound of the putt and the feel of my hands was, I've hit it dead solid. So then I was calm, that, okay, the ball would have good speed, then halfway there, right over the exact line I was looking—I said, well, I've got a good line. And all of this is taking three, four seconds, five seconds, maybe? But it seems like I'm having time almost to myself to editorialize. So I've gone from, I've hit it solid perfect, it's got a good line, to, that's gonna be close, and the last ten feet I said, holy cow, that ball can't miss.

It just hugged the ground on the line, and when it goes in it was . . . you know, my vertical leap was three inches, but that was more than it's ever been in my whole life. And Fuzzy comes over and hugs me and whispers something in my ear, you know, typical Fuzzy style.

But I remember going to the press, and I just remember thinking, now here my wife's on the green with me, and with raising my kid, she wasn't always with me, she probably was there about half the times I won. And she was there with me to enjoy it, this older couple that was friends with my mom and dad came into the press room, they were like . . . they'd never been to anything like this. I'm sort of thinking, I never went out ahead like this, I was second in L.A., second in Tournament of Champions, and it was nice to win in a totally different part of the country that was so storied, and all of those things were kind of running through my veins.

And one of the reporters said, have you ever made a putt like that to win before? And I said no—actually I've made it thousands of times as a kid on the putting green at Hyde Park, literally at dark, hitting these putts across the green . . . this is to win the tournament. That was truly living a dream, with the setting, the scenario, and so that was exceptionally special, for all those reasons.

Gosh, we had a great time. I waited till everybody was gone, we were there until dark. We took the older couple, the Garretts, we drove them to where their car was parked in public parking, I'm in my courtesy car. And we said, you follow us back to the hotel, and they did. We all went up and caught our breath, and now it's about eight o'clock. And we took them, my friend that I grew up with, Mike Blackburn, he's my teacher, I took him out there almost as a . . . you've helped me all year, let's just come out to San Francisco and have a good time, so he was there for the week. He got to sit in, he was sitting next to Paddy on the eighteenth green when I made the putt.

So between my lifelong friend and teacher, and my wife, this older couple, my son, my caddy, Bob Arch, who's a good friend of mine, we all went to dinner at one of the famous restaurants down at the wharf, I forget the name of it. And I walked in, I just called and made a reservation, I didn't say anything, I don't think I used my name. We walked in, and as I walked in they had a bottle of champagne for me, and we just sat and drank and ate and just had a wonderful time.

Then, that next morning, my wife and I and my little boy got up and we, unscheduled, rather than fly home, we said, let's take advantage of being out here. I got a rental car and we drove to . . . the national park . . . it's the equivalent to Yellowstone—not Redwood, I'm blanking on which one it is, I'm embarrassed. Anyway, we drove to the national park, we just walked through the tour stuff, looked at the waterfalls, took our little boy, at the time Tyler was three, and he loved Indians, and we went to the craft stores, and we stayed at the lodge there, and it snowed the next morning.

And as we were driving out of the park it's snowing, and I guess we left out of Fresno, or whatever the nearest airport was, and flew home a couple days later. It was just a magical week, it was the final tournament of the year, I—twice in my career won the last tournament of the year. I won the last tournament in '83 at Pensacola. Just a storybook way to end the year, and in a playoff, a putt of that length, and in that setting at the Olympic Club with the gallery, all that went with it. It was exceptionally special.

When I was fourteen, at the Donald Ross course I grew up on in Hyde Park, they had the city championship. And the city championship in north Florida is a giant thing—former winners are major people, Steve Melnyk won it three times, Bert Green, who used to be a tour player, won it. All the good players in southeastern Georgia would come down, and it was a full 160 kids from ages whatever up to nineteen, up till your nineteenth birthday you could play.

And Melnyk had won the tournament the previous three years, and the trophy had been retired. There were a couple of kids that were eighteen that were expected to win and all, and I shoot like 74 the first day, in the last week, the last day. And I shoot 70 or 71, made an eagle, I holed out a five-iron on a par four. And my oldest brother, Jim, who's always been my biggest fan, had come home from school—this is in June, he came from school, and he was caddying for me.

I remember it vividly, I made like a thirty-footer on fifteen, made about a twenty-footer on seventeen. I get to eighteen, and I've got the tournament won, I'm two shots ahead, and the kid I'm playing against hits it in a ditch, of all things, drops. To make a long story short, he chips in, I've got the tournament won, we're putting up side by side with him, off the green in this little depression, the course where I grew up in, my mom and dad were standing there watching, my brother's caddying for me, and I've got a two-shot lead. So it's over to me.

But he chips it in, and I'd already chipped to about twenty feet, so if I don't make the putt I don't win. And that's probably as much luck as anything else, but what it did was, it's something I was able to draw on for the next thirty-five years, that when I was in that situation I was successful. That was a real neat deal for me.

There's some other days that have been more meaningful to me [beyond golf], but I pick those days because they stand out to me, both in the sense of accomplishment and where they happened. The eighteenth green at Hyde Park is, on the public course, three hundred yards from where I grew up, from the house I lived in. The Players Championship is in my hometown, and then San Francisco, the venue itself . . . Olympic Club, like I tried to describe to you, if you've been there, you know what I mean, the venue of that setting on the eighteenth green.

All the things with [Ben] Hogan and Fleck, and just the

memories you have as a kid knowing golf. I think everybody dreams of winning tournaments and playoffs, and trust me, it's just as much fun to win by five shots. But I think that's the romance of golf, to do it that way. So that's why those jump out.

And I also think that what comes to my mind [about] those . . . the biggest reason, now that you've asked me, is that my family was there to share it with me. And even though [in] San Francisco all my kids weren't there, my wife and one of my three children were there, the little one, so that was real, real special.

STEVE MELNYK

Like Bruce Fleisher, Steve Melnyk stepped up to the first tee at Augusta after winning the U.S. Amateur early in his career and was paired with a member of the Big Three. But Melnyk's first round at Augusta led to a different twist: a lifelong friendship with Jack Nicklaus. Later, during the 1986 Masters, that pairing came full circle when Melnyk, working the Masters for CBS, helped call his good friend home from Amen Corner during Nicklaus's unforgettable charge.

I grew up in Georgia idolizing Bobby Jones, that was just someone that all amateur golfers in the state, and of course in the country, model themselves after. And then I won the U.S. Amateur in 1969, so with that in mind with Jones, Augusta National, and the Masters, it would probably be my first round in the 1970 Masters. I was paired with Jack Nicklaus.

Interestingly, I met him for the first time on the first tee. And we both played well, but more importantly we struck up a friendship that has lasted now over thirty years.

Well, I made the Walker Cup team, so I knew, having made the Walker Cup team, I would play in the Masters—that's back when they invited a rather large constituent of amateurs. Now they've reduced it to five, which I think is a mistake, but back then there were twelve to thirteen amateurs who played on a regular basis at Augusta.

But I won the amateur at Oakmont, played as good a golf game as I could play. The field included Tom Watkins, Lanny Wadkins, and Tom Kite, and I was fortunate, in fact I had an eight-shot lead with nine to play, and I won by five.

What happens when you win the Amateur, obviously doors are open that you never can conceive of, and I grew up in a small town in south Georgia, so I was candidly ill equipped for a lot of this stuff, looking back. I had all the sophistication of a pair of brown shoes and a black tie—Bob, to say I was unsophisticated would be kind.

But it forces you to grow up in a hurry. You're thrust into a national spotlight, in forums that you're not ready for. I was making grades and was smart along those lines, but I was not smart in terms of the ways of the world. I had not flown on an airplane very many times before . . . things like that.

So anyway, I had played in some PGA tour events prior to the Masters, which kind of got my feet wet. But nothing perhaps prepared me for what was the best week you could have. I do remember this, and I'll tell you this vividly. I stayed at Augusta National, and I stayed there for ten days. I got up there early, and luckily I had a member's room, so I didn't stay at the Crow's Nest.

But I paid—this is what they charged me: a dollar for breakfast, a dollar for lunch, two dollars for dinner, and a dollar a night to stay there. Well, my bill for ten days was $78, I'll never forget it. It was like being at a hostel—I can handle that bill.

And they took such good care of me. Candidly, they take better care of the amateurs than they do the pros. It goes back to Jones's tradition, and that's why it's so meaningful. I could pick a lot of other days that have been significant, but given all the things I've just mentioned to you, I think that would be the most important one.

And I'll tell you this quick story. We walked off—first of all, Nicklaus had the honor and hit it a gazillion miles down the fairway, and I hit this toe-hook popup that didn't make it to the top of the hill. It was so ugly. I was shaking so bad I didn't think I could keep the ball on the tee. We walked off the first tee, we walked down the hill, and I turned to him and I said, I gotta tell you something—I'm scared to death.

I put my hand out, and I'm shaking, and he turned to me, and he put his hand out, and he's shaking too, and he said, I'm scared too, let's go have fun. And it was great, I birdied the first hole, I birdied the third hole, I was two under par after three. And I thought, man, this is easy. I went on to shoot 73. I think he shot 71.

And it was as good a day as there was . . . that's something you dream about.

Practice rounds were fun. It was just great fun, you paired up with your friends, other amateurs, professionals you knew, you had fun. The golf course was easy, you shot low scores, you think, this can't be this easy. Then the first round, the pressure is so suffocating, you say to yourself, when you get to play a shot at the green, I didn't know there was a pin position over there, things like that, I didn't imagine the greens would get so fast overnight.

And the enormity of it all is . . . I can't even describe.

I was thrilled when I saw the pairing from Tuesday night and tried to find [Nicklaus] on Wednesday to introduce myself, but that's back when Jack would come up early and then play rounds and then go home. I think he got back like late Wednesday afternoon, he hit a few balls, so I never had the chance to meet him, thinking that would help with some of the stage fright.

I will tell you this. I was so—you've heard this before—maybe disappointed when I met him face to face because I was so much bigger than he was. In my mind's eye he was Paul

Bunyan. You know, he was five-ten, five-ten-and-a-half, and has this high squeaky voice. But he's not. And that was at the time when he'd lost so much weight, he'd gone from being "Fat Jack" to being a pretty dapper dresser and looked pretty good and things like that.

And to say we had a large gallery was an understatement. I'd never seen so many people in my life when I got to the golf course. I thought I was gonna kill a few when I teed off—it's an experience that you're just not equipped for.

I made some mental errors, and he encouraged me through the whole way. He just could not have been nicer, it's as though he spent most of his day making sure that I was okay, that he stayed out of my way, he kept the crowd from moving when I played. He was as helpful as he could have been within the rules of golf.

And later, in fact after the round, he actually gave me his yardage book that he kept for years, and I wrote down stuff that I still have today. I showed it to my kids the other night, as a matter of fact. It was just way before the days of yardage books and stuff, he'd walked 'em off, you know, stuff that he relied on for years.

And you know, as I said, it began a great friendship.

It was a little bit of a letdown [after that]. I guess I was so pumped and primed, and played reasonably well, that's back when the scores were not very low because the greens were Bermuda and had poannu in 'em, so the scores were never as low as, say, they are now. And scoring was tough, so 73 was a pretty good round starting out.

I made the cut and played okay, I think I was low amateur, which was a thrill. It just . . . kept looking back at that time. Interestingly, I came back the next year as an amateur and got paired with Arnold Palmer. And Arnold was intimidating. Jack was terrific, he was imposing—Arnold was intimidating, and Arnold didn't speak much. That's back when he was still the

King—you spoke to him, he didn't speak to you, that kind of thing.

He wasn't rude, I'll never say he was rude, but he just intimidated—he had that look. And if you said something to him, I wasn't sure whether (a) he didn't understand me or (b) he thought I was the dumbest person there ever was.

The crowds were different . . . that was the Army. They were wild—they wanted him to do well. He was . . . I won't say in the declining, I guess he was in sort of a decline, but they still hung on to the hope that he was gonna hit some dramatic shot or hole a four-iron or hole a bunker shot. They were more boisterous, where Nicklaus's crowds were more reserved. You watched Nicklaus to see great play, you watched Arnold for excitement.

And I will say this, I also shot 73 with Arnold, but I made six birdies, it was a weird round. And the only thing he really said to me, when we got in the scorer's tent, he signed my card and he looked at me, and he goes, do you always play like this? I had no comeback.

And then, of course, I went back, I ended up playing five years there, always made the cut, went back as an announcer with CBS for ten years. It's just a special place. My boys got to play up there last Christmas, so Augusta National and the Masters and Jones are just special.

I think the single most precious memento or trophy I have from my entire golf career is a letter I got from Bobby Jones after I won the Amateur. And I don't say or share that with many people, but you can throw out all the other things, and the fact that he took the time to write me when he really was not well. I think he died shortly thereafter . . . it's the most precious thing I have.

It was right after I won the Amateur, it was like in early October of 1969, and he said, "I watched with interest your play at Oakmont," and he talked a little bit about how much he liked the golf course, how tough a test it was, and he admired the way I conducted myself, and things like that. I mean, he said all the things that, to a southerner, and to someone who admired Jones, just made your heart skip. . . . [The content was] just, "I hope that my health will allow me to welcome you to Augusta National this spring, we look forward to having you as a Masters participant." I've had it framed, and it's still in that frame.

I never met him. I'm so disappointed that his health failed him, he never made it to the Masters in '70, and I think he died at the end of '70, I'd have to go back and check that. But he just couldn't get around.

They tell me that he would dictate letters, and he would sign letters, and it would take him an interminable length of time to put the pen in his hand. He took his left hand and put the pen in his right hand and molded his fingers around the pen, and the signature on my letter in particular reflects that of someone who barely was able to write. I mean, it's excruciatingly painful just to look at the signature even today. . . . He signed it Bob Jones—never Bobby, he was always Bob.

I'll tell you one other side to that . . . it's years later now, and I was up in the mountains of North Carolina and was shown a home where Jones lived in the summertime. And it was just like you'd imagine it would be—quaint, comfortable, but not fancy, great view of the mountains. And I tried for years to buy the house, some people bought it who were nongolfers, and they really didn't know what they had. But it's up there today, in Highlands, North Carolina. They still have it.

At that point [the people at Augusta] were very nice. They introduced me as low amateur, I was awarded, it was basically a sterling silver box, which I have today. But really at that time it was more the Masters champion, the focus was on the Masters champion. I was just there, it's just part of the tradition. I mean, it was great to be there on the putting green, and the previous winner put on the coat of the winner, and that was pretty neat. I think it was the year [Billy] Casper beat [Gene] Littler in a playoff.

My greatest day as a pro . . . well, this will surprise you, it came recently. I left the tour in '82, I broke my elbow, this is at age thirty-four, I came out of retirement at age fifty, when I turned fifty I played in the U.S. Senior Open and the Senior British Open, and both my sons, each of my sons, caddied for me in the tournament. That's probably my favorite day. The U.S. Senior Open was at Olympia Fields, and the Senior British at Fort Rush.

[It's] just that I was so proud to have—in the first case the Senior Open—my oldest son Dalton caddy for me. In fact, we played with Graham Marsh, who went on to win the tournament. And at the British Senior later that summer my youngest son, Butler, caddied for me.

I thought that because I left so early—in fact, one of the kids was not even born—that I would never get to enjoy that. While these senior players that play on a regular basis get to enjoy it in a more frequent manner, I missed that. But anyway, I got to do that, and it was a thrill for me, and a thrill for them, and it was pretty special.

They get to see you compete, even though I certainly wasn't ready to compete at that level. They saw me, you know, as one of the other players, and they got to sort of be inside the ropes and see what it's really like in the crucible of competition. So it was good for them too.

It's more a learning experience for them—I mean, my future's clearly behind me, I've moved on into business, they know me as a businessman, not as a golfer. In fact, last night, it's funny you called, I was flipping around the channels, I got bored with the football game, and there was the '73 Masters, and I was on. They watched me, they were saying, look, Dad, it's you, look at those pants. And I tried to explain that polyester was big back then—it was ridiculous. So that's their frame of reference. Anyway, it's special to have them out there with me.

I played some practice rounds with Raymond Floyd, Bob Murphy, Vinny Giles played with us one day, Jay Sigel. Now, I've been accused of being a little conservative, but to put it in perspective, I was the only player at that Senior Open to still have persimmon woods. I've been accused of being just a little bit right of Jesse Helms, but I take that as a compliment. Anyway, that was the fun part, I still have my old persimmon woods from when I played the tour, and could still hit it just as far as those other guys. My kids couldn't relate to that.

As an announcer? Yeah, the '86 Masters. That's easy.

What struck me at the time, because I covered Amen Corner, was [Nicklaus] kept making moves, he had birdied nine, ten, and eleven, bogied twelve, and I said, don't count him out. I remember saying that on the air. And as he went past my hole, we watched it on monitors, and it's as though, Bob, he orchestrated every movement on the back side as the roars went up, and it got deathly silent or quiet before he played. And it's like, when he moved, everybody else moved, when he stopped and played, no one else played. It was eerie.

He shot 30 on the back side with a bogey, with his son carrying the bag. Maybe that's why when my kids caddy for me I still think that's so special, because when he hugged Jackie when he walked off the eighteenth green, I just lost it. It's a good thing I wasn't [CBS announcer Pat] Summerall. It's horrible—we kid Summerall that he cries at Kmart openings, so I don't know what you should do there.

But clearly that was the best day. In fact, when I rode home from Augusta down to Jackson, I said at the time, I wish, or I hope that I pick up the paper tomorrow morning and read that Nicklaus has retired—that's it, I'm going out on top, that's as good as I can do.

I've played enough golf with him to know there's simply no quit in him, and he simply doesn't know he can't do the things that he does. Even on the twelfth hole, I don't know how well you know the hole or the back side of Augusta, but he played it way left of the flag stick. And I said at the time, before he got to the tee, having played with him there a bunch of times, he won't aim at the flag stick. He may work hard at making three, but he won't make a big score. And sure enough, he aimed it left and chipped up and missed the putt for par, but it didn't hurt him so much. And I knew the way he played.

He did all the right things, which he's always done. I've always said publicly that he won so many tournaments and so many majors not because of his ball striking but because of his course management. And that's what he did there.

I knew his tendencies, and I knew his mind-set. And I knew I could almost anticipate what his course management would be. He simply wouldn't let himself make foolish shot choices. If the flag stick happened to be way left on the eleventh hole, I knew he wouldn't aim at it. Sure enough, he aimed at the middle of the green at eleven and made a twenty-footer for a birdie. But that's the way he played.

And he laid up a lot of holes. For a guy that was as long as he was, he laid up more and played more conservatively off the tee than anyone I know. I keep trying to tell my kids this, I say, you know, he always kept the ball in play. He never beat himself. And so I could just see what was happening.

And of course, he'd had such a great history prior to that—he'd won five tournaments prior to that event in '86. Then a couple of years ago, when he played well, that didn't surprise me. He doesn't know he's now, in this case, he's sixty years old. In his mind he still thinks he's forty.

I just knew that he was ready to play well. I had talked to him during the tournament—I respect his privacy in terms of his pre-round preparation, but I could talk to him enough to both give him space and know that he was ready to play well. Now, all the elements have to sort of work with you to do what he did, shooting 66 the last day and shooting 30 on the back side, nevertheless he was capable that week. And of course, he finished it off.

I'm thrilled for him. I guess we have similar views of the game—I think, and this sounds self-serving, I think I truly treasure the traditions of the game. Right now, I serve on a couple of USGA committees and things like that, and knowing Nicklaus and how he felt about Augusta and Bobby Jones and how special that event was to him, we talked about that a lot, sort of personally, away from the golf course and stuff. I just knew what it meant to him. And that was the tournament that he always thought he could and should win. So nothing he did there surprised me.

We worked together at ABC, he helped me settle a lawsuit, he gave a deposition for me—he's just one of those guys that I might not see him for nine months, and I see him the next day, and it's like I saw him yesterday, that kind of deal.

I was never intimidated by him after I got to know him and wasn't afraid to call him "Carnac," which was his nickname, or give him shit when he needed to be given shit. I've been guests at their house, and Barbara Nicklaus is so special, and she's had a wonderful softening effect on him, because his ego can get carried away sometimes, and she'll quickly put him in place.

They raised great kids, they've got a bunch of grandkids, and I think one of his real joys in life now is that he's been able to create businesses where he can bring his kids into the business, it's just sort of a way to keep the family unit fairly close. So I think it's a thrill to him to be able to have Jackie and Stevie and Michael—and of course, now Gary's out on the tour, which has gotta be a thrill for him. I think he missed out on that when the kids were growing up, and I think this is his way to sort of make good.

As far as the overall state of the game goes, I think there's a real conflict now between the skill levels of the PGA player and the skill level of the twenty-four million people who play golf. And sometimes they clash. There's this hue and cry about equipment and the ball going too far, but Bob, you're talking about two or three hundred people that that might affect.

And you know, if there's a real sort of divide within some of the folks of the USGA between wanting to protect the game, the ball going too far, and the springboard effect of the club, etc., and the average guy, I come from that side, because we've owned and operated golf courses, we built nine golf courses, that's what I did in my business. And so I just say to them, look, I've got an eighteen-handicapper over here, and if he thinks he can hit it five yards farther, he's gonna enjoy the game more, he's gonna play more, and we're all gonna benefit. So there's the other side of the coin.

And I think that's the continuing debate among the USGA now, and how they handle that. This could be an endless argument here about what role the equipment plays—I'm a big advocate of saying that the athletes today are huge contributing factors to the fact that the ball's going farther. They swing the club faster. I mean, when I played, nobody worked out. Today everybody works out. And I think they've tended to ignore that for the most part.

I think the younger members of the executive committee are cognizant of that. But then there's the older crowd, who shall remain nameless, who can't seem to relate to that, who can't seem to recognize that. It's a real problem.

But I think over time it will sort itself out. I mean, what difference does it make, on the one hand, when you look at it, the scores on the tour, the scores and events are not dramatically lower. The ball may be going farther, but there are other ways to set up a golf course that might attack that.

In fact, I was up at Pinehurst last week with my younger son, and as I went around number two I was thinking, you know, this is perfect. You can hit it a long way here if you want to, but you bring a lot of trouble into play. At the Open this year there was no rough around the greens, and for the first time ever a real short game came into play as opposed to pitching out of deep rough every time. In fact, I make the contention that having deep rough around greens saves bad shots, where at Pinehurst the marginal shot runs way away from the green because there's no rough to save it.

And I think the USGA had a real eye-opener at Pinehurst this year. I would not be surprised this year if, at certain courses, you'll see a different type of setup. I hope so anyway. Augusta National has no rough. If you miss the green, the ball's gonna run into trouble. Now, you do have a lot of people around the greens, but at those greens where there are no people, it's fun to see a guy have three or four choices for a shot to the green.

LARRY MIZE

Playoffs, of course, have set the stage for some of golf's most dramatic moments, especially at the majors. The 1987 Masters produced a three-way matchup between Greg Norman, Seve Ballasteros, and Larry Mize that had drama to burn. In the end, it was the unsung, unknown local hero who took the green jacket, and that final day became Larry Mize's greatest day in golf.

It would have to be the Masters in '87. . . . I feel like I'd get shot if I don't talk about that.

I'd taken the week off previous to the Masters in '87, the last tournament I'd played in was the week before that, the Players Championship in Jacksonville. And I'd had a nice week, I'd played solid. I think I finished around twelfth or something. I had a nice week, so I came into Augusta feeling confident. I was playing well.

And you know, I don't think you ever expect to win, or at least I wasn't expecting to win, but I was thinking that I had a chance to have a good week and maybe win the golf tournament.

I got off to a good start the first day and shot 70, which put me in second place. And so I played in the last group on Friday, which was a lot of fun. I was playing with John Cook, he shot a 69. We played together the first day and shot 70 and 69, he shot 69, and then we played together Friday. I shot 72, I'm not sure what John shot, but we did not play together anymore.

So Saturday I shot another 72—actually, the last seven holes on Saturday was, I think, a key to giving me the momentum I needed going into Sunday. I was two over par for the day through eleven holes, and I hit my tee shot in the water at twelve, the par three. So obviously, [that's] not what you want to do, but I dropped it back about ninety yards to give me my full sand wedge and hit it up there about ten or twelve feet to the right of the hole, and made the putt for bogey. And that was a big bogey, because it gave me some momentum, I felt really good I only made bogey, and not double, after hitting it in the water.

So that put me three over for the day, and then I made three birdies coming in, from thirteen on in. I think I birdied thirteen, fifteen, and eighteen. So that got me back to even par, and it got me right back in the middle of the tournament. So that was a real key there, making the bogey on twelve and birdying three holes to shoot even and get to where I'm just one or two shots back and right in the thick of things. It gave me some momentum, and it gave me some confidence going into Sunday.

I really felt like I played well all week. You just need things like that to happen to win a golf tournament—you need to make a couple of putts here and there at the right time. And making that par putt on twelve was the big putt, because that gave me the momentum to not be too deflated after not playing that great that day and not scoring that great. That was a big putt there . . . it just gave me the momentum.

I remember that, you know, I was in second place after the first day, and I was still in good shape after the second day, I'm not sure where I stood. But you know, at this point in time you're just trying to play solid and stay in contention, because it's early in the tournament. So I don't remember much other than . . . you know, it's funny how that just stands out, what I talked about from twelve on in. I was about to shoot myself out of the golf tournament there.

Well, I'd never been this close to the lead, I'd never been this close going into Sunday. I'd had some good tournaments, I'd finished eleventh my first year, and you know, the previous year, 1986, I shot 65 the last day, which was a lot of fun to move back into about sixteenth place, to get top twenty-four to get back for '87. So I'd had some good rounds, but I'd never been this close to winning the golf tournament.

I was a little bit nervous. I remember going to bed Saturday night, I slept good, but I laid awake for a few minutes in bed, you know, excited about my position and the chance I was gonna have on Sunday.

I felt really comfortable on the course. That was my fourth time I played in the thing, fourth tournament and [fourth] time at the Masters, so at this point in time I did feel very comfortable on the golf course.

I was paired with Curtis Strange, which was a great pairing, Curtis and I are friends. I kind of made some birdies and bogies, it was a little bit of both on the front nine. I think I turned one under, and I can remember walking off the tenth tee with that big scoreboard there on eighteen, seeing my name up there like one shot back right there in the thick of things, and that kind of got the nerves jumping even more.

I told myself, you know where you stand, let's focus on the golf course and quit looking at the leader board, because it was too early to look at it, and I knew where I stood anyway. You don't have to look at the leader board, you know what you have to do.

The back nine . . . it was pretty much the same all day, birdies and bogies. I bogied the tenth hole, and then came back with a nice par at eleven. Actually, it was a big key, because I made about a fifteen- or a twenty-footer coming from the same line that I had the chip shot on later. So I made the nice putt there.

And twelve was a key hole, again. I hit a good six-iron up there about fifteen feet and made a birdie. And then I hit a driver and a four-iron on the green at thirteen and made another birdie there. So that gave me the lead, and of course, that was great, and it was a lot of fun.

Unfortunately, I bogied fourteen and fifteen and gave the lead right back. I knocked it over the green at fourteen and didn't get up and down, and fifteen I hit it over the green at the water on sixteen. And that was a learning experience for me there on fifteen. The pin was on the left side of the green, and I shot at the pin. And you don't shoot at that pin unless you've got a wedge in your hands, in my opinion. So I shot at the pin, and it went a little long and left, and if you go long and left on that hole, you're going in the water [toward] sixteen.

I learned that day to go at the center of the green, which is what the guys did behind me. Seve and Norman both went to the center of the green, hit it just over the back of the center, chipped it down and made the putt for birdie. That was definitely a learning experience there.

I felt pretty good—I think some of it was just the nerves at Augusta. I think that fourteen, the bogey there with the short game was a little bit of nerves. I think fifteen was a bad decision, that wasn't really the nerves. But I still felt really good with my game, I mean, I was playing well, I felt like I was doing everything good—it's just keeping your nerves under control to where you can execute and perform.

I think that's the big key . . . or really anytime, and especially at a major, and definitely at Augusta. It's a real intense, fun—I mean intense in a good way, but it's a real intense back nine at Augusta when you've got a chance to win.

I was disappointed that I'd just made the bogies, so I was just talking to myself, telling myself, that's okay, let's just birdie the last three holes. I was just trying to press on forward and pick myself up and not let it get to me.

And you know, I played the last three holes pretty good. I hit it on the green at sixteen, but I left myself about a twenty- to twenty-five-footer, and I two-putted there. And seventeen, I left myself about a twenty-footer there. I really was pretty comfortable, my nerves were pretty well under control. I don't remember anything really standing out, I was really just trying to give myself a chance to make birdie on the last three holes.

And I parred seventeen, and then eighteen I hit a good tee shot, and it was funny—Curtis was first to hit, he hit a three-wood. I had a driver out, and I saw where his three-wood went, and Curtis and I were hitting about the same distance at that point in time on that day. And I saw his three-wood went far enough, so I changed to a three-wood, which was . . . I think it was a good thing he hit first.

I hit the three-wood just to the right of the bunker, and hit a nine-iron on the green about six feet away. And I knew I had to make the birdie, so I was nervous over that putt, but I had a really good putt and knocked it right in the hole. That was a big thrill for me, to birdie the last hole to give myself a chance.

I remember Jodie Mudd got off to a good start, I think he eagled number two, eagled or double-eagled. I think he eagled number two, and he jumped up on the leader board. There were a lot of names up there with chances to win, you know, the scores weren't very low, we tied at three under, and that was the playoff.

So there was a lot going on . . . of course, Norman fell back a little, but then he charged on and made some birdies coming in. And Seve was right there, you know, Curtis was there, Bernhard Langer was there, [Roger] Maltbie was there, [Ben] Crenshaw was there—I just remember it was really jammed up, there were just a lot of people there.

But the course was just playing so difficult, the greens were so hard and fast that there were birdies and there were bogies, and a lot of holes you were just trying to make par and get off of it.

Of course, I'm in the playoff with these two great players, but the way I played all week, and especially the birdie at eighteen, gave me a lot of confidence. So while I was excited and nervous about the playoff, I really felt good. And I guess, as they say, I had my butterflies flying in formation.

So I hit a really good drive on the first hole, on number ten, and caught the downslope, and I ended up putting it by those guys by about thirty yards, I got the advantage of that bounce of the slope. I was last off, they both had hit, and I was last to hit, and I hit one right down the left side, because the wind was in my face, and I knew I had to burn it down the left side or I might leave it up top.

And I didn't want to do that, because then I've got a long shot in, and I had a three-iron in during regulation. To give you an idea, in the playoff I hit a seven-iron in, so I really ripped the drive down the left side, I hit it great. And then Seve hit just to the right of the green, and Norman hit a good shot, landed by the pin and went just on the back fringe. So I'm sitting there with a seven-iron just trying to hit a good shot in there and just hit it in there about ten or twelve feet underneath the hole to the left, just in perfect position.

It was a lot of fun. The crowd was going crazy, they were a large support for me, being the hometown kid, the underdog in there. So it was a lot of fun, the crowd was really behind me.

And you know, the playoff, Seve three-putted, Norman two-putted, and I missed my putt, so Norman and I went on to the eleventh hole. Actually, I guess my chances got better, because I'm one great player down, now there was only one great player that I had to beat, so the odds were getting better in my favor.

Well, you really don't think about [how famous they are].

And maybe the good thing last year, in 1986, Greg and I had gone through a six-hole playoff at Kemper. So I'd been in a playoff with Greg before, I'd played with those guys a lot before, so you're really not thinking about it. I'm just focusing on my game—I know that they're great players, but I'm just trying to win the golf tournament myself.

The gallery was pretty much mine . . . it was a pro-Larry gallery. I definitely had the hometown thing going, the underdog thing going, so the crowd, the majority of the people, at least the boisterous ones, were pulling for me. It was more of a cheer for me, which was a lot of fun. It was pretty neat.

On eleven, there was no downslope for me to get a big kick off of, so Norman outdrove me. But I went back to my good position, about twenty yards back, and then I had a five-iron to the green. The pin was cut on the left over by the water, and you know, trying to get in there close, but I think in the back of my mind making sure I didn't hit it in the water. I hung it out to the right, which back then was my tendency, to kind of hang it right a little bit, so I did. I hung this quite a bit right, about 140 feet right of the hole.

And then Norman was up there, I guess he hit a seven-iron or an eight-iron, I think a seven-iron on the right fringe of the green about fifty or sixty feet away. And you know, my whole thought now was to be really focused and put the pressure back on him, because he was still a long way from the hole.

So I wanted to hit a good aggressive chip shot, and the nice thing about it was there was no decision—there was only one way to play the shot, I had to play a bump-and-run. The green was too hard, so that's nice, because having to choose between a shot, sometimes you can get indecisive, and that was no problem with this shot.

And I just tried to play a good, aggressive chip shot. I hit it perfect, and it came off good, and it just looked good all the way. I just kind of froze and watched it, and then when it went in, I couldn't believe it, and I ran around jumping and screaming like a crazy man. It was exciting for me, but then, you know, I had to calm down and get prepared to go to the twelfth hole. You always have to expect the worst, so I had to calm myself down and prepare for that and, you know, watch him putt.

And when he missed his putt, he came over and congratu-lated me. It was just a tremendous thrill for me to win the Masters, and to know that I get to go back there every April and play in the tournament. It's a pretty neat thought.

You know, there wasn't much to say really—he just con-gratulated me and said, good shot, you know, just congratu-lated me on the win, and that's . . . there's not much else to say. I know he was disappointed, and I thanked him, and that's about all you do in that situation.

They take you right into the Butler Cabin, and then you do the CBS thing, they interview you. And icing on the cake, I got Jack Nicklaus, who was my idol growing up. Jack Nicklaus put the green jacket on me in the Butler Cabin. So that was a big thrill.

And then from there we went out to the putting green, where they have the ceremony out there, where Hoyt Hardin, the chairman, spoke, and then I think it was Jack Lewis, he was the low amateur, was introduced. And then they introduced me, and I had to say a few words, and I just . . . I can't re-member, I know I thanked the crowd, because they were great all week, and just told them what a big thrill it was for me.

And they went through the ceremony for the photographers on the putting green of Jack putting the jacket on me a couple of times. I know they got me kissing my wife, Bonnie, and I was holding up my son, then our one-year-old David, so I got some fun pictures of that.

From there, Bonnie ran home to put on a dress, because the champion eats dinner at the club that night with the membership . . . I take that back, from there I went to the press room, did all my press room things, and interviews afterward with TV and everything like that.

And then I went in there and they gave me . . . they might have given me a shirt, or maybe Bonnie brought me back out a shirt, I can't remember. She brought me a shirt, and I guess I borrowed a tie, and then I guess I put on my jacket, and I eat with the membership, my wife and I do, so she came back in a dress.

So it was getting pretty late, I don't know what time we started eating, we ate there with the members, and people came by and congratulated me, and that was fun. I don't know how much I got to eat, because people were coming up to me and congratulating me.

But it was fun, and we didn't get out of there until eleven-thirty that night. And Bonnie and I drove home, and of course, my parents live in Augusta, and we stay with them every year, so everybody was still up, and some friends were over, so we probably got to bed around two o'clock after we'd done pictures and everybody congratulated me.

I had to get up the next morning and do an outing the next morning at Fort Gordon, the military base there. I drove to Hilton Head, so it was kind of a busy Monday, and I was definitely a little pooped—actually, then I had to get up Tuesday morning and do the *Good Morning America* shows and everything, so I was pretty exhausted, I hadn't had much sleep. My 76 in the first round at Hilton Head I guess was understandable.

It was just a fun time . . . I'd love to do it again.

I don't really think it did start to hit me for at least a month or so. It was such a . . . for a while there afterwards I got so nervous teeing off because they would announce me as the 1987 Masters champion. And obviously I was not used to that, so when they did that, I would be more nervous than normal teeing off, just because of the introduction. So it was about a month after that it started to sink in. And it just gradually sunk in over time after that. It didn't sink in all at once.

It was more opportunities for me to play overseas, financially it was a tremendous tournament for me to win. The recognition that I received, I guess all of a sudden people knew who I was, the recognition was . . . actually that was probably the biggest change, the recognition part was the biggest change.

As far as who I was as a golfer, it shouldn't have changed me, but for a while I did go through an adjustment period, thinking that I had to either kind of play differently or live up to it, or something like that. I had to perform a little better, and well, it was just, actually after about two years I was reminded that I was still the same person, that I'm still the same golfer that I was before, and nothing had really changed other than I had won a tremendous tournament.

I was putting more pressure on myself, I was probably a little more frustrated, and my temper was coming back up. And basically it was my faith in Christ that kind of got me straightened out, let me know that I'm not significant because I'm a Masters champion, I'm significant because, you know, God loves me through Christ, through Jesus. So that was really the key that helped get my head screwed on right.

I know that when I won the Johnny Walker World Championship down in Jamaica at the end of '93 . . . it can't compare to [the Masters], but it was a lot of fun, because even though it was a limited field it was a real good field, about thirty guys or so, and I won by ten shots. You know, going out there with a three-shot lead on Sunday and shooting 65 and winning by ten and just pretty much blowing it open was a lot of fun.

I guess I've won eight times throughout the world, four on tour and four others, but that one stands out, just from that perspective. I mean, I've won by . . . I guess I won in Japan by three shots or something, but never by ten, and the round that

I played that Sunday has gotta rank up there pretty high as far as playing a round under pressure.

I think the main thing was my focus—I was just really focused. I did not get distracted, I did not let the pedal up, I didn't look ahead or look behind, I stayed in the present tense, and that's what you always want to do. And those days are rarer than you want 'em to be. It was just one of those days, I guess, as they say, I was in the zone and just kind of took it deep and kept on going.

I think I probably enjoy it as much now and maybe even more, because I'm able to see it clearer. You know, I'm not trying to do anything with it, I just know it was a tremendous victory for me, and I can really enjoy it. As far as the context, I don't know, it still is amazing that I won the golf tournament, but here again, I'm gonna try and do it again, but I think I'm able to see it clearer and have it in a little better perspective than I did when I actually won it.

It's always fun to beat great players . . . let's face it. I guess it's extra special that I won the Masters in beating two great players like that in a playoff. Maybe I see it clearer that way, I didn't think about that as much at the time. But to win the Masters at that time, and to win it by beating two great players like that in the playoff just kind of adds to it. Getting the coat from Jack, he was wonderful in giving me the thing—he said something like, you know, you handled yourself like a true champion. I never spoke to him during the week or anything, just kind words at the end, which was always nice. But you know, kind of everything just makes it special.

JACK NICKLAUS

Despite the litany of achievements that barely begin to describe Jack Nicklaus's amazing career, it's not hard to guess his greatest day. The 1986 Masters has become one of golf's defining moments in the twentieth century, as much for the emotion Nicklaus showed on the eighteenth green with his son Jackie, who was caddying for him that day, as for the remarkable win that he pulled off at the age of forty-six by shooting a 30 on the back nine at Augusta National. Nicklaus has talked about that day many times, but he offered his most thorough rendition of that victory in his 1997 autobiography My Story, *from which this account is excerpted.*

Poorly as I'd played throughout most of 1985, my early-season 1986 performance was worse.

My driving was nothing to write home about, but it was sensational compared to my iron play. Time and again I would stride up to the ball with an eight- or nine-iron in hand figuring how to best position it for a birdie putt, only to walk off the green with a bogey or worse. Out of seven tournaments I entered preceding the Masters, I missed the cut in three and could do no better than a tie for 39th in the other four. Flying up to Augusta for my customary on-site practice the week before the tournament, a statistic I happened on in a magazine painfully reflected the condition of my game: 160th on the money list with $4,404.

By then, though, I was feeling better about my prospects than in many months.

Although Jack Grout was still mending from open-heart surgery, he had felt strong enough by early March to accompany Jackie down to Miami for a day to watch me play at Doral. Asked afterward for a diagnosis, my old friend and teacher minced no words: way too handsy.

The more I thought about this judgment, the more evident its truth became to me. Although at my best my hands and wrists played a key part in delivering the club head to the ball correctly, they did so reflexively, never through conscious direction. Accordingly, my sense of their role in the swing had always been one of passivity compared with the motion of my arms and the work of my lower body. This was a product of Jack's endlessly repeated doctrine of my youth: "reach for the sky" swinging back, and reach for it again on the follow-through.

With Jack's help, I began reaching for the sky again the Monday after Doral, and although I missed the cut in New Orleans ten days later, I felt better about the way I struck the ball. Another missed cut followed at the TPC [Players Championship] a week later, but by then even more light had appeared at the end of the tunnel. But the question remained: would I have exited the long, dark passage by the Thursday of Masters week?

My first three rounds of the Augusta National that week were 74–71–69. I played about as well as expected to from tee to green, and pitched or chipped nicely the few times I missed the greens. Thus the progressively lower scores were mostly due to steadily improved putting.

All spring I had used a new aluminum-headed, large-faced, offset, center-shafted putter that my equipment manufacturer of the time had developed. I had not recently putted particularly well with it, but as the club felt progressively better and better in my hands, I went from putting poorly the first day to okay the second on dry and crusty greens, then pretty well on Saturday. Somebody asked me in the press session after that third-round 69 about when I had last broken 70, and I responded that it was so long ago that I couldn't remember, which was the truth.

After fifty-four holes I thus stood at two under par. The bad news about that number was that it left me four strokes back of Greg Norman. But there was also some good news. Even though the list included Seve Ballasteros, Bernhard Langer, Tom Kite, and Tom Watson, there were only seven players between Norman and me.

The natural tendency when trailing going into the final round of a tournament is to focus mostly or entirely on stroke deficit in evaluating one's chances and deciding strategy. I'd learned a long time ago that an equally important factor is the number of players needing to be overtaken. That evening, weighing how I was by now playing and putting against the number of golfers ahead of me, I felt good about my chances.

Soon after breakfast Sunday morning, Steve [Nicklaus's second son] called from Hattiesburg, Mississippi, where he was working the event for PGA tour members [who had] not qualified for the Masters. Well, Pops, he asked me after we'd talked a while, what's it going to take? I told him I believed 66 would earn me a tie and 65 would win. That's the number I've been thinking of, said Steve. Go shoot it.

By the time I stood where my drive had finished amid the pine trees off to the right of the eighth fairway around three o'clock that afternoon, the possibility of doing so seemed pretty remote. After comfortably parring the first hole, I'd birdied the second with a nice pitch and putt after pushing my drive into the trees on the right, but then three-putted the tough par three fourth hole after my two-iron tee shot landed just short of the cup and trickled forty feet back down the green.

At the par three sixth I felt I'd given away another shot when I missed the putt after knocking a five-iron four feet past the hole. And then came a stroke of good fortune that reinforced my sense that this might still be my day.

Had I been in the lead or closer to it, I would have punched an iron shot back to the eighth fairway through a six-foot opening between a couple of large trees about twenty feet ahead of me. As things stood, I felt I had to begin putting better numbers right then if I was going to get in the hunt. This was a par five hole where I'd always looked for birdies or better, and my yardage checks confirmed I was within three-wood distance of the green. Studying the gap, I figured that if I could keep the ball down and fade it slightly while still striking it solidly, I might just get home.

I pulled the three-wood from the bag, set up extra carefully, made what felt like a good swing, but pushed the ball slightly. About a foot to the right of the tree forming the side of the gap I was aiming at stood another fat pine. My ball shot through that little aperture and finished just to the right of the green, from where I pitched to about ten feet and two-putted for par. It was a tremendous gamble followed by a huge piece of luck, and I still get cold shivers whenever it comes to mind.

Because of its precipitous back-to-front slope, Augusta National's ninth green is one of the trickiest to putt of perhaps the trickiest eighteen putting surfaces in golf. My pitching-wedge approach had left me about eleven feet above and to the right of the hole. I'd walked over and was beginning to set up to the ball when a huge roar came from the direction of the eighth green.

Aha, I told myself as I backed off, that's either Kite or Ballasteros making eagle. Then, almost before I could get back to my putt again, along came another enormous yell from the same direction. Aha, I told myself, that's the other guy also making eagle. And, indeed it turned out that both players had done just that by holing pitch shots, Tom from about fifty yards and Seve from eighty.

The hullabaloo naturally had stirred up the huge gallery around the ninth green. To settle things down, I turned to the folks nearest me and said, okay, now let's see if we can make that same kind of noise here. People laughed and applauded, and when I got back over the ball I found myself more relaxed and very positive about both the line and speed of the putt. I made a good stroke and watched the ball roll dead in the heart of the hole for a birdie three.

I really should have hit a three-wood instead of the driver off the tenth tee, and I got another break when the gallery blocked the ball from going far enough right to tangle with the trees separating the tenth hole from the eighteenth. I followed up with a nice four-iron to about twenty-five feet, and felt even more comfortable over the putt than I had the one at nine.

The eleventh hole, the beginning of Augusta's Amen Corner, becomes more dangerous the shorter the drive you hit, due to the pond tightly fronting the green. I crushed my tee shot, leaving me with only an eight-iron second that stopped about twenty-five feet past the pin. Sandy Lyle, my playing partner, was on the same line, and after he moved his ball over one putter-head length, I decided to roll mine just inside his marker coin. It was a perfect read.

Periodically after Angelo Argea stopped caddying for me in the late seventies, one of my sons would volunteer to take the bag, particularly in the majors, and Jackie was looping for me this time. Jackie jumped high in the air from a standing start as the ball disappeared in the hole. Birdie, birdie, birdie. Three under par for the day, five under for the tournament.

As I walked onto the twelfth tee, I received an incredible ovation from the thousands of people gathered in the wooded area that forms the peak of Amen Corner. Few of them, I imagined, had expected this rally by the old guy, but it was clear how much they appreciated it and wanted it to continue.

If I needed any further charging up, it was the twelfth hole that provided it. The wind seemed to have come up a little, meaning that the club I probably needed to hit was the six-iron. But I had a problem with that—if I aimed over the center of the front bunker to be sure of not going right and down into Rae's Creek off the green's steep front bank, but pulled the ball left or hit it a little strong, I would either end up in the back bunker or face a very difficult chip from the bank behind the green.

Eventually I decided on a firm seven-iron, and the wind came up when I began swinging, causing me to pull the shot a fraction. Finishing as it did on the back fringe, it wasn't that terrible a shot, but after I hit a pretty good chip that took a bad bounce, then an even better putt that caught a spike mark, the bogey I walked off with made me mad. Come on, Jack, I told myself, don't do what you did yesterday after you birdied twelve and became defensive. The only way you're going to win this thing at this stage is by being aggressive. Go for it, big fella.

The pep talk seemed to work immediately, because at thirteen I drew an extremely solid three-wood tighter than I'd planned around the dogleg elbow. This left me with a three-iron to the green that I wanted to fade in, but had to draw because of a little branch sticking out from the trees that line the entire left side of the hole. The ball stopped about thirty feet past the pin, from where I two-putted for my fourth birdie in five holes.

A glance at the scoreboard as I walked to the fourteenth tee showed me that the contenders by that point had been reduced to four: Ballasteros at seven under, Kite at six under, Norman at five under after double-bogeying ten, and myself at five under.

At the fourteenth hole I hit a three-wood off the tee, then played a little six-iron that looked great in the air but ran just over the green into the back fringe, leaving an awkward chip that I rolled down perfectly for a tap-in par.

Since turning for home I had been conscious that whatever the other holes brought, I would have to eagle the par five fifteenth if I was going to win the Masters. A fine drive was necessary, and I hit one, absolutely nailing the ball into the light breeze, leaving myself 202 yards to the hole. I hit a solid four-iron, the ball never leaving the flag and landing just short of the hole, then rolling down about twelve feet to the left.

After we got down to the green and began our surveying, I suddenly remembered that I'd had a similar putt for eagle in an early round in 1975, but hadn't hit it hard enough. As I finished aligning myself over the ball for about six inches of break, I switched focus totally to distance, telling myself, let's make sure we get this ball to the hole—just hit it hard enough. *Plunk*. Eagle three, five under for the day, seven under for the tournament. Whoops, I said to myself, here we go.

Although I don't remember registering what must have been the huge roar when the ball dropped, as I was walking after my tee shot on fifteen, Seve was holing a putt of about eight feet for an eagle three at thirteen. Glancing at the scoreboard to the right of the thirteenth green as I headed to the sixteenth tee, I saw that he was now the only player ahead of me, and by only two strokes. The thought that went through my mind was, well, he still has some golf ahead of him.

The club I most like to hit at the par three sixteenth at Augusta is the six-iron. On that day, with 179 yards to the cup and the breeze in my face, I knew as soon as I stepped on the tee that it had to be the five, and a solid one too. Put it up in the air, was my last thought before swinging, and I guess I did so just about perfectly, because, although the bunker that was short of the green prevented me from seeing the ball soon after it began rolling, the ever-louder crowd saw on videotape that the ball had missed the hole by about half an inch, before trickling about two-and-a-half feet past and to the left.

It was a tricky little putt, though, and Jackie and I took all the time we needed deciding how much from left to right the ball would break. When it fell in the heart of the hole, I was glad I hadn't putted before we reached total agreement. Six under for the day, eight under for the tournament. And now, for the first time, I was absolutely certain that I could win myself a sixth Masters. So much so, in fact, that as we walked to the seventeenth tee, I told Jackie, hey, I haven't had this much fun in six years.

As I was beginning to address the ball with the driver at seventeen, a big gallery reaction from the direction of the fifteenth fairway told me to back off. It was a strange sound; loud, but somehow more like a moan than the roar that Masters galleries famously let loose when a contender does something dramatic. I told myself Seve had either holed out from somewhere off the green at fifteen or hit into the water, and I would have liked to have known which before I teed off. But unduly delaying play is against the rules, so I got on with my business, which was to drive up the left side of the fairway to set up the best angle to the green. I made what felt like a good swing, but pulled the shot a little too far in that direction.

As I walked to the side of the tee, someone in the crowd announced that Seve had hit his second shot at fifteen into the lake fronting the green. Later, seeing a replay on television, it seemed to me that he just quit on the swing, perhaps because he was uncertain whether the four-iron he was using was the correct club. Whatever, he ended up with a bogey six.

When I got to my ball, I found it in light rough midway between a couple of pine trees, with the branches of one of them necessitating that I knock the approach down a little bit. The distance was 125 yards, which normally would have me reaching for the nine-iron. With so much adrenaline flowing, I decided on the pitching wedge and played exactly the shot

I'd visualized, a crisp semi-punch that stopped the ball about ten feet left of the pin.

As on the previous hole, the putt was a difficult one to read, resulting in much conferring between caddie and player. Jackie said left edge. Remembering the putts here, perhaps influenced by Rae's Creek, always seemed to break more right than they appeared to, I figured just outside right. That's what I went with, and the ball broke beautifully dead into the center of the cup.

Miraculously, stunningly, at nine under par I now led the 1986 Masters.

From my birdie putt at nine to the one I'd just made, I had played the most aggressive golf in my career in a major since my make-or-break final round at the 1972 British Open. Walking to the eighteenth green, I decided on a strategy change. You've had an incredible run to get where you are, I told myself, so don't screw it up now by trying to cap yourself with a birdie at eighteen. Just go ahead and play the hole intelligently. If you make birdie, great, but par will be just fine.

That translated into a three-wood from the tee, which I hit solidly into ideal position just to the right of the bunkers guarding the left side of the fairway. Throughout most of my career, the cup on Masters Sundays had been cut in the lower tier of the two-level green directly behind the front left bunker. This time it was located in the right rear segment of the upper tier. The math indicated I had 179 yards uphill into a slight breeze. The club I'd wanted to hit walking to the ball was the five-iron, and that's the one I quickly decided on and pulled.

The swing I made was one of my best of the day, but as the shot reached its apex, I felt the wind hit me in the face and knew the ball would finish short of the green's upper tier. It actually flew farther than I figured, landing about two-thirds of the way up the green, but then rolled back down about forty feet short of the cup.

I will never forget the ovation we received on our walk up

to the green that day. It was deafening, stunning, unbelievable in every way. Tears kept coming to my eyes and I had to tell myself a number of times to hold back on the emotions, that I still had some golf to play. But, as at Muirfield in 1972 and St. Andrews in 1978 and Baltusrol in 1980, it was awfully hard to do.

Getting down in two from forty feet on Augusta National's huge and difficult eighteenth green was far from the position I wanted to be in, but it was what I had to deal with to possibly win a sixth Masters. I kept telling myself, don't leave yourself a second putt, don't leave yourself a second putt. And, most fortunately, I did not, closing out a back nine of 30 and a round of 65 with a tap-in of about four inches, a distance I've generally been able to handle.

The affection Jackie and I then showed each other seems to have become one of sport's most indelible moments, and it will surely remain one of my most cherished memories through all of my remaining days. Jackie simply could not have been more helpful or supportive in the way he handled the mechanics of an always stressful and grueling task, nor in the timeliness and insight and sincerity of his encouragement. It was just a wonderful experience to have one of the people I care most deeply about share by far the most fulfilling achievement of my career.

And what made it even more wonderful was that Jackie also enjoyed it so much. I was so proud of him, he would tell the press later that evening. Finally, when I putted out at eighteen, he told them, "Dad, I loved seeing you play today. It was the thrill of my life. I mean, that was just awesome."

From the scorer's tent we were taken to Bob Jones's cabin over by the tenth tee to watch the eight players behind us finish the tournament. By the time we got there, Watson and Nakajima, the pair immediately behind Lyle and me, had putted out, and Ballasteros and Kite were coming up the eighteenth fairway. With the wind knocked out of his sails on fifteen, Seve had three-putted at seventeen to drop to seven under par.

But Tom was still at minus eight, meaning he could tie me with a birdie. Ideally positioned off the tee, he hit an approach that landed on the front of the green's upper tier, then ran to within about twelve feet of the cup. As I watched his putt after about six feet I thought he had made it, but at the last second the ball swerved to the left and stopped on the lip. His score was 67, which in many years would have won the Masters for a golfer in contention starting the final round.

As the putt missed, someone in the room said, okay, that's it, it's all over. No it isn't, I quickly replied, you've still got Norman. Donnie Hammond and Bernhard Langer, the next-to-last pair, were no longer a factor, and neither was Nick Price, Norman's playing partner. But Greg had surged to nine under par with four straight birdies from the fourteenth through the seventeenth, the last of which I'd seen on television. If he parred eighteenth, we would be tied. After mostly sitting since I arrived at the cabin, and aware that my back was beginning to stiffen, I got up and started walking around while still looking at the screen. Greg might birdie to win outright, but the odds were favoring a playoff. If it came, I wanted to be as ready for it as possible.

Greg's tee shot at eighteen split the fairway, but was far enough back to indicate that he'd hit the three-wood. I figured he would play either the four- or five-iron, and he went with the former. I could tell from the way he almost lost his balance that the swing wasn't a good one, and the ball flew into the gallery well right of the green. Long experience told me that he needed a miracle to birdie from there, but I continued pacing because he could still par the hole. He made a good attempt at about the only shot that would work for him, pitch-and-running the ball to the back of the green about fifteen feet above the cup. Considering how he'd putted the previous four holes, I felt there was a pretty good chance that he'd make this one, but as soon as the ball started rolling it was apparent that he'd pulled it slightly.

Amazingly, stunningly, I had played the last ten holes of the Augusta National in birdie-birdie-birdie-bogey-birdie—par-eagle-birdie-birdie-par, and it had won me a sixth Masters.

I would have been on top of the world for a long time after that victory without any of what followed it, but the reaction of hundreds and hundreds of people, from close friends to complete strangers, and from everywhere golf is played, with calls, telegrams, cards, letters, flowers—even champagne—simply would not let me down from my high for weeks and weeks afterward.

We stopped counting the pieces of mail when they reached five thousand. Mountains of them arrived each morning at the house and office for many days, some addressed just "Jack Nicklaus, Florida, America," and each of them seemingly nicer than the previous one.

Most of them mentioned Jackie's and my moment of affection after I putted out on eighteen—it really seemed to have touched a lot of hearts. I've never been a great reader of anything, but I read every single one of those telegrams, cablegrams, cards, and letters.

Perhaps the one that sticks in my mind the most was the telegram from Arnold Palmer: That was fantastic! Congratulations. Do you think there's any chance for a fifty-six-year-old?

ARNOLD PALMER

The one constant in Arnold Palmer's greatest days in golf is the charge, and Palmer made perhaps his ultimate charge at the U.S. Open in 1960 at Cherry Hills, shooting a 65 on the last day of the tournament to come from well back in the field and win. Palmer made his move in the first seven holes of the final round, making birdies on six of them and then parring the last five holes to hold off a forty-seven-year-old Ben Hogan and a twenty-one-year-old Jack Nicklaus. That defining round helped set the stage for a remarkable career in which Palmer literally put golf on the map as a major sport in the latter half of the twentieth century. He won sixty tournaments on the PGA tour and another ten on the Senior Tour, but Arnie's real legacy is the combination of skill, style, and charisma that made him a pioneer and a true legend of the game.

I was playing very well at the time [going into the Open], I recall quite well, because I played Oklahoma City, and I played well there. And I was pretty high, and I got to Cherry Hills, and I felt good about everything.

But the first three rounds were just very disappointing to me—I played pretty well and nothing happened. It seemed like I was just sort of treading water, not doing much. And I knew that there was a chance that it would break open, but I didn't know when.

And it did, of course, in the last round, that's really when things started happening. You know, I wasn't surprised—as I say, I felt like my game was good, and I was just disappointed that it hadn't happened before the last round.

An example was the first hole of the tournament. I suppose I was excited about getting started, and I hit a bad tee shot and hit the tree, and the ball fell down in a stream running down the hill. And I made six on the very first hole. That kind of put me off a little bit.

But then it just sort of came back together . . . the problem was, nothing happened. I think I shot two 72s and a 71 going into the last round.

Well, I shot 65, and I did not putt particularly well. The first hole I two-putted, I chipped it in, which was sort of the thing that ignited the whole thing on one hole. And then I made a couple of fairly good putts. But then, after that, starting at the eighth hole, where I missed about a three-, four-footer there.

I made a par at nine, and then the back nine I played, with the exception of the eighteenth hole, I hit every green and just missed putts on most of the holes. I made one birdie on the par five, and I missed the green at eighteen and chipped it up, made about a three- or four-footer for a par. But the rest of it was sort of routine. There was nothing exceptional on the back nine.

So the action all happened on the front nine, in the first seven holes.

Well, I felt pretty good about it when it started happening the way it did. You know, I knew that the guys that were leading were in back of me, and that they would be looking at what I was doing, and that would have some effect on them. And of course, that's pretty much what happened.

You know, they kept putting my score up, and some of the reporters came out that had made some disparaging remarks to me earlier. And of course, my remark to them was, what are you doing out here?

Anyway, that was pretty much it.

I was very aware of what had happened—I had won the Masters, and I won the Open. And I was headed to the British Open, with great anticipation and expectation. I felt like my game was good, and I'd been thinking about the four majors, which I had talked to Bob Drum [the golf writer for the *Pittsburgh Press* who was Palmer's close friend] about. And of course, that became even more of a front-line conversation.

And it worked out pretty well, except I didn't win the British Open.

I was very excited, of course, winning the [U.S.] Open was one of my major goals, and I was very aware of all the things that were happening.

I suppose, to some degree, I was disappointed that I wasn't winning more [after that] . . . more Opens, more Masters, the whole thing. Of course, in '60, '61, I had a good year, but I didn't . . . I won the British Open, but I didn't do as well as I thought I should do.

I always felt that I was very fortunate to be where I was, and to be doing what I was doing, and to have all the nice things that were happening happening. So I didn't concern myself with the risks, the failures, things that didn't happen. I always felt like, well, tomorrow's another day.

I suppose that at that time I didn't think of it in that context [as a greatest day]. I could cite the British Open at Birkdale, or at Troon, or the Masters a couple more times too. I was thinking that I had won, and I had that personal satisfaction.

I guess you have to think . . . I think about the things I did as a child when I was playing golf, and playing by myself at the club, and imagining the shots that I was making, and put myself in the position of playing in the Open, and having it happen. And it happened.

Certainly winning on the Senior Tour is great, but I think

it's just an opportunity for a second shot at doing the things that you love to do. I'm always happy to have won the Open and the PGA, which I consider probably the biggest and the best tournaments.

And I suppose winning the Open at Oak Hill in a playoff was one of the big thrills. It was a playoff against Casper and Bob Stone, and it was a tough day. And I think about winning the Open, which was very gratifying. What we did on the Senior Tour did pump the game up a little . . . that's the good news. So I think that's the greatest day on the Senior Tour.

JERRY PATE

At the age of twenty-two, Jerry Pate had the golf world by the string, winning the U.S. Open in 1976, his rookie year. Pate went on to become a major force on the PGA tour for the next half-dozen years before a shoulder injury at the age of twenty-eight curtailed a promising career. Pate lived the high life while he was on top, displaying a combination of skill, style, and panache that made him one of the more memorable characters on the tour.

Obviously, the greatest day in golf for me, I would have to say . . . man, you know, it's kind of hard, because you've gotta look back and determine what point in your career elevated you to the next level. Was it winning the Florida Amateur, was it winning the U.S. Amateur, and then was it winning the U.S. Open? And that kind of happened systematically in that order.

But I would have to say, probably, still, would be winning the U.S. Open, in 1976, at the Atlanta Athletic Club.

Two weeks prior to that, actually the Monday the week before the Open week, I had to qualify in Charlotte for the Open. And there were probably about 130 or 140 entries playing for like four, five, or six spots. I can't remember how many there were. Let's say half a dozen, six spots.

And I was second in the qualifying, which got me into the

Open—I was not exempt. And the week before that, the Sunday before that Monday I qualified, I finished up at the Philadelphia Classic that was at White Marsh Golf Club, and I bogied seventeen and eighteen to fail making a playoff by one shot. Tom Kite and Terry Beal went into a playoff, and Kite ultimately won. So I finished third there.

And the week before that was the Memorial, I believe, which was Jack Nicklaus's tournament, maybe the first year he held the Memorial, the first official tournament, and I finished about eighth. So I had a good tournament there. So I was sort of on a high, I was playing better each week—this was my rookie year, you've got to realize. So just making cuts was something I was proud of at that point in time.

When I came to the Open, I started thinking back to the year before. I had played the U.S. Open the year before in Chicago, and shot 79 in the first round after starting out birdie, par, par, birdie. I was playing with [Hale] Irwin and Gary Player, and I was leading after the first four holes. And then when I realized I was leading, I got nervous, I just came unglued and shot a 79 that day.

The last three days I think I beat just about everybody in the field. Maybe [John] Mahaffey and Lou Graham, who ultimately tied and played off on Monday. But I played extremely well on Friday, Saturday, and Sunday, and I made the cut, like 79–69 is what I shot, which I believe was 148 at that time. And I made the cut, and I went on and played my last two rounds at like 71–73 or something.

But back in those days you could shoot 70 in the U.S. Open and you were obviously a threat to win. So when I arrived in Atlanta, and I had just finished well in Philadelphia the week before, I just finished second in the qualifying to get in the Open, so my confidence level was extremely high. I always played well on tight golf courses or golf courses with tight fairways, and the Atlanta Country Club was not necessarily a tight golf course, but it had some difficult driving holes where you really had to be a straight driver, and you usually always have to be a straight driver to win an Open.

I felt like, well, if only I could get off to a good start the first day and shoot a low 70s, and I believe I shot a 71. In fact, I think I bogeyed the last hole to shoot 71. The first day I was playing with Charlie Coody and maybe Bruce Devlin, I know it was Charlie Coody. Isn't that terrible that I can't remember—I mean, it's only been almost twenty-five years. And then the third day I was paired with Rod Funseth, because you played with the same guys the first two days. Rod Funseth, who's dead now, he never even warmed up, he just walked up to the first tee and hit it.

And then the fourth day I was paired with Mahaffey in the last group, which was pretty exciting, to be a rookie on tour playing in the last group on Sunday in the U.S. Open. When I started the first hole, I drove it right in the center of the fairway, and I missed the green. The pin was tucked on the front left, and I missed the green left, the ball buried on the back slope in the front bunker.

And, I mean, it was looking like I was gonna make six. I had an impossible shot. And somehow I just took the club straight up and just stuck it down behind, on top of the ball, right behind it, and it just popped up real high and came down and just barely carried the lip of the bunker, released, trickled down the green, and rolled up about a foot from the hole for a gimme.

So I parred the first hole, and then I parred the second, and then I birdied the third. And knew right then I had a shot at winning, and so that way I was just chasing Mahaffey the whole day. He had the lead, but I was just right on his heels.

It wasn't until the fifteenth hole . . . I bogied fourteen and then the fifteenth hole was about a 220-yard par three downhill. I hit a one-iron about six feet from the hole, and I made birdie. That got me to within one of Mahaffey. Then the next hole, sixteen up the hill, he three-putted, and I two-putted for par, and we're tied.

And then we went to the seventeenth hole, par three, where I two-putted for par, and he three-putted, so now I had a one-shot lead going to eighteen. And at eighteen we both drove it . . . he drove it more to the right, it appeared, off the tee, than I did, but I hit it farther off the tee, and it was a dogleg to the left off a blind tee shot, and I didn't really think I was in the rough. I thought maybe it was in the rough, but when I got there it was well in the rough.

When we came up to the first caddie, I had the ball marked, and it was about ankle-deep. And then we went on, and I looked about twenty yards ahead, and there my ball was sitting right up on top of the grass, a perfect lie. I was just lucky that I had a perfect lie. I had about 190 yards to the hole, I had a four-iron in my mind, and my caddy kept telling me it was a five-iron. And back then, of course, the balls didn't go anywhere, you had those little small-dimple balls, clubs were shorter, clubs had more loft on 'em. So hitting a four-iron today would be like hitting a five-iron back then.

I had a four-iron out, and my caddy told me to hit a five-iron—John Considine, in fact, he still works for me today, not as a caddy, he works for me in my business. He said, no, it's a five-iron, you only have about 180 to carry the front, and the pin's on ten, just hit the five-iron. You can carry the five-iron 180 easily out of the rough, it's gonna fly on you.

The only problem he was worried about was hitting it long, being to the right, and not having enough club to the green, kind of angled away to the right. There was water up to the right side, and if I went long and left, or left, I would be in a bunker, so left wasn't a problem as much as it appeared on TV. Long wasn't a problem, there was a big bunker, I think there may even have been two bunkers. They've redone it, I can't remember that hole.

So I hit a five-iron, just real nice, high, and soft, and it came down and landed about two feet from the hole—I sank the putt and won by two.

Really what turned my whole tournament around was Saturday, playing with Rod Funseth. I three-putted the first hole for bogey, and then I parred two and three, and the third hole was a very difficult par three, about 200 yards, and the USGA had shaved the bank down in front of the green. It had a long sloping bank in front of the green. The green sat up about ten feet in front of the water, maybe fifteen feet above the water.

And I hit a three-iron that hit on the green and kind of kicked to the left and rolled and rolled and rolled and rolled over the edge . . . pretty much like Tiger's ball did in this last tournament. It rolled and rolled, and next thing I know it rolled down in the lake, so now I have to play short of the lake. My first shot I was hitting a six-iron, so I started out bogey-bogey-par-double-bogey. I three-putted one, I three-putted two, I parred three, and I double-bogeyed four on Saturday.

It ended up, I think I shot 68 that day. I turned it around, including an eagle on the hole on the back nine, hole twelve, a par five. And I really played well after that—I was four over after the first four on Saturday, and it looked as if . . . there he goes, there goes the rookie, on Saturday. I was in the next-to-last group, I think, on Saturday, playing with Funseth. And then Mahaffey was playing with someone else in the last group, I can't remember who it was, and on Sunday I was there in the last group with Mahaffey.

Just putting it behind me [was what made the difference] . . . telling myself that I was good enough to bring it back, and playing one shot at a time from there in. I was taught that by my dad, you've gotta focus on the moment, and play that one shot at a time.

I was the guy in pursuit, so when you're chasing the leader, you're in a more relaxed position if you're a tenacious player and an aggressive player, and most golfers are pretty tenacious. You want to go after the leader, and it wasn't until the seventy-second hole that I had the lead. I was tied for the lead, and it wasn't till after I walked from the seventeenth green . . . I didn't have the lead but one hole. How about that?

Then I birdied it to take a two-shot lead, and Mahaffey made bogey, and [Tom] Weiskopf and [Al] Geiberger in front of me made par, so they were all tied with Mahaffey, Geiberger and Weiskopf and Mahaffey were all tied. And Mahaffey bogied eighteen, and they parred, so Weiskopf and Geiberger were second, tied, and Mahaffey finished fourth, I believe, as it turned out.

That last shot, I'll never forget it as long as I live. Walking with me in the group was Harry Easterly and a guy named John Loppheimer, who went on to become the commissioner of the LPGA tour, and he went to work for Mark McCormick IMG, in fact, he still works for Mark McCormick in their London office. And John Loppheimer, they were walking with me, Harry Easterly was the rules official . . . I remember hitting the shot, and the crowd was going crazy, and it was starting to get dark, because they had about a two-hour rain delay that day. We got started late, it was at least seven o'clock at night, maybe a little bit later.

I recall walking up the fairway and looking at the big leader board and trying to figure out where I stood in the field. I watched Weiskopf and Geiberger ahead of me make putts for whatever, I thought they were possibly birdies. And everybody kept saying, no, those were for pars, and I asked John Loppheimer, are you sure all I've gotta do is two-putt to win? And he said, all you have to do is two-putt. I said, now make sure before I putt this first putt, you know, can I two-putt and win, or do I need to make it and win. And he said, no, all you have to do is two-putt.

When I walked up on the green and everybody kind of gave me a standing ovation—I mean, the ball was two feet from the hole on a flat putt, there was no way, you could almost die of a heart attack and roll it in and get it down in two. And I realized at that moment that I'd won the Open, and I was so nervous.

I mean, it was sort of like the feeling you have, and the only way I've ever had another feeling like that was the first time when I had my driver's license, I looked in the rearview mirror, and there was a blue light that had me pulled over. I didn't know what to think and what the consequences were gonna be, but I knew that I had taken a different course in my life, and my life was about to change. When you get your first speeding ticket, your life's gettin' ready to change—you know, your parents when you're sixteen? And I'll never forget the feeling when I stepped up to that green and people gave me a standing ovation, and everyone knew I had it won.

I remember it was time for me to play, Mahaffey went ahead and putted first, and he had wedged on the green and was on in four, and he made about a ten-footer for a bogey. And now it was my turn to just kind of eke it down in two from two feet. I remember gripping my putter and regripping it as I stood over the putt, and my whole body seemed numb, I was so nervous I could hardly feel my putter grip.

There's no other way to describe it . . . you know, you're just so nervous, and I guess it's anxiety or whatever, you cannot describe it. I've never ever had that feeling since, even though I've won some big tournaments, and hit some great shots in golf. After that I was sort of relaxed. I remember much later I shot 63 to win the Canadian Open, my second win, which was really as important as my first win, because it proved to the world of golf that winning the Open wasn't a fluke, that I could really play, and I shot like 263 or 266, which is a pretty low score—I think I had the scoring record at the Canadian Open there for a while.

But I wasn't nervous when I won in Canada like that. In fact, Jack Nicklaus was in the last group, he shot 65 and I shot

63. It was like a duel of birdies that day. But I was never as nervous in my career as I was in that putt. I knew that I had won the U.S. Open . . . that's the best way I can describe it.

I remember walking into the scoring tent, and my wife was there, she was all crying, and I can remember vividly what she had on. I remember signing my card there, Tom Weiskopf and Geiberger came up, they were waiting in the scoring tent, they thought we'd have a playoff the next day. I remember exactly how Geiberger had that little floppy hat on, and Weiskopf gave me a nice pat on the back, shook my hand, and congratulated me, and they walked out.

I can remember John Mahaffey, who was about in tears, and it was kind of sad, because John was such a great player and a good guy, and I felt like . . . and really, to be honest, for a couple of years he was mad at me for beating him, but I guess he got revenge when I three-putted the seventy-second hole at the PGA Championship and forced a playoff with he and Watson. And he won on the second extra hole against Watson and me, so he got his reward there winning a major championship.

But I really felt that there was some sympathy for Mahaffey, and when I was interviewed—I want to say by, it was either Jim McKay or Bill Fleming, one of the guys back then that used to work for ABC Sports, I think it was Bill Fleming, Mc-Kay was up in the booth—he asked me, did I feel sorry for John. When I saw the interview, I sounded cold, I said, well, I didn't say, no, I wasn't sorry for him, but I really did feel sorry for him. But I said, well, it's a seventy-two-hole tournament, unfortunately John had a bad break on the last hole. But you have to play all seventy-two holes to win.

I don't know what else you could say, but I really felt good about what I had done, because I thought I was a good player, I never dreamed I could win an Open my first time as a pro. But on the other hand, I guess I was egotistical enough to believe that I could, because I was low amateur the year before and felt like I had a shot at winning that year. So I don't know, it's just funny how circumstances happen.

The qualifying was very nerve-wracking—I would say the only comparative pressure would be qualifying for your card, really, more for the tour, not just one event. I guess you can blow it off, if you don't qualify for the U.S. Open, there's always next year, it's just one event. If you don't qualify for the tour, it's a whole year without playing the tour, and you have to wait until next year . . . it's a different feeling.

It was a total different feeling of being nervous, because the U.S. Open is the biggest tournament in golf, and I'm thinking, oh my God, I just won the biggest tournament in golf as a rookie, which was quite an accomplishment—only Bobby Jones and Nicklaus had won at that age of twenty-two. It's a little like Tiger winning the Masters when he was twenty, that was quite an accomplishment for Tiger Woods. You know, it's hard to describe that feeling, being so young and lucky and gifted, it's obviously not all luck, you've gotta have the talent, to be gifted and have the cards fall in the right place for you, hitting the right shots at the right time.

I used to get really tickled because people used to always laugh and say, well, he pulled that five-iron, no way he could have hit that five-iron at the hole. And I said, look, if you take a twenty-two-year-old kid and put him out there with a five-iron in his hand, he's not aiming at the middle of the green with a five-iron. In fact, I've been known to aim at the pin with a one-iron, much less a five-iron, and I think today you don't have anybody aiming at the middle of the green, they all go for the flag on every shot.

But what was really satisfying when I won the Players Championship in 1982 was when I came to the last hole of the Players Championship with a five-iron in my hand, and I hit it about two feet just to the left of the pin. And when I got in the press room, people were asking me about that shot, what a remarkable shot on the diabolical Pete Dye golf course. And I said, well, I guess I pulled another five-iron, huh? That kind of shut 'em up, after that they realized.

And you know, in my career, I had the four hole-in-ones at the U.S. Open, I was one of the guys that did that. I was the fourth person, I guess, to have a hole-in-one at Cypress playing on sixteen, I had a hole-in-one with a one-iron there, which was a pretty dramatic shot. You know, I had a few other remarkable shots in my career, that hole-in-one at Augusta a couple of times, shots where I hit the ball close to the hole during competition, under pressure.

But hitting a golf ball has always come sort of second nature to me, I've always had a slow and a smooth, rhythmic swing. So under pressure, the smoother your tempo is, the easier it is to get away with a bad swing. You've got time to regroup during your swing process and square the club blade up. I've been blessed with good tempo, which is not really . . . even though my dad used to tell me all the time, keep your tempo, think about your tempo, I could say either I was born with it or he taught it to me. I would say it was a combination of both, I don't think it was just second nature, I think it was something that he taught me to do, and something I tried to work on and maintain in my swing throughout my career.

Well, obviously, it was certainly a great milestone, not just a stepping-stone. It allowed me immediate access to anything in golf, it allowed me immediate access to just about any person in the world. I mean, I could literally pick up the phone and call the White House and get a response from . . . the president.

When you're twenty-two years old and you win the U.S. Open . . . I mean, look at Tiger Woods. Who could he not call and get a response from, right? Of course, we didn't have the media attention then as we do today. Tiger's success has been hyped up, but it was pretty special to be twenty-two years old and just won the U.S. Amateur and the U.S. Open, which at that time, I mean, Nicklaus and Bobby Jones and I all won the Amateur at twenty, and we all won the Open at twenty-two.

And then you turn around thirty days later, you knock off the Canadian Open, beating, in 1976, Jack Nicklaus [who] was no slouch. He was probably at the height of his game, and you knock Jack Nicklaus off with a 63 on Sunday— right then people realized that I could play. I was number one in the tour qualifying school. Everybody talks about how hard the tour qualifying school is, out of 420 guys, I was number one there. So that, in itself, my record was starting to show that I was, you know, a contender.

So that's where it changed my life, it opened up doors to the golf world, and just to the world, period. When I would go to Los Angeles, I would go to Bel Air Country Club, and all the movers and shakers and the people in the know would want to play golf with you, invite you to have breakfast or lunch, or come stay with 'em. You know, I was immediately on Bob Hope television specials, I did *Hee Haw,* I did sports banquet shows all over the country. I was asked immediately to guest-commentate in the booth on eighteen when I finished my round, at CBS or NBC, walk up and do a little commentary, just what was going on during the day. I used to stand in, guest analyst.

I immediately was put financially in an area that was so much ahead of my peers, from golf, that it was threatening to my relationship, and it caused a lot of harm in my relationship with other golfers. Immediately I started playing practice rounds with Jack Nicklaus and Arnold Palmer, I played practice rounds with Weiskopf, Lanny [Wadkins], Ray Floyd, Johnny Miller, and Trevino, all these guys were the top guys on tour at that time. They were the veterans and I was the rookie that came out with Curtis Strange, Gary Coke, Andy Bean, Jay Haas, and George Burns. They were all my contemporaries.

And there were guys, such as Ben Crenshaw, who won like a couple of tournaments but had not yet won a major. Guys like Bill Rogers, Bruce Lietzke, and Bobby Watkins, guys that were friends of mine, but they had not won. So it was probably a little bit intimidating to them that I had so [much] success . . . and also, it just built my ego bigger than life, and it probably hurt me.

There's no question, it's an ego builder when you go everywhere, and people are absolutely bowing down to you, every want and need. And I could do no wrong really in the eyes of a lot of people, even though I was just human. So you start believing your own stuff.

And then I went on and played a couple years and didn't win, then I came back and won the Southern Open twice, the Memphis Open, the Pensacola Open, and then I won the TPC [Players Champion]. When I won the TPC in '82 I was only twenty-eight years old, and here I'd won eight tournaments, a team championship, I had fifteen seconds, including three majors, seventy-five top ten finishes, and I'm twenty-eight years old.

I've got my own plane, I've had for several years, a King Air 200, which back then was almost a million-and-a-half-dollar aircraft. And the only other two people that had a jet on tour, or a plane on tour, were Palmer and Nicklaus. And we all had our own planes, and I was flying on every corporate CEO's jet in America, G2s and G3s, and traveling to Europe, riding around in Phantom 6 Rolls Royces to and from the course to the British Open, and taking helicopters to the Jackie Gleason Inverrary and Doral before Raymond Floyd ever thought of it, and when Greg Norman was a guppy, he wasn't a shark. And again, I'm only twenty-eight years old.

By that time Greg Norman had never even won a tournament, nor had Nick Faldo, on the PGA tour, or Nick Price, or the guys you see today that are almost my age. So it really put me up on a pedestal. And all along, I mean, people like Curtis Strange had not won the U.S. Open, I was ahead of Tom Kite on the all-time money-winning list at that time, and here's a guy that went on to lead the all-time money-winning before Norman passed him.

Money-winning doesn't mean anything really, it's irrelevant—I mean, David Duval won more money in the first two weeks he played this year than I did in my career. So to measure somebody's success today by money is ludicrous. You measure it by their top ten finishes, and where they played in the majors, or where they finished in the big tournaments.

But this is really where it took me. And there was a lot of jealousy among other players, I can remember really insulting Curtis Strange, who—in college Curtis and I were very, very close. I would say Jay Haas and Curtis were closer friends because they played at Wake Forest, but Curtis and I were extremely close, and to this day I really admire and respect and think the world of Curtis and Sarah, but I'm telling you, there was about seven or eight or ten years where Curtis was mad at me.

And I finally went and asked him why, and he told me, he said, you had a practice round set up with me one day after you had won the Open, and Jack Nicklaus asked you to play, I think it was, either Arnold or Jack, I think it was Nicklaus, and you blew me off and went and played with them. And I got to the course and saw you were right on the course and you had blown me off. And I said, you know, Curtis, I apologize, and I was so egotistical and into trying to be the best player in the world . . . please forgive me, but you probably would have done the same if Jack Nicklaus would have invited you to play, you would probably have gone to play with him.

Back then, it was more of a game of trying to climb the ladder to the top, and I had gotten to the top. And once you get up there, it's pretty lonely. And I think Curtis probably found that out, when he won back-to-back Opens, you could see his career's out in the pasture now. He's retired his career, he doesn't have the drive and desire, he's still a great player and a good person, but that one particular comment he made to me . . . boy, it just absolutely hurt my feelings for a long time.

And the sad thing is, I had hurt his feelings for a long time as a friend. Not purposely, though, and I'm sure this is what's happening to Tiger Woods, and he's gotta be real careful, although he's got some people like [Mark] O'Meara that've helped him and some other guys that have been close to him. I think that once you win enough, people kind of accept that, oh, well, he's all right, winning seems to put bad things behind you.

But I was so egotistical and cocky that I wanted to be the next Jack Nicklaus, that I didn't care if I said something that hurt somebody's feelings, because I really wasn't saying it to be mean. And I wasn't saying things to get ahead, I was just used to it. I grew up in a big family with six kids, and four boys, and I mean, it was like a verbal battle all the time who was best. You know what I mean . . . you understand where I'm coming from?

And I really didn't mean it personally, as a personal thing to other people. I just probably made guys that were my peers mad. The guys that I went to school with in college, there were still guys out there, but I think people that know me today know that as a person I've always been a giver—I mean, I guarantee you I'm not a taker. Even though it might seem like it when I was in college and coming up the ladder on the tour, that I seemed like a taker because I wanted to achieve greatness and wanted to win.

But I look at a person that's a taker as somebody that cheats to get ahead. I definitely would not do that and would not want to hurt someone to gain fame or success or fortune for me. But my point is that I was very competitive verbally, and that was really all insecurity on my part, that was my insecureness, that was my weapon. I was probably a pretty insecure person, I really couldn't sit there and look myself in the mirror and justify—Jesus Christ, how did all this happen to me so fast?

Two years before, I was in college, just kind of a mediocre player at the University of Alabama, which has a mediocre golf program. Even though we had a great coach, all of a sudden I had jumped up to the big league, but not only the big league on the tour, I was one of the best, the top ten players on the tour.

And hell, by 1982, I was probably ranked the number-one player in the world when I went out with my shoulder injury. I was the leading money-winner that year, I had just won the Players Championship, second at the Masters by a shot—well, I was third, but I got beat in a playoff by a shot by Stadler. Second at Doral, second at Colonial, just won the Memphis and Pensacola the fall before, was in the top six on the money list the last couple of years in a row, so I was getting ready to finish sixth, sixth, and first on the money list.

And boom, out went my shoulder joint, and it was the end of my career. By the time I was twenty-eight years old, I was done. Even though the public thought I was continually active for a lot of years, it was because I kept my face out there, I did television commentary, or I was playing enough that people—or they had commercials still running, I was doing Canon camera commercials, or Wilson sporting goods commercials, other types of things that kept my exposure up.

But really, by age twenty-eight I was done. I tore the cartilage in my left shoulder joint on one swing. I remember exactly when I did it, and how I did it, hitting one-irons—you know, don't ever practice one-irons. They're too hard to hit even when you have to hit 'em. People don't even carry one-irons anymore, they carry two-irons that are bent like a one-iron.

That's what's so funny about the game, people maybe hit the ball farther—hell, the clubs are the same, they've just got different numbers on the bottom.

But I tore my shoulder out in '82, and had surgery in '85, '86, and '87. I went a couple of years, and nobody really wanted to operate on me, they weren't sure what was wrong, and then they finally diagnosed it as torn cartilage, and then a torn rotator cuff. Then I had multidirectional instability in my joint. I'm okay today, but it's just a lot of tears after being twenty-eight and thinking now you're just getting ready to be in your prime, and you've already accomplished as much as anybody would ever dream of accomplishing.

And you think, from twenty-eight to thirty-eight, Lord-a-mercy, for those ten years I felt like I could have won twenty tournaments or more, easily. I was just warming up, and then—boom, that was the end of that. So there's a lot of unresolved issues there with me personally, from a golfer's standpoint. From a career standpoint, I think as far as a person, I think it took me till I was probably thirty-eight, forty, to realize it just wasn't meant to be.

And I had a lot of resentment really, for a long time, from about twenty-eight to thirty-eight, I carried a lot of baggage around and wasn't happy with myself. And then I jumped into doing television, and doing the golf courses, which I love to do, and I got involved in other things and businesses. I owned and operated some golf courses, I got into real estate development, did a lot of different things.

But you know, financially, I've always had some success, but personally, it was sort of a downer for me to not be able to achieve the goals that I thought I could achieve. I always wanted to win the Masters, growing up in Alabama and being born in Georgia. It just wasn't meant to be.

In fact, I'm trying to graduate from college. When I left my senior year, I went to school my senior year, I just lost a lot of my credits. And I'm just a few hours short of getting my college degree, and my senior project is to write a book.

I think it'd be interesting, because during that run, in the seventies and eighties, Lord, I had Bob Hope come ten straight years to the Pensacola Open, President Ford came and stayed at my home and played the Pensacola Open, and all the famous . . . the people, from the Dan Rostenkowskis to the Baron Hiltons to the Jimmy Buffetts and Charlie Prides and Glen Campbells and B. J. Thomases.

Oh gosh, Roy Clark was there eleven straight years, brought his band and flew in and did a celebrity show until 1989, and so from '78 to '89. I mean, these were friends of mine that came in and played in a celebrity golf tournament and had a wonderful time. George Lindsey came in and emceed it, every year they came to Pensacola, really just in support of me and loving golf, and knowing that I enjoyed golf and I had fun playing. I started the orange golf balls, and I did the jumping-in-the-lake trick.

I guess I was probably the prelude to Payne Stewart's antics with his knickers. I was the guy that came along after Trevino, and I guess Fuzzy [Zoeller] was still running his mouth in those times and saying crude things. But I was a little more in a colorful mood by using golf balls that had a lot of . . . I don't think I ever said any cuss words or anything that ever insulted anyone, but I would dang sure talk to the gallery. And I had fun with the gallery.

And I think that also was a little unnerving to my competitors and guys that were my contemporaries. Because I would go out and play, and walk down and talk to my caddy, talk to the gallery, you know, have a good time, smiling. I enjoyed it, I loved playing. I loved the competition. I loved mixing it up. I was the kind of guy that liked to play and get in a fight, and liked it. I didn't like getting beat, but I didn't mind mixing it up.

I'd always smile and give people that grin, and go on and hit the ball in there close to the hole. And a lot of the guys were sitting there with straight faces, with a scowl on their face, trying to concentrate, and they didn't think I cared. But believe me, I cared immensely about my game. It was just my style.

And then when I went to the orange ball deal and won at Memphis, I did the dive in the lake. And then when they had the diabolical stadium course that Pete [Dye] and Dean Beman built that everybody was ready to hang Pete and excommunicate the commissioner, I went and threw Dean in the lake and threw Pete Dye in the lake and dove in behind 'em.

That kind of set the tone of stadium golf and showmanship, that golf was not merely a sport, it was entertainment. That's what Trevino did, and that's what Chi Chi [Rodriguez] did, and I got many a call, believe me, not only from Tim Finchem in the last . . . four or five years ago I got calls from Tim, but many a call from Dean Beman, and sincerely saying that, you know, you need to get well, the tour needs you. They really need somebody out there to have fun, because this is entertainment. We're not just looking for guys that can shoot low, we're looking for guys that can entertain our viewers.

I enjoyed it . . . I loved it. And I think that was very intimidating to other players at times. I can remember playing with Trevino and Chi Chi, when they'd beat your brains out. Trevino would, and I could see why Trevino could beat Jack one-on-one because Lee would get out there and have fun doing it. And I think some people that are real serious in their actions on the course. Sometimes when someone is out there that looks like they're goofing off, it really is a little bit unnerving.

It was just my style to do that, I wasn't doing it to unnerve anybody. Heck, when I grew up, there'd be eight people traveling on a trip to south Florida from Alabama to go see my grandparents for Christmas in a station wagon with a maid in it, and I was in the middle of the family. I always used to have to sit in the front seat between my mom and dad 'cause I got everybody stirred up.

Interestingly enough (celebrating the U.S. Open victory) . . . after the ceremony, they used to have a tournament called the Amana VIP in Amana, Iowa. And it was the prestigious thing to go to back then for players, because they had a wonderful pro/am on Monday, and they had a wonderful celebrity party and show on Sunday night. And that's where I ran into and met Roy Clark and Charlie Pride.

And I got on Raytheon's plane right after the Open, with Ben and Polly Crenshaw, he was married to Polly back then, and Suzie and myself, and when I won the Open they invited me up to play in that tournament. So we jumped on their plane in Atlanta and flew to Cedar Rapids, Iowa, and we had the celebrity show, and we were late there, it was about ten o'clock we got there, and they were entertaining onstage.

And they introduced us, turned the lights on, and said, Jerry Pate, U.S. Open champion, big deal, so I'm like a kid. And the show went off, and after the show they had people just sitting around, having coffee or cocktails or whatever, and I'll never forget, Roy Clark and Charlie Pride had an annual poker game that went on.

And I didn't know how to play poker, and they said, come on, kid, come on and play cards with us. And I went in, and another guy, Woody Woodbury, was there, he was playing, and a couple other guys. There was some guy named Gus from Dallas or something, an Amana dealer. I'll never forget who these people were.

And I sat down, and they were playing hundred-dollar minimums in draw poker, and I couldn't even sort my cards. After I played three or four hands and threw in, Roy Clark looked at me, and he said, you need some more money, son? And I said, I sure do. He said, well, do you have any credit? And I said, I just won the Open. And I'll never forget, he said, I like your style, son.

So we stayed there until about three in the morning, drinking and playing poker, and I don't know how much money I lost, it turned out I don't think they ever made me pay. But Roy and I became immediate friends, along with Charlie Pride, and the next day Charlie and I were paired in this celebrity pro/am at this golf course called Stateline in Amana, Iowa.

That was the damndest tournament you'd ever see—they must have had ten thousand people come out from Iowa and watch all these celebrities and pros play. It was every Monday after the U.S. Open, every year, and they had great players. Julius Boros would play, and [Gene] Littler and [Bob] Goalby and on and on, I mean, back then Crenshaw played in it.

Everybody played in it, because they would pay your way, George Forsner was chairman of Amana, it was a big deal. They'd pay your way to come up there, and they'd always give you nice gifts, they were just wonderful people. And Lou King, who ultimately became the director of PGA America, was running it, and he was a great marketer and promoter of this Amana VIP program. Lou was the one that invited me up there, he and I became lifelong friends after that.

I played with Charlie that day, and Charlie Pride, every five minutes, he'd always go, in that soft Mississippi drawl, y'all know who this is, this is Jerry Pate, the U.S. Open champion . . . y'all get his autograph. Everybody was trying to mob Charlie, and he was putting the heat off of himself, saying, get his autograph. We had more fun playing that day, it's just memories I'll never forget.

CALVIN PEETE

Picking up where Lee Elder left off, Calvin Peete became the predominant African American golfer on the PGA tour during the 1980s. Like Elder, Peete transcended race as he went on to post a dozen wins and become the second-winningest pro on the tour during that decade. Peete's greatest day as a golfer was winning the Tournament of Champions in 1985, but for him that victory was overshadowed by his numerous accomplishments both in and beyond golf.

I didn't start golfing until I was twenty-three years old. . . . I hope you're recording this, because this might be my best interview. The things that I did in golf, my exploits, my accomplishments, winning the TPC [Players Championship], winning the Tournament of Champions, being second-winningest pro in the eighties, and [leading in] driving accuracy for ten straight years, that's not an accomplishment to me. That was a goal.

When you're looking at a goal, that's not an accomplishment. The accomplishments come beside—my greatest accomplishment is when I was able to send four kids through college, through the exploits of golf. My oldest son, finishing Northwestern with two majors, and doing very well. My middle son finishing the University of Virginia, getting his master's. My oldest daughter finishing at a black college, a historic black college, and I'm very happy about that—at least I got one through a black college, and that was Alabama State University. My youngest daughter just got out of school last year, graduated in July, from the University of North Florida. . . . My youngest son we were glad to get out of high school.

But you know, when you really start talking about greatest accomplishments, I have so many, Bob. Let me say this to you—I watch this on videotape, doing a clinic, kids coming, five-, six-, seven-, eight-year-old kids. And to see this little black kid hit his first tee shot, his first golf ball, and loft it out there about thirty yards, a pitching wedge I started him with, and lofting it out there about twenty-five or thirty yards, and to see that smile on his face when he turned back to me. And I say, now, can anything beat that? That's hard to top.

I mean, I could talk about the TPC, but I went out to do that . . . this, I didn't go out to do, with that young kid. So what is my greatest accomplishment? That, to me, is a loaded question.

I ain't no phony, and I ain't gonna jive you, because I have so many. Coming from my background, inner-city kid, eighth-grade dropout . . . was a millionaire before I got my GED, and that was only to influence my kids and let them know that, hey, how I feel about education, you know?

So, accomplishments is when I look back at my family, and I look back at what I have given, not what I've accomplished for myself, because what I've accomplished for myself, that's what I set out to do . . . okay? That's not an accomplishment.

When you set out to do something, it's like in your business . . . you didn't just stumble upon this (*laughs*).

So, you know, I tried to express that to the media, and I know that's a very relevant question. But there's really no real answer to it . . . your greatest accomplishment. We have so many, I mean, my wife, my children, and my friends, and so many other things, my father, my mother, my sisters, my brothers, I mean, we could go on, when we start talking about accomplishments, I'm a part of all of them.

We've gotta talk about the game? And life? Well, let's be explicit about it . . . (*laughs*). I'm only bullshitting you . . . (*laughs again*).

All of my career, as far as golf is concerned, is nothing but accomplishments. When you start from the bottom, you have nowhere to go but to the top. I didn't pick up a golf club until I was twenty-three years old. Within ten years I was on the tour, playing golf with the best golfers in the world. Within four years I was winning against them, and within another five or six years I was rated as one of the best golfers in the world.

It's really hard to tie it down . . . but I would say winning the TPC in 1985 against the strongest field in golf, whom I really admired and idolized as a young golfer coming up. The Jack Nicklauses, the Arnold Palmers, the Seve Ballasteros, the "Sharks" [Greg Norman], and all the other great players whom I admired. I sailed, to beat them in the strongest field, not to mention the Tournament of Champions in '86 the following year, but to win the Players Championship, as far as competitiveness is concerned, that is the highlight of my career.

Everything I've accomplished in golf stands out. As my teacher would say to me, when I was in the sixth, seventh, and eighth grade, you're the most unlikely to succeed. And that's because of the fact that I did not have great attendance in school—I was smart, but school was boring to me.

And now, to relate that to golf, okay, I didn't pick up the game until I was twenty-three years old, and really, after a while I really began to feel for myself, why do I have all this information and all this knowledge and nobody else does? Why am I rated as the straightest-ball hitter in the history of the game when there's people that studied this game? I mean, they went to the greatest teachers in the world.

It's like, how am I able to do this? I have no answer, Bob.

My brothers and sisters used to say things to me . . . you were destined for success, because anything that you were looking for, you really took it seriously. And that's the thing that I really tried to convey to kids. I do motivational speeches, and I say, hey, look, you must be dedicated. That's what I really try to [say] to kids, is that motivation—that you must persevere, you must be dedicated, and therefore we all have that insight, of what we're capable of doing. And that you're capable of doing to your best, and then move on to something else.

But don't take on something you know you're not capable of doing just because somebody else says it's okay. It's the same thing I really say to them about drugs—don't mess with drugs because some dude says it's hip or it's cool. That is not of your doing . . . leave it alone.

So those are some of the things that I realize, as a young man growing up—what I was able to do and what I was not able to do. And I'm very fortunate in being able to decipher that at a very early age. I don't have to try tennis, okay? I know I would love it, but I don't think I could do it to the perfection that I want to do it at.

I took up bowling, and I bowled a 600 series—I mean, I'm talking about after six or seven months of bowling, and I was into golf at the same time I was into bowling. It was a question of, do you want to be a professional bowler or do you want to be a professional golfer? But when I watched bowling on TV, I didn't see no brothers out there, back in the sixties . . . you know where I'm coming from?

But then, two years after picking up a golf club, 1966, this is '68 when I saw Lee Elder in the championship for the American Golf Classic it was called—it's Firestone now, but at that time it was called the American Golf Classic. He and Jack Nicklaus were tied for the lead, and they went three or four holes, five or six holes, whatever it was, before Jack eventually won the tournament from all over the golf course, and Lee was just right down the middle, right on the greens in regulation, just could not capitalize on the putts.

But I was so impressed with the brother, Bob . . . I was impressed.

And that's where I got my inspiration from . . . hey, there's a brother out there doing this, why can't I? And I didn't see no brothers in bowling . . . I mean, just to be frank.

When I came on the tour . . . let's see, did I meet him before then? Yes, I did, it was like '69–'70, we all played in a tournament that is very close to our hearts, which is the Ted Rose Memorial. Ted Rose is one of the pioneers, perhaps the best black golfer of all time, that never really got a chance to prove himself. [There was also] Gil Stiller and a few others, who were really good golfers but never got a chance to really excel and express themselves on the golf course.

We met in that tournament. And the director of that tournament was announcing, "Now on the tee, Calvin Peete," playing out of desperation, or whatever. And Lee may have asked him, who is this guy, I've heard a lot about him, and I heard [the director] on the loudspeaker, this is the guy that's gonna beat your ass when he gets to the tour.

Don't write this shit (*laughs*).

But that was my first introduction to Lee Elder. And from then, and this is . . . I'm talking about back in the early seventies—'72 I turned pro, '75 when I joined the tour. Within ten years of picking up a golf club I was on the tour. So therefore most of the guys that I was introduced to, I already knew: the Tom Kites, the Tom Watsons, the Jim Simons.

As a matter of fact, in my first professional win, I won it from Jim Simons, the All-American . . . I was bad on him. I played in several U.S. Opens, as an amateur, still in college. And I played in a couple of Masters. You know, this was a top player, you know, and I beat him in a playoff. That really ruffled my wings.

And so, to know that I know these guys, and I can compete with them, and for them to know me . . . when I came to the tour in '75, I was no stranger. It's just that a lot of blacks didn't know me, because, as I advocate to young black players, you do not learn to play professional golf at the level that you want to play with on the tour at the municipal golf courses. You've gotta get to the country clubs, you've gotta have access to the country clubs, because those are the type of golf courses that we're playing on.

It's hard—therefore you've gotta know somebody. See, golf is a network also. And this is what the kids gotta do, or the parents, or the junior golf instructor, or whomever is instructing these kids or guiding these kids, he's got to let that portion of the upper echelon know that this is the kind of kid that we like to have. Great kid, good personality, good game . . . we want to take him a little bit further than the municipal golf course.

So fortunately for me, growing up in south Florida, as far as my career is concerned, I had access to great country clubs, because there was no discrimination there. This was a resort area—if you've got the bucks, you can play. So I was very fortunate, but there's a lot of black kids in other areas that do not have access to country clubs, and that's the way you learn to play.

You can the learn the game, the basic fundamentals, on the practice tee of the municipal golf course, but when you start saying that I want to play golf at another level, if I'm gonna take it to another level, you've gotta get to the country club.

And that comes from my community, that comes from support by politicians, our local politicians in our community. That's where we've got to go. That's the level we've got to get to with our kids, because they all are not gonna come up in the ranks like Tiger Woods.

So that's the only disappointment I have, as far as the Tiger Woods syndrome is concerned, is that we do not have five or six Tiger Woods. I mean, the phenomenon of Tiger Woods, if you can call it a phenomenon, he's not really a phenomenon, is he grew up with a golf club, biting on it in his sleep, gripping it, just like a baseball bat or a basketball.

But how many of our kids are biting on the club at this point? Not enough, not enough—so that's the only disappointment.

Greg Morrison of the old *Mission: Impossible* was a very good friend of mine before he passed. He told me the same thing. In my heydays, back in the eighties, he came up to me and said, hey, man, you're a hero whether you like it or not. You're a role model whether the hell you like it or not. And that's the same thing that I task those athletes with. Every time we get together, I tell 'em the same goddamn thing, you know, you can take all your money and you can run off and hide if you want to. But you still, when you come out into the public, you're a hero for those kids. Don't mess over the kids.

I want people to respect me, as a good brother. I want my wife, I've been married twice, I want each of them to respect me as a good husband as best I could. And to my children of my first family, to respect me as a good father. And I've got a three-year-old and a six-year-old, I just want to try to instill the same values in them that I instilled in my first family. And they've done very well.

Other than that, Bob, as far as the people who watched me golf, it's whatever they feel about me—and let me try to reiterate that. It's not what they feel about me, it's what they feel about my exploits, because they don't know me. I'm only speaking of the people personally. . . . I want them to respect me for my competitiveness, and my congeniality on the golf course, and my camaraderie.

GARY PLAYER

*Growing up in South Africa, Gary Player was a young man
with a big dream. Overcoming formidable odds, Player had
his greatest day when he fulfilled that dream at the age of
twenty-nine by winning the PGA Open to complete the Grand
Slam. But Player was hardly finished—he went on to pursue
his larger dream of becoming the best golfer in the world, winning tournaments and championships around the globe. To
top off his fabulous career on the regular tour, Player proceeded to win the Grand Slam on the Senior Tour.*

Yes, well, I don't have any reservations about that . . . as a
young man, I had a very tall ambition, and for a young boy
from South Africa, small in stature, I had the dream, the ambition, of winning the Grand Slam of golf.

You know, I go to England, and I'm the youngest man to
ever win the British Open at that stage, twenty-three. And then
I go across to America, and I win Augusta, fighting Palmer
down to the last hole. And then I go and I win the PGA at
Ridermink, and the amazing thing is that I had missed qualifying for the British Open the week before. So I went to America, back to the States, with my tail between my legs.

And I win the PGA . . . now, when you think, the fourth one
is always the hardest to win. I mean, Tom Watson never won

the PGA, Palmer never won the PGA, Trevino never won the Masters, Sam Snead never won the Open, and you know, that's the tough one to do, the fourth.

So now I've got the U.S. Open, and Nicklaus, thank goodness, entices me and persuades me to go practice with him the week before the U.S. Open, become familiarized with the place. Which I do, and then I win the U.S. Open, and that, you know, concludes . . . I'm not saying I don't consider the U.S. Open the most important tournament. But it concluded the Grand Slam.

Well, you know, being twenty-three, you go in with an optimistic outlook. I'd realized that nobody had ever won the British Open at twenty-three, and I had this on my mind. You know, I've always had goals, which I find terribly important. I win the British Open, and I was so excited, I sat at the prize-giving, I had my Tournament of Champions jacket on from the Desert Inn. And I sat at the prize-giving, all on my own for about twenty minutes waiting for everybody to arrive, I was so excited.

And then I go across and I won Augusta, and as you know, Arnold and I fought it out all week. And you know, there were 100,000 people there, and 99,998 pulling for Palmer, obviously, nobody had known me. The only people pulling for me were my wife and my dog, which is understandable.

And I go along, and I win that and get my first green jacket, and I bring the green jacket home, can you believe it? And Clifford Roberts phones me up and says, have you taken that jacket home? And I said, yes, I have . . . [and he says], nobody ever takes it off of the grounds. And I thought very quickly and I said, well, Mr. Roberts, you'd better come and fetch it.

And he kind of liked that. He said, you know, don't ever wear it, and here I'm sitting next to my phone, and exactly ten yards away it's sitting in my cupboard, in a plastic bag with my honors, I was a four-letter man in college . . . in a plastic bag with my honors . . . and my honors blazer and my Masters jacket are right there together in a plastic bag, having never been taken out.

Well, you know, it's interesting, everybody said Palmer blew the Masters because he took a six on the last hole. But I'll never forget *Sports Illustrated*, they were very kind to me, they said, well, Gary Player won the Masters because he had a seven at thirteen, and I remember the gallery . . . I drove in the trees on the right at thirteen, and all I had to do was go up the fourteenth fairway, and there was so many people there, and they didn't move 'em out of the way, and I got a little bit impatient. I mean, if it was today, I'd just wait until they moved 'em all out of the way and chip up the other fairway and just wedge under the green.

So I had said, well, to hang with this, and I'll try to just chip it back up onto the fairway. And as you know, I don't know if you know Augusta, from the right-hand side it's all downhill to the creek. I chipped into the creek and made a seven. Then I got a six at fifteen, and then I went on to win.

And because Palmer did it on the last hole, they said he blew it, but they didn't know I went 7–6. I was up and down in the trap from the seventy-second hole, and Palmer, he flubbed it across the green, double-bogey.

It was very interesting . . . I'd just spent two nights with Billy Graham at his home in North Carolina, prior to Augusta. And he said to me, one of the things you've got to realize to win Augusta is you've gotta have some adversity. And my goodness, he said, I don't care if you win it or you don't, you're favored going into Augusta because you played so well at Wintertour. But even though you're favored, you're going to have difficult times to encounter.

And when I got that seven and that six, I just thought of what Billy Graham said . . . and I was very strong going down the line.

When I won the Open, I went back to the hotel, and the hotel had hired a band, and they played a South African song, and they had a big cake for me, and all my friends came over. It was marvelous.

And then when I won Augusta, Clifford Roberts and Bobby Jones invite you to have dinner in the clubhouse. So that's a wonderful way to rejoice. Well, I said to him, I said, Mr. Jones, you know, on the third hole, it's very difficult to get a birdie . . . don't you think that little neck on the left-hand side of the green is too narrow? He said, you're not supposed to get a birdie, it's a par hole.

And I've never forgotten that.

And then, he couldn't cut his meat, he had arthritis so badly. So I cut his meat for him and lit his cigarette for him, I remember doing that, he was such a very, very nice gentleman.

The third is the PGA. Now, I'm playing in the British Open at Troon in Scotland, and I miss the cut. And I go and leave immediately to go back to the PGA to get acclimatized, and I go back with my tail between my legs. And man, I just . . . you know, I've always been a positive thinker, and I changed my game around, and I just played fantastic and won the PGA with a nice score on a very tough golf course at Aronameck.

Well, Aronameck had a bunker on the right-hand side of the fairway, and a bunker on the left. They've subsequently changed it, you know, and I took a four-wood, and I aimed it at the bunker on the right and hooked it, knowing I couldn't reach the bunker on the left. So I still got a fair amount of distance out, but I couldn't quite reach the bunker, so I always kept the ball in play.

And I putted very well, and I came down the last nine holes with a great ding-dong battle with Bob Goalby, and won it on the last hole. And I put my drive in the trees on the last hole on the right, and I hit this big slice with a four-wood. I had a very favorite four-wood, I sliced it around the trees onto the front edge of the green and two-putted to win.

Well, I celebrated that one—I had a lot of friends there as

well, and the members that were at the PGA and the U.S. Open, I became very friendly with them, because I spent extra time there preparing for the PGA and the Open, which I never normally did.

Well, you know, I'm listening to everybody talk about how so many players missed the one and never achieved it. And particularly, I heard so much about Sam Snead. But you know, I realized I had to have the mind to do it. I went into probably the best frame of mind I've ever been in at a golf tournament ever at that U.S. Open.

I went to a Catholic church every day, and I'm not a Catholic. I just prayed for patience, courage—not to let me win, but just courage and patience. And I had great visualization. I used to walk to the scoreboard every day, and they had the U.S. Open scoreboard there, this was when they had the winner of 1964 still on the scoreboard, still in gold letters because it was the last year, and it was Ken Venturi. They had all the names of the winners there, and I just stood and I visualized my name on the board, I did it for a minute every day. I just visualized and brainwashed myself. And then I tied with Kell Nagel of Australia.

But I was so fit, I was squatting, in 1965, with 325 pounds, and my body weight was 160. And I was so strong and so fit, I even played in black clothes, can you believe that, in St. Louis, in July, or whenever it is? I'd melt away today if I did that.

It was terrific, because I got on so well with the members there, and they put a big plaque in their garden which stands there today, because, you know, I gave my total purse to cancer and junior golf, because my mother died of cancer, and I love juniors, young people . . . youth. And then I got very friendly with the members, and they wanted some of my clubs and my clothes and everything, and they put this museum in their clubhouse for my winning.

The third was the PGA . . . celebrated with a lot of my friends.

Being a fitness fanatic, I was always very confident of winning. That was the big thing. I always went into every tournament thinking I was going to win. I'm sure Nicklaus and Palmer did the same thing, that's why we had such great rivalries. And you know, I've always had this positive attitude in doing that.

I didn't ever work on trade-offs or any of that, I just had . . . it was like a railway line, with one idea in mind.

Well now, I go to the U.S. Open, and it's very hot, which is to my advantage, because I am super-fit there. And two, you know, so many people had said . . . I started with weights in 1953, they always said Gary Player will be finished by the time [he's] thirty.

Well, you know, I'm working out with weights, and I'm very fit, and I don't know if you realize, but I won the Grand Slam before I was thirty years of age, when I was twenty-nine. And I'm sure that Tiger Woods will probably do that as well.

But anyway, you know, I was fit and strong, and then I tied for the tournament. I had a two-shot lead with three holes to go, and Kell Nagel went birdie-par, and I went par-bogey. But I was very superconfident of winning the playoff, because he was forty and I was just twenty-nine . . . and man, I was fit. And in that heat, that extreme heat in St. Louis, you know how hot it can get, that was a very big plus for me.

You know, when you feel fitter than another person—it's amazing what fitness can do, and I was so determined, because I made a promise to Joe Dye, who used to be the president of the USGA. And when we played at Pittsburgh several years before, I said, whatever the third prize in the U.S. Open is, whether it's a hundred thousand or a million, I'll give back my prize money to the USGA for cancer, because my mother died of cancer and because I love junior golf.

And I was in that position to win now, and fulfill that dream of my mother and junior golf, and I got extra confidence and extra focus.

Well, the playoff. I holed two long putts in the first five holes. And then at the fifth hole Kell Nagel hooked the ball in the rough, and you know how heavy the rough is. He tried to get it out, he hooked it, and he hit somebody else in the gallery, and oh, he got into all kinds of trouble on that hole. So I just surged ahead from there.

When your mind is focused and you're feeling positive, you say, well, I've got this final dream within my reach. I've worked like an animal, and I've exercised, watched my diet, made great sacrifices, and I'm in great shape.

When you think of the American pro, he's right near his home wherever he is in the States, and you know, I was ten thousand miles away, and it was taking over thirty hours to fly to America in those days. And I was living in motels, and being away from home, and I made these sacrifices, which made me very determined not to let it slip.

Well, I bent over to get the ball out of the hole [on the last hole], and I stayed there for about thirty seconds and said a small prayer of thanks . . . fulfilled, dream fulfilled. The first man, the first modern-day golfer to win the Grand Slam, third man in history.

You know, I beat Nicklaus—if you ask the average American, they'd all say Nicklaus did it before me. Nicklaus is such a tremendous golfer, but you know, people don't know much about history, they just automatically think he did it before me, and that's understandable.

Well, I was so . . . you know, I've always admired the USGA, and I've put on a tie and a suit and a jacket to go receive my U.S. Open, because that was my final victory. And I just think a dress code is so important to prize-giving—this is something that died. Some of these guys go to the prize-givings with their hat on—I mean, I just cannot understand it. My father would have given me the backhand if I'd gone to a prize-giving with my hat on. Now they have dinner with their hat on.

Well, it was just fantastic ... the USGA gave me a nice standing ovation. And the members there were fantastic, because after all, I'd been there for a week prior to the Open and got to know so many of them. And I had chats with them, and I had dinner at the club, and it was like being in my own club.

Oh, I knew what I'd done when the putt went in on the last hole. Oh boy, I sure did.

My ambition was always to try to be the best golfer in the world, not the best golfer in the United States. I wanted to go and win national championships in Australia, and I went on to Australia and won seven Australian Opens, which is a record. Nicklaus is second, and Greg Norman is third—Nicklaus has six, and Greg Norman has five.

And then I wanted to go play in Brazil, and I won their Open, and I won the South African Open thirteen times. And I went around the world, playing all around the world, trying to win everywhere. You know, it made it easier, because when I won all those tournaments, I had airfares paid for me, and guarantees—and it wasn't much, but at least I didn't have to pay my own airfare.

Well, there's nothing that compares to the Grand Slam, but you know, for me to win the Australian Open, or the World Match Play Championship, for example, I beat Palmer in the final round of the World Match Play, I beat Nicklaus twice, [by] six and four, and that's thirty-six-hole matches. You know, to win that World Match Play five times, that was a big thrill for me to win that, because you had all the best players in the world there.

So all of my victories ... a victory was always important to me, but obviously the four major championships always stand out alone.

Well, I've won the Grand Slam on the Senior Tour as well. I've won the British Open Senior three times, and that's played on the toughest [course] of all the senior tournaments that we play around the world. Around the world, the British Open

Senior is on the best golf course, on a real links golf course that they play the normal Open on.

And then I won the U.S. Open Seniors twice, and I won the U.S. Seniors PGA three times, and I won the Senior TPC once. So, you know, I've won nine majors on the regular tour and nine majors on the Senior Tour.

The nine majors on the Senior Tour have given me just as much pleasure, because, you know, it's a different age in your life and a different stage. You know, it's like a lady, if you go to the ladies' tour, they're gonna tell you their nine major tournaments are the most important in the world, obviously. And if you go to Europe, they're gonna tell you their tournaments are more important than America or Australia or Japan . . . it's natural.

Well, the Hall of Fame doesn't mean anything to me compared to the Grand Slam. There are guys going to the Hall of Fame having won one major championship, there are guys going into the Hall of Fame never having won a major championship. I mean, what's so fantastic about that? I mean, it's not . . . to be in the Hall of Fame is nice, but I mean, geez, there's no comparison between being in the Hall of Fame and winning the Grand Slam.

You know, I'm not . . . you know, life goes on. The time of the youth is now. I had my youth. And I don't expect the youth to make a fuss over me, because they can never appreciate . . . how can you tell a young man what it was like to travel forty hours in a jet with six children, and live in a motel with six children every week, and be away from your home and your country and your parents and things like that? How do you explain that to a young man who's playing for $5 million a week and is spoiled rotten?

Do you think he would understand it? Why even try to explain it to him?

How can you explain to the youth that Arnold Palmer and I used to play the entire tour for not even $1 million when they're playing for $5 million a week? And they fly their own jets, and they have contracts worth tens of millions . . . you cannot explain it, and so I don't try.

So all I want on my epitaph is that Gary Player won the Grand Slam of golf on the Senior and regular tour, and you know, we know he can play golf, but he tried to contribute to society. That's the important thing.

In fitness, in manners, in diet—you know, America's got a serious problem. The biggest problem facing America today is obesity. Fifty percent of the American population suffer from obesity. Twenty percent of the youth suffer from obesity.

You've got a diamond, a great diamond . . . America is the great diamond of the world. You better keep polishing it. You understand what I'm saying? Look after that great country. You've got a nation that's overweight, it's hard to be productive, and it's hard to polish the diamond.

Well, you need athletes . . . I'm going to be writing a book on the youth. It's too late for grownups, it's too late to convince America that this junk food, and the mothers who are really poisoning their children, they don't worry how they eat, they feed 'em being fat as pigs in front of them and they don't do anything about it from when they're young. And I want to write a book on exercise and on diet, because I love America, and I want to try and give something back other than just winning golf tournaments. So I have some great plans on doing a book when I'm ready.

And see, I can substantiate the book, I'm not like some of these people that talk about diets and they're thirty pounds overweight. I'm in shape—at sixty-four, there are not many people in the world that can beat me in a fitness contest.

So this is gonna be my big contribution, is either a movie or a video or a book . . . I'll find somebody to sponsor that sometime in America.

NICK PRICE

Renowned for his swing and his shot-making ability, Nick Price chose two greatest days. The first was his first victory in his rookie year, when he held off a pack of pursuers that included Jack Nicklaus, Hale Irwin, Ray Floyd, and Johnny Miller to win the World Series of Golf. His second greatest day took place a little over a decade later: in 1994 Price brought his career full circle by capturing the trophy that had eluded him in 1982—the British Open.

There's two, really, that were really important for me. The first one was the 1983 World Series, the other was the British Open in '94.

It was my rookie year in America, and considering what had happened at the British Open the year before, where I had squandered a three-shot lead in the last six holes, it was very important to me, even though this was over a year later, to win. I got into contention again to prove to myself and to other people that I had the ability to finish off.

And the World Series at that time carried a ten-year exemption on the PGA tour, it had a $100,000 first prize, which was one of the biggest first prizes of the year, outside of the major championships, probably one of the more important events, because of the quality of the field. You couple that, I led from start to finish, and then I had three of the world's best players at the time breathing down my neck coming into the Sunday— it was Jack Nicklaus, Isao Aoke, and Hale Irwin.

And the significance was, I beat them by four, finally. So not only did I prove to myself and to other people that I had the ability to play under intense pressure. Where I had failed in 1982, I came out with flying colors in 1983. And that, I think—had I not won that, it may have had a lot of long-term ramifications and effects on my game, and also on my self-being.

But to come out that way just proved to myself that by winning I could sustain and I could play under self-pressure. Just the fact that all the factors that you go and do isn't wasted, I think that's the hardest thing. I think to go out and practice and go through the motions and go out on the practice tee and hit hundreds of thousands of balls each year, and in the back of your mind you're afraid that you may fail, that when you get to the winning post you're going to trip over and fall, horses are gonna go past you. It just gave me an enormous amount of self-worth, in terms of putting so much into it in terms of the time.

I have always been the kind of person that I did not want to be just another golf pro. I wanted to distinguish myself as someone who maybe wasn't given a whole lot of talent but worked hard, and the work paid dividends for me.

During the week—I was in my first year—it was the first year of the all-exempt tour, where they took the top 125. And at that stage I was lying about 108th on the money list, and we were probably about three-quarters of the way through the year. I was starting to play better, but I was stalled . . . I think if I hadn't made another dollar through the World Series, I thought I'd finish, I worked it out, about 121st. So it wasn't as though my well-being or my exemption on the tour was in jeopardy, but there was so much to play for, for the week.

And particularly when I started playing well, and that

ten-year exemption started looming. That was something that really was . . . at that stage you don't get too many opportunities to win an event as your first one that carried a ten-year exemption, so that was certainly at the forefront of my mind all week.

I had seen Firestone on television on many occasions, and it was the kind of golf course that I felt very comfortable on, because it wasn't gonna be a golf course where a particularly low number was shot. It was going to be—somewhere in the single digits under par was going to win. And I think when I did win I did get to double digits, I shot ten under, and next best was Jack Nicklaus at six under, and then Johnny Miller five, Ray Floyd and Hale Irwin were at four under.

But that was one thing that sort of stuck out more than anything else when I played the golf course, was the fact that there was a really good opportunity for me here to do well and make some money and elevate myself up the money list. And I'd had three or four top-ten finishes where I'd had opportunities to win, probably my best opportunity before that on the tour was at the Kemper Open, when Fred Couples won and I finished two shots back of him. There was five of them that went to the playoff, and Fred won, but that was certainly my best opportunity to win at that time.

Coming into Sunday, I had all these guys breathing down my neck, and Tom Watson was another shot back. There were a lot of good players around me, so it was important for me to finish strongly.

I just played very solidly all week, I didn't do anything in particular exceptionally well, except my iron play was very . . . what had probably been the weakest part of my game, which was my iron game, was becoming the strongest part of my game that week. My game plan was to hit the ball—because Firestone had small greens in those days—was to try and hit the ball in the center of the green. There's a lot of long iron shots that we had there, it was a real acid test for my game, to put it in a nutshell.

But I think on the second round, I holed an eight-iron on the ninth hole from 157 yards. And those kinds of things didn't happen, you don't hole many iron shots, at least I don't, and when those sort of things happen, you feel that the writing's on the wall for you, the golfing gods are smiling and things are gonna happen. There were a lot of little things like that that happened, but that was probably the major thing.

The most important thing to me was that I was not going to fold . . . whatever you want to call it, that I was gonna be rock-solid. And I missed one green coming down the stretch, the last seven holes I missed one green, which is the fifteenth, which is a long par three, and I nearly holed my bunker shot. I think everyone was expecting me to start to fold a little bit and start making some mistakes, and I hit that bunker and nearly holed it, and that seemed to settle what nerves I had at the time, and then I went on to par the last three holes and win by four. That was also another significant shot at the time.

Every time you look at the leader board, you see the names Nicklaus, Floyd, Watson. And these are guys who were idols of mine, and here I was, twenty-five years old or twenty-six years old, probably four of the most distinguished players of the generation ahead of me breathing down my neck. And that was certainly staring me in the face at every leader board. But I proved to myself that day that if I just focused on what I was trying to do, I could achieve.

I think the win gave me so much confidence, and the knowledge of knowing that I could win.

And then I went through a tough phase, because I just couldn't replicate that again for about seven years. I came very close on numerous occasions, but I just never pulled it off. And I think probably the thing that, the one part of my game that was the weakest during that, was my putting, which I worked on really hard. And when I started playing really well from '91–'94, that's what the difference was, I thought of making putts under pressure, where in times gone by I hadn't been.

I remember very well, because Steve Melnyk interviewed me on the eighteenth green, and I was obviously at a loss for words, I couldn't really think of anything to say. I was just in the situation and what I'd done, and conscious that this feeling of pressure had been taken off me. And he asked me, what did it feel like? And the first thing that came to my mind was, because I'd played so well, I couldn't believe how easy it had been.

You know, when you sit in the hotel room on the last night before a major championship and whatever, you have visions of all sorts of things going wrong, and all sorts of things happening, other guys holing bunker shots and making long putts against you, and of just sort of maybe holing a four-footer, a knee-knocker on the eighteenth to win by a shot. Well, as it turned out, I played the last two holes in relative comfort, knowing that I could go bogey-bogey and still win by two.

I think when I said to Steve Melnyk, I can't believe how easy it was, it came over in the wrong way. And a lot of people who didn't know much about golf felt that that was kind of an arrogant, or . . . I'm trying to think of the right word to use, it was kind of an I'm-here-to-stay sort of thing. But it didn't come from me that way, what I meant to say was that it just shows, I'm trying to explain to people that if it all goes well and you do do the right thing, winning is not the hardest thing in the world. It was just based on my own internal picture.

That was probably the most humorous thing—I took a bit of stick, I got a bit of slack from people about that. But as soon as I explained it to people, told people the position I was in, told people, look, this is how I was feeling going into that day, and then everything fell into place for me. And it was relatively easy.

I had four or five of my close friends around, and we went out to dinner and drank some wine and just had a lovely evening. I celebrated for a long time after that.

It basically gave me my plane rides, and assured me of a career, which, even at that stage, when you're twenty-six, you're on a year-to-year basis, and you're never sure where you're gonna be the next year. And if you don't play well, you're out, you're back to Q-school, and that just meant I didn't have to go back to qualifying school for the next ten years, which allowed me, I think, to work on my game probably a little more freely than having the pressure of knowing that if I did have a bad year, I would be out on my ear.

And I think that's what really helped me to become the player I did, because there were times when I was refining things in my golf swing and in my game that, had I had that Q-school looming over my head every year, I might not have tried, and maybe not have accelerated my progress so quickly.

The British Open was very unusual for me, because when I left, I had won, I believe, the Western Open two weeks before. And I normally take a week off between . . . [the U.S.] Open and the British Open, it gives me the opportunity to refine, to work out a few of the areas that I have things that maybe don't feel too comfortable in my game. And that week that I go over before the British Open, I'm at home, I try to get all those little kinks ironed out.

I felt when I left here on a Sunday to go to Ternberry that my game was in as good a shape as I've ever had it. I had worked on my chipping, I worked on my little runup shots, my bump-and-run shots, I'd worked on my driving, and I'd worked on everything that sort of niggled me. And I say that having won the week before, but even so I made some mistakes there that I wanted to eradicate. You want your game to be as tight as possible going into a major championship, and I certainly felt I'd done all my homework when I left here on a Sunday.

When I got to the British Open, when I got to Ternberry on a Monday, I went to hit balls, and it was as though every single thing that I'd worked on had left me. It was terrible. I'd left my golf brain in America, and here I was in Scotland, and I felt that, you know, what had I done wrong? And I actually, for a period of time there, I was panicking, something had set in.

But as with everything, you know, you can't lose the form that you've had for seven or eight months or whatever, two or three years, or your lifetime, it doesn't go in one day. You're just having a bad day. So I tried to look upon it as a bad day, and then Tuesday was much, much better, and then Wednesday there in the practice round I played a lot better.

And it was still frustrating, because on a scale of one to ten, having left on a Sunday, my last practice session being on a Saturday before I left to go to the British Open, my game, I felt, was at an eight and a half or a nine out of ten. And when I got to the practice tee the next day, I felt like I was about a two. And then when I got to Wednesday, my game actually got to a four or a five, so at least I was in a position where I felt that I could play well.

And then every day my game got better. But it still never got to the level that it was at when I left, which certainly, feeling-wise . . . but each day got better. I think that was probably what helped me on Sunday so much, because I knew that when Sunday rolled along, and I think I was only one back for the lead, maybe two, I felt that I was gonna have a really good opportunity to win my first Open championship. So that was when I went into Sunday, when I walked up to the first tee, that if I didn't make any foolish mistakes and I didn't three-putt unnecessarily, or miss an iron shot from the middle of the fairway because I was being too greedy or too aggressive, that I was gonna have a good opportunity.

And it all came down to the last nine holes, which is when so many determine the champion for the tournament. Nobody in the field on the front nine had really poked their noses in front and said, hey, I'm the man to beat. And when we turned on the back nine, Jesper Parnevik was about two holes ahead of me, he was the first one to take the bull by the horns. And he started running with it, he made some birdies, and immediately he started doing that, I said to Squeak, my caddy, he's the man we're gonna have to beat today.

And maybe his birdies picked my game up a little bit, because everyone was sort of wallowing, nobody was doing anything of significance. But he did, and I think that's what spurred me on. And then I birdied twelve, I got two behind him, he shot into a three-shot lead. I played thirteen and fourteen very aggressively, and I hit both my shots over the green, which is the last place you want to do that.

But I chipped well on both occasions, once to about three feet, and then the next time to about two and a half feet to save par. And my short game was rock-solid, and I knew that I had that in the back of my mind, that I could be aggressive, and if I missed the green, I would be able to get it up and down and save par, which is a wonderful feeling to have. You just feel like you can go flat out at it.

On the thirteenth hole, I hit a very good five-iron to about fourteen feet and missed the putt, and then playing sixteen, seventeen, and eighteen, which on that particular day was downwind, I knew that I would have to have a special finish. I would have to do birdie-birdie-par, or a par-eagle-birdie, or a par-eagle-par finish. I would have to play the last three holes in two under par to have an opportunity to get in the playoff, because when I was on the sixteenth tee, Parnevik was actually playing seventeen, and being downwind, it was more of a par four that day than it was a par five, we were hitting a drive and a long iron to it as opposed to a drive and a wood on a normal occasion.

And sixteen was probably the best hole I played all week. There was so much said about seventeen and the eagle I made there, but the way I played sixteen that day is what won me that Open championship. I hit a good driver down the middle of the fairway, and I had about eighty-eight yards, and the pin was in a very, very, very precarious placement. It was just over on the left-hand side, and it was just over a bern. I don't know how familiar you are with the hole, but there's a bern, and anything that is short would just roll back into the bern, and that was a five, maybe even a six.

But just to the left of the pin and about eight or nine yards behind the pin, there was a little mound on the green, and I used that as a backstop with my sand wedge. I hit my sand wedge, pitched it pin high, it had one bounce, rolled up this little bank, and then it took the split and spun back ten or eleven feet from the hole. And I made that putt for birdie from pin high, just about pin high on the left. I didn't shoot at the pin, but I used that bank to bring the ball back and give myself a shorter putt than if I had gone straight at the pin, because if I had gone straight at the pin, the ball would have finished twenty-five feet beyond the hole. That was about the best I could have done without being foolish.

So when I holed that putt, I felt like I had played that hole with all the experience and the professionalism that I had learned in my career, whereas maybe lesser players would have shot at the pin, hit it twenty feet by, made a great putt, and not holed it. I used this little bank, and . . . it's just experience, I think.

And then seventeen, again, I had the opportunity to shoot at the flag, but I remembered that short and to the right you had some little moguls there, some little humps and swells which would have made chipping from there very difficult. So I purposely hit my second shot, I chose, I was in between clubs, I was in between a four- and a five-iron, I knew it was gonna be a really good five-iron to get the ball to pin high, but if I hit a good four-iron, it was gonna go past the pin. So I decided to go with a four-iron, to give myself a flatter putt coming back, and an easier shot, so even though I was hitting the four and I wasn't going for the flag, I knew that I was gonna have an easier putt or an easier chip from the back left-hand quadrant of the green, as opposed to being anything short.

And I hit the four-iron really well with a little bit of a cut on it, and actually it didn't bounce as far right as I thought it would, but it ended up about . . . I think it was sixteen paces from the hole. And exactly as I thought, I had a putt that was downhill, not that severely downhill, but only had about eight inches of break on it, which is not a lot of break for that length of putt, and a little bit of a two-tiered green, not much of a tier to putt down, probably about six or eight inches' difference in elevation from the top tier to the bottom.

And I hit this putt, and I picked the spot I wanted the ball to run over the top of the tier, and the ball ran right over that spot, and as it started taking the break, I knew it was gonna have a really good chance to go in. At this stage I was still one behind Jesper, who was now playing the eighteenth hole.

Anyway, my ball hit a spike mark about two or three feet short, two and a half feet short, just as it was starting to lose speed. And it bobbled a little bit, and I thought that the spike mark was going to knock the ball out of the hole. But it didn't, it managed to go in on the right side of the hole, and I mean, I was jumping around and very excited, obviously, my caddy and I were giving ourselves hugs and slaps on the back.

As I picked the ball up in the heart of the hole and started walking to the edge of the green, Squeak, my caddy, came up and said, Parnevik's bogied eighteen. So instead of being now what I thought would be tied for the lead, I was now one ahead. And the difficulty that I'd had all week was making par on that eighteenth hole, it was just played very difficult. So now my heart's pounding at two hundred beats a minute, and I've gotta play the eighteenth hole, which is the one that I've had the toughest time with all week.

I slowed myself down, and again, drew on my experiences

in the past, and took a couple of deep breaths, and focused on my target, and hit this three-iron down the fairway probably 275 yards, which is one of the longest three-iron I've ever hit in my life, leaving myself a seven-iron for the middle of the green, and two-putted from twenty-five feet. So it was a perfect way to play the last hole.

But I think seventeen no one could have predicted—as I said to myself on the sixteenth tee, I knew that two birdies would get me into the playoff. And I finished 3–3–4, and had I finished 3–4–4 or 3–5–3, I would have been in the playoff, so I did one better. That's sometimes what happens with your strategy, is that you have a strategy set up, and you say, that's the way I'm gonna play, and of course, under that intense pressure, I still had the ability to think clearly. I think that ability to think clearly under pressure is what separates the winners from the runners-up.

For me, personally, this was a different period in my life, and I don't think you could have compared—even though it was the same player, it was a different player. I think what I had learned from my earlier experience in '82, my experience in '88, and the way that I had played in '91 and '92 and '93 and '94, this was a different Nick Price. Because I'd learned how to play the game properly—I'd learned how to win. And when I played well now, I was winning, I wasn't finishing second, third, fourth, or fifth. That was the difference. And I knew that if I played well and didn't make mistakes, I knew I was gonna have a very good chance to win the Open.

There was something . . . I don't know, maybe I'm a slow learner, once you go through those emotions and those ups-and-downs when you're in contention in major championships, I had learned and had used the experience, my previous experiences, particularly my one at the British Open, I think.

But I did think about those when I wasn't playing. But when I was playing, I was so focused on what I was doing that those didn't even enter my mind.

In fact, at the prize-giving, after I signed my card, we had about fifteen minutes of standing around, my wife was there, and David Ledbetter, I had fifteen minutes before the prize-giving. And I looked at Jesper, who was standing there, obviously very dejected, and I thought . . . I've been there, I've seen that. I've seen that movie. He made a mistake, just as I had made a mistake.

And I think in hindsight it wasn't a good thing that happened to him, but he turned it into a good thing. And I think that's what I did. It would have been very easy for me in 1982 just to waft away or slip away into oblivion and become just another journeyman professional. But I used that experience, and I said to myself, if I've been in contention in a major championship at twenty-five, I've still got another fifteen or twenty years left of my career. I can get into contention again, and the next time I do it, I'm not gonna make the same mistakes.

I don't think, up until the '94 PGA, which I won three weeks or four weeks after that British Open, I don't think I had ever played as well in a major championship as I did in 1982. That was, tee to green I played phenomenally well that year, and the only one that I would say that I played better in was the PGA at Southern Hills.

I think what surprised me more than anything else was how low the scoring was that week. We did have very good weather conditions, it was warm every day, I think there was only one day that I wore a sweater, so it was a beautiful week for golf. The course was in phenomenally good condition, I think they had set it up where the rough was a little on the light side, it wasn't very heavy, and that was why the course was having good scores shot on it, the greens were immaculate.

But having left Florida, just to put you into my mind-set, I left Florida on a Sunday playing so well, and then arriving on a Monday, I really didn't feel on Monday and Tuesday that I had an opportunity, that I was gonna have a shot at winning.

I felt like, if I played well, I was gonna have a top-ten position. But by my practice round on Wednesday, where I played so much better, I did have a chance, and it was a question of, even though the top half of my game wasn't as good as I liked it, the bottom half of my game was certainly a lot better than I thought it was gonna be off of the previous two days.

And I knew that if my game was tight—and a lot of times people will say, what do you mean? You've gotta look at the bottom half of your game and how many mistakes you're making. You can be playing really well, but with the bottom half of your game you can be hitting some wild shots, and those will make you double-bogeys.

Whereas when the bottom half of your game is tight, you leave yourself in a position after maybe a poor tee shot to get the ball close to the green, or if a good tee shot and a poor second shot, you give yourself the opportunity to get the ball up and down. You don't hit it into a position you can't make par from— I think that's what, the whole week, the bottom half of my game was very strong. And it allowed me to make the birdies that I did make count—in other words, instead of making three birdies in a row and then double-bogey, bogey, you know, I'd make one birdie and then go with four pars. That consistency is something that you need over seventy-two holes.

Someone had written, in 1982, that I'd had one hand on the trophy, and then I'd watched that hand sort of fall away. And I thought about that for a long time after, and I always thought, am I gonna get both hands on the trophy? And for some reason, when I saw that trophy, it triggered something in my mind, because the speech that I gave was not premeditated at all, it was something . . . when I say premeditated it was, because I was thinking about when I was standing there, but it wasn't something that I'd thought about for months before or years before. But it was in the back of my mind, when I saw that trophy it triggered that—one hand on the trophy.

And I thought about 1988, and I said, well, I had another hand on the trophy in 1988, so when they gave me the trophy, my words were, in 1982 I had my left hand on this trophy, and then in 1988 I had my right hand on this trophy, and now finally I've managed to get both hands on it. That was probably the best way to explain it, because when you can feel the thing, you know, you wanted to have it with both hands but the other hand just couldn't get on there. So that was a very important, I think a very pertinent and heartfelt line in my speech. And I think a lot of people knew that I'd paid my dues.

That's something about the British Open—you have to have a few close shaves before you win it. And I think Jesper Parnevik will win it, it's just a matter of time.

We had a lovely party at dinner, a party in the hotel, where I had a lot of my friends and associates, there were probably about thirty-five people at that party. It was a very special evening, my wife's parents were there, unfortunately my mother wasn't there, but we then left on Monday morning and went down to see her, and my brother who lived down in the south of England. So I spent the day with them, which was also . . . it just meant so much to me then, it really did.

I just took that confidence, when I came back from the British Open, either the warmer weather or the comfort of being back in America, I'm not sure what, but I went back to hitting the ball the way I was before I left for the British Open. I worked extremely hard the two weeks before. I nearly won at Memphis. After the British Open I had a week off, and then I played at Memphis two weeks before the PGA, and that's always been one of the courses I've done very well on. I actually got down to the last hole, where I had a putt from about eight or ten feet to get into the playoff with two other guys, and the ball just lipped out. There were three in the playoff, I ended up finishing fourth, but one shot out.

And then I was scheduled to play the next week, before the PGA, and I withdrew, because I didn't want to be tired for the PGA. I felt, with all the attention I'd had on me and all the interviews that I was giving, that I needed to go back home and just relax and get ready. I went back home and practiced very hard the next week, and worked on my short game, and I don't think I will ever dominate a major championship like I did that PGA in '94. I just played so solidly all week, and to me it wasn't a question of—especially on the third day—it wasn't a question of whether I was going to win or not, it was how many I was going to win by. And that's how I felt.

I was in such control and just had all my ducks in a row. I just had—every department of my game was very, very strong that week. When I did make a mistake, I'd chip or recover exceptionally well. And the only mistake I made on the last day was I three-putted the eighteenth hole. If I two-putted that, I think I would have won by six, I think I won by five. I won by five, but realistically it was six shots.

And that probably was, I don't want to say the pinnacle of my career, but I want to say that was probably the most in control I've ever been at this game in my life. I've had a lot of good play since then, but nothing has really come close to that peak that I hit there.

It would be similar to sort of the peak that Tiger Woods is going through right now, although his peak might be a little higher than what I was. If you want to run a comparison between he and I, he hits the ball a lot further, he has a much better ability to actually pulverize a golf course than I have, because he hits the ball longer and higher and whatever.

I think that was about as close as I'll ever play the game to . . . not perfection, but flawlessness.

To me it felt like all the hard work, every single little thing that I ever thought about, swing thought, mental thought, physical thought, you name it, I mean everything that I'd ever worked on in my career was worth it. Every single thing.

The fact that I had some flaws in my swing, and I'd worked

very hard on those, and those were now minimal. The mental part of the game, I'd worked very hard with Barbara Teller since about '88 on trying to focus better and be more concerned about my next shot as opposed to the ones that are going up in two, three holes' time, or the one that I've just hit—to have the ability to just forget, and just focus on the most important shot that I have to play, the next one. And that's what I did so well, I think that's what I did better than everyone else in the field that week.

You couple that together with the way I was swinging, and that was the result—a win by six shots. It was really the highlight of my golfing career. There's not too many people in the history of the game that won back-to-back major championships. And to deal with the media pressure, as well as the fan pressure, for you to perform, is one thing.

But then on top of it to keep your game, and to keep focused on that, is something that's very important. It's very easy to say, there, I've won the Open championship, which I so wanted for so long—I could have easily just sort of slipped back and said, well, I'll just take it easier for the rest of the year. I got up the next week or two weeks later and nearly won at Memphis, and planned the week off. It was all strategy, and everything that I did panned out, everything that I did there, I couldn't put a foot wrong.

But it wasn't that it was lucky, it was premeditated or something that was planned. So to go to the PGA and still have that desire to go and win again was something that was very important to me.

You have to look . . . I think a golfer has to look at his career as in a lifetime. You don't measure a person's career by a three- or four-year stretch. You look at his career over a lifetime, over a period of fifteen to twenty-five years. And if you have a look at my career over the last twenty-three, twenty-four years, you'll see that there's been a steady progression to a certain level, and I peaked at that level. And even though I've dropped off a little bit, I'm still at a level that a lot of players . . . a level that I really wanted to play at.

When I play well, I win. It doesn't matter where I am in the world, against whatever competition—when I play well, I win. That's something where I could not have asked for anything better. And I'll tell you what, I've had a hell of a lot of fun doing it, too.

CHI CHI RODRIGUEZ

Before he became famous as one of the chief raconteurs and showmen of the Senior Tour, Chi Chi Rodriguez made his name as a hard-charging, gambling golfer who always kept his fellow pros on their toes with his daring tactics. For his greatest day Rodriguez chose his first tour victory, which took place in 1963.

My favorite day in golf was when I won the Denver Open, that Sunday when the guy that gave me my first job as an assistant pro, gave me the first down payment for my first car, gave me my first steak . . . when I won he was my first teacher, and with that money I bought my mother a home in Puerto Rico.

The thing that I remember most is that last hole. I had a two-shot lead, and it was the narrowest hole in the world, with trees right and left and out-of-bounds right. And everybody thought I was going to hit an iron off the tee, and I took a driver, and I hit it about 330 yards. I hit a wedge about eight feet and two-putted and won by two strokes.

In those days they used to give everybody a coat, and they had made coats for about ten players . . . none for me. I said, well, which is the biggest coat that you have, and they said, well, we have made one for Joe Parrish, and I said, give me that one, and that's the coat I wore.

It had a lot of dogleg holes, but it was the kind of a course that you could lay up and do well, you know, I was always being some kind of an aggressive player. Most guys were hitting irons, I was hitting drivers on most of 'em—that's why I won. I think I played the last day with Dave Hill, and Dave played wonderful, he could have won, but I was luckier. I think I played with Art Wald the last day.

I just called my mother after the tournament, I said, you're going to Puerto Rico, you're not gonna live in the Bronx anymore. I think two weeks later she was on the way to Puerto Rico.

That was the one that made my mother happy for the rest of her life. She said, I was expecting that, son, I know you're a good son, and God always takes care of me. That's what she always said when I gave her something, she said, God always takes care of me. I said, how about me, Momma? I don't count?

Nothing will experience . . . going into the Hall of Fame, and getting awards, and all that stuff is great for your . . . those are material things. But winning the first one was a spiritual thing, you know, that's a great big difference.

I never thought much of treasuring material things. The best award I've ever had is a little plaque I have in Puerto Rico where all my peers, all the kids, the young guys, when we were kids we grew up together, we played for five cents and stuff. All ex-caddies, when they moved to New York, they formed a little club, and they used to play tournaments against other nationalities in New York.

And they gave me a dinner, and they gave me that little plaque, and that little plaque is the best for me that I will ever have. It was from the guys that I came up with, they could hardly afford the dinner that they gave me, and they could hardly afford the plaque, they gave it to me with the flag of Puerto Rico. It's a beautiful little plaque.

HAL SUTTON

In his two decades on the tour, Hal Sutton has won a PGA Open and seven other tournaments, but his greatest day came during his Ryder Cup experience. After playing on two losing Ryder Cup teams in 1985 and 1987, Sutton experienced total redemption as a key member of the 1999 Ryder Cup team that galvanized the sports world by making one of the most stirring comebacks in golf history on the final day of match play.

Okay . . . my greatest day in golf was winning the Ryder Cup.

Well, it was a bad to a real good—we were down, and to come from behind like we did, I mean, if we'd have written a script, we'd have written it differently, but I think that we would have written it wrong. I mean, from just a sports enthusiast standpoint, there's no greater deal than to come from that far behind. To get down that much and to come from behind is pretty great.

And to be on the team with all the guys I was on the team [with]—I'm probably biased, but by the same token I think it was probably one of the greatest teams that's ever been assembled. A group of great guys, and a great captain, and for us all to pull together like we did when everybody said we weren't gonna be able to pull together, that it was twelve individuals, was a meaningful experience for Hal Sutton.

It was a goal of mine all year long to make enough points to be on the Ryder Cup team. So I played accordingly, as much as I had to, in order to score enough points and be secure in that. There was a great deal of satisfaction involved in making the team.

As far as highlights of the tournament, I mean, I thought it was a great honor to be called on to play in these five matches. I was really, really tired, but somehow, when you get into an experience like that, you reach down inside and you call on things that you didn't even know you had. And I played with two great players as partners, I played with Jeff Maggert and Justin Leonard.

Probably the only regret that I have about the Ryder Cup is that I didn't get to play with Payne. I would have really liked to have been Payne's partner, I think he and I would have made a great best-ball team. But it didn't work out that way.

And then the Sunday where all six matches were up so much early on, the momentum switched to our side, and it was just probably the greatest feeling I've ever had walking around that golf course, feeling what was happening happen.

The first match we played, we were the last match that played that day, and it was Jeff Maggert and I playing Lee Westwood and Darren Clarke, and that was two of their better players. We got down early, in fact, in every match I played I was down early, except for one, I think. And we got two down early, and we ended up coming back and winning pretty good.

Jeff was a great four-ball partner, or foursomes partner, I should say, because we played every other shot in that format. And he and I both drive the ball pretty straight and hit a pretty good iron shot, so we stayed in every hole, in other words. That's why we were effective as a foursomes team.

That afternoon José [Maria Olazabal] and [Miguel Angel] Jiménez beat us two and one, I think—they just played really good, they birdied like three out of the first five holes, or four out of the first six or something, and got us down, and we just never could recover from that.

You know, we stayed even with 'em after that, or we gained one, I think we were three down at one point, and I had made several long putts to keep us at that. I mean, they were making 'em from everywhere, and I was having to make 'em from everywhere. We could never get the putt in ahead of 'em—I made a lot of long putts with them, but it was like I was inside them, so we couldn't switch the momentum.

The next morning we played Colin Montgomerie and Paul Lawrie, Jeff and I did. And it was a great match all the way, we were down, one down all the way, until we got to seventeen, actually, we got even, and then eighteen we won.

It was just a great match. It was four great players playing right to the very end, and that's the way the match turned out. It was the first match of the day, it was a neat feeling to start out Saturday that way, but we didn't get on top of it. Ben [Crenshaw], that afternoon, switched Justin in place of Jeff . . . I guess a lot of people questioned that move, I think Jeff was getting tired, and Justin, Ben was betting on Justin's putter getting hot that afternoon.

It was a hard-fought match—we had to get it up and down out of the bunker to stay even on the last hole to tie the match. It was just . . . we could never get up on them, and they could never get up on us, basically.

And then Sunday's match, I played Darren Clarke second match out, and he holed it from twenty yards right of the green for a birdie on number one and got me one down. And then I got back to even on two, and then I was never down after that.

Well, you know what, I played well all week long, to be honest with you. I didn't make any adjustments in my game, I just kept trying to do the same things I was doing. I putted well that week, I drove the ball well that week, hit some really good iron shots when I had to hit 'em. You know, guys that win all of their matches in the Ryder Cup have to get a little bit lucky to do that, first of all, because, I mean, when you're playing against—when you get there, that's twenty-four of the best players in the world.

And usually every one of 'em are pretty much on top of their game, because they had to score enough points to get there in the first place, and that just ended in August. You played late September, you're only a month after that. So I felt very fortunate to be able to get three and a half points out of it—to get any more than that I'd have had to be really lucky, I think.

I thought the course [The Country Club, Brookline, Massachusetts] was a great tournament venue for the Ryder Cup. It offered some excitement, it offered some par fives that people couldn't reach in two, it offered some really precise shot-making, which made people make bogies and things like that, but also gave people the opportunity to make birdies. And I think it lent itself to a variety of different shots, and in match play that's what it needs to do.

If everybody had to play every hole the exact same way, well, then, it would get monotonous, even playing match play. But having those par fives that some guys could get to and some guys couldn't get to—for instance, the sixth hole, where some guys could drive it, other guys didn't chance it. You know, different things like that made it exciting.

Well, I've never in my life in all the majors, and I've won a major, never felt the pressure that you feel in the Ryder Cup. I don't know, I can't even describe it to you—you just don't want to do badly. I mean, you're playing for your country, you're playing for guys that you normally play against, you don't want to be the bad spoke in the wheel, so to speak.

And so what ends up happening is that everybody wants to play their best, they want to do their part, they don't want to let the rest of their teammates down, they don't want to let the rest of their country down. You know, when you're play-ing individually, the only person you're really letting down is yourself, and you can deal with that.

In golf you lose 99.9 percent of the time—being second is los-ing, in other words. So, I mean, we deal with losing more than we deal with winning. But, I mean, when you start playing match play, it's just you against that other guy, and so it's . . . you've only gotta beat one other guy, and that makes a big dif-ference, you know? So I think that's why you feel a lot of pres-sure, not wanting to make mistakes, wanting to do your best.

You know, the whole week . . . it was a different feeling among my peers when I got there than I'd ever felt with them at a regular tournament. I mean, we began to get closer from the first night we were all together. And by the time Saturday night had passed us, we were all like brothers, basically—I had never sensed that, going into that week, that we could all get that close.

I think with everything that had transpired prior to the Ry-der Cup, you know, everybody had thought that some guys would only play if they got paid, and that we were a bunch of money-hungry guys—you know, if they didn't pay us, they wouldn't put forth their best efforts, or they wouldn't even play. And I mean, there was just a lot of . . . I won't say mis-quotes, but a lot of misunderstanding about how guys felt.

I think some of those guys were just trying to set a precedent that things do have to change, you know, that guys have given this week of their time for nothing, and let you all make all this money. But at the same time you're gonna have to look at us, financially—it was mixed emotions among all the twelve members of the team. Some guys felt that way, some guys didn't feel that way.

And I think because of the difference in the two, everybody felt like we were separated, so to speak, and we could not play as a team together. And to see that all come to a head, and all of us say, okay, all that's behind us, and we have gotta pull this off, was one of the greatest feelings I've ever had.

I don't think everybody was together completely until that Saturday night that we all had the meeting. Ben and Julie [his wife] had done a video, where there were a lot of famous people, celebrities and government officials and everything else in this video. There was a lot of humor and a lot of seriousness in this video.

We all watched that video together—I mean, a lot of important people saying some really neat things, and personally, to each and every one of us. And then the humorous side of it was that they had gone to each college where everybody went to school and had the cheerleaders do a personal cheer to that player. That was the humor side of it, because, you know, you can imagine guys going back a long ways [from the time they were in college] . . . not just myself, but anyway.

And then, on the serious side, when it was over with, there's a little . . . a deal that everybody always does at the Ryder Cup where we sit around in a roundtable discussion, and everybody, including the wives, says what the Ryder Cup has meant to them and what the experience has meant to them. And you know, at that point there was a lot of seriousness going on, there was a lot of everybody kind of spilling their guts on what was going on way down deep inside 'em, how they felt about the whole experience, you know?

And I think as everybody unfolded how they felt, everybody began to pull together and say, okay, some of the guys that I felt like were maybe a little bit out, they're a part of this inner group. When everybody saw that, we played . . . everybody played brilliantly. They saw the American firepower on Sunday that everybody thought was there, you know?

I think it was because of everybody really getting to know what was in somebody's heart.

Well, we knew early on that . . . I mean, actually, I think partially the reason Mark James has been so upset since then is because of the way he paired everything. He actually paired it where the momentum could switch to our side. I mean, the key is that Tom Lehman and I won because we were playing Lee Westwood and Darren Clarke, and that was truly two of their better players.

Had he paired it the way he really should have paired it, he would have paired those two guys in the first five or six matches. But then he paired the three guys that hadn't played at all—and I'm not saying they're not good players, because each and every one of them are, but they had not been in the competition until that morning. So when he paired 'em like that, he was . . . Tom and I set the precedent by taking two matches up front, and then we felt like the other guys could take their matches off of those three guys, well, then, we're ahead, immediately.

If we take the first five matches, we've erased the lead and we're ahead—which was exactly the way it transpired. We actually had it 12–10 before they ever scored a point. And as we were walking around the golf course and we see that all six of those matches are four up or more, I mean, we're pretty well, everybody . . . the stage is set.

And you know, that was a neat sensation. The crowd sensed it, the European team sensed it, and the Americans sensed it. And from my standpoint as a player, as one of the teammates on the American squad, it was unbelievable. I mean, you know, as I'm telling you about this I have cold chills going down my spine.

The crowd began to get into it . . . I mean, you know, I'm sorry, I was born at night, but I wasn't born last night. These people had forgotten how they act, I mean, sure, we got excited, but we made history at that point. We were making history, there'd never been any team to come from that far behind.

Part of the reason why they were upset is they were on the losing end of that history being made. And I understand that, I've said that before. In losing, in all sports, we make excuses as to why we didn't get the job done. I've done it a million times myself, I'm not sitting here saying they shouldn't have done that. I understood it.

But anyway, as far as the celebration went, we all were sorry for that, we wished it hadn't happened, but the moment overcame us. And it's overcome them—I stood in the middle of the seventeenth fairway in Muriso Village when Seve [Ballasteros] closed Curtis [Strange] out, and it was total celebration. And we had to wait. So . . . fifteen minutes we waited in the middle of the fairway. So I don't forget all of those things—they do.

Well, the celebration afterwards was probably the neatest experience I've ever had. I mean, there were thousands and thousands of people gathered around there, and I mean, I couldn't believe that you could get that many people on the eighteenth green. I've always thought that eighteenth green was pretty small, but I've got a different picture of it after we put that many people on the green.

And to see each one of our teammates so happy about that—I mean, I promise you that the excitement that every one of those team members showed, they would have never shown for a personal win. And then in the aftermath of days passing, I mean, the night we spent there and we all celebrated together, it was just a feeling that I really can't describe.

It was a sense of accomplishment, a sense of satisfaction, a sense of closeness. I don't know how many adjectives I can use to describe it, but anyway . . . and then after this, and I have to add this, with Payne's death, left a void.

Because I felt like he was a brother, you know? And I felt like part of that closeness is gone. I don't even know how to describe it any differently than that, I'm sitting here looking at the Ryder Cup team picture as you and I are sitting here talking, and I see the excitement on every guy's face there as we're all touching the cup.

And I mean, it's just . . . I don't even know how to put it into words, I'm sitting here looking at Payne's face, and I mean the accomplishment . . . this man won two U.S. Opens and a PGA, and I can assure you I've been around for all of 'em. Nineteen years of his career, and there's no time that I've ever seen any more excitement on his face than right there in this picture.

You know, I can tell you about all the other eleven men on this team . . . David Duval, who was criticized greatly through this, I mean, the accomplishment that that man felt when this was over with, the transformation that that man made during this tournament will be probably the single greatest growth spurt in his life.

Just from being misunderstood about how he felt, not fully understanding the importance of the Ryder Cup . . . to get that complete picture at the end of that tournament. I'm sure he felt like he was in one of the greatest growth spurts of his life.

Tiger, the same way really. Tiger's right here, he's got the greatest smile on his face you've ever seen—I don't know what to say. I mean, these guys . . . we all grew. I don't know how to put it any other way—we grew, we learned things, we were part of a growth spurt in each other's life there.

There was just the greatest sense of pride that you could have possibly have imagined, and not only between us, the players, but between the fans. I mean, I can't tell you how many times I've had people holler out at me, Hal, thanks for the Ryder Cup. Not just my part in it, but other guys, I'll be playing with other members of that team, and they'll holler out, Tom, thanks for the Ryder Cup.

They just . . . so much pride across America, that that Ryder Cup was won.

Well, first of all, I think maybe one of those reasons [I choose that as my greatest day] is because of the amount of pressure involved in the Ryder Cup. I was on two losing teams, both on their soil and on our soil, and for me, and another reason is that twelve years had elapsed since I've been on a Ryder Cup team. And I've . . . personally speaking, I mean, there were moments in my career when I thought I'd never have another opportunity to play on a Ryder Cup team.

So from a personal standpoint, the satisfaction that I felt—first of all, just being able to make the team, and then secondly, to be able to play a vital role in us being able to get it back. That's probably why I place the amount of importance on it that I do.

Let me tell you, all of my life one of the gauges of whether I felt like a player was a great player was by how many Ryder Cup teams that guy played on. And the more Ryder Cup teams you play on, I mean, when you look back at Hogan's career, you look back at Byron Nelson's career, you look back at Sam Snead's career, you look back at Jack Nicklaus's career, you look at Arnold Palmer's career—all of those players have been on the team three to five, six, seven times, whatever.

And to me . . . and some of those experiences were winning teams, most of 'em were for those guys. Because back then it was just America against England and Scotland and Ireland, and America didn't get beat much. But then when they added Europe to the equation, I mean, it equalized everything. So it's been nip and tuck ever since.

I was on the first two losing teams, in '85 and '87, and that was a bitter pill to swallow. I'd say the first time we lost on their soil, I think was '85.

I went through a multitude of changes in my life in that time—I wouldn't even know where to start. Well, I tell you what I did learn, from 1985, I was 1–3–1 in 1985, and I felt like I was a contributor to the loss that week. I certainly lost more points than I won, and I did not play well in '85. And I made my mind up, and I knew the reason why I didn't was because I was trying to keep something bad from happening all the time, instead of trying to make something good happen.

So in '87, when I went to the Ryder Cup, I made up my mind that I was gonna make something good happen. And I played well in '87, I scored three and a half points in '87, and

I did it by saying, okay, I'm gonna make birdies. These guys are good, and we've gotta make birdies to beat these guys, so I was trying to play aggressive golf. And I took the same attitude in this year's Ryder Cup, and said, I'm going for broke, I'm not gonna play safe all the time. We're gonna have to make birdies to beat these guys, and that's the way I'm gonna play.

So I learned from my first Ryder Cup experience. Now that twelve years—I don't know if I learned any more in that twelve years about how to play Ryder Cup.

I felt like I was always trying to make the most of the moment. And, I mean, that's really what you've gotta do, whether you're putting for birdie or whether you're putting for par. You've gotta treat 'em all the same—they've gotta go in.

You know, a lot of times that's hard to do, we go through various stages in our life where we're not feeling as confident and we know we've got par in the bag, we're not trying to make that birdie because we don't want to put bogey in the equation. But I made sure that I kept that up for that three days, and I was trying to say, okay, I don't care if I make some bogeys, we've gotta make a lot of birdies.

Photo Credits

Billy Casper: *photo courtesy of ALLSPORT / J. D. Cuban*
Jim Colbert: *photo courtesy of ALLSPORT / Scott Halleran*
Bruce Crampton: *photo courtesy of ALLSPORT / Gary Newkirk*
Lee Elder: *photo courtesy of ALLSPORT / David Cannon*
Bruce Fleisher: *photo courtesy of ALLSPORT / Gary Newkirk*
Ray Floyd: *photo courtesy of ALLSPORT / David Cannon*
Hale Irwin: *photo courtesy of ALLSPORT / David Cannon*
Lee Janzen: *photo courtesy of ALLSPORT / David Cannon*
Tom Kite: *photo courtesy of ALLSPORT / Gary Newkirk*
Tom Lehman: *photo courtesy of ALLSPORT / Craig Jones*
Bobby Nichols: *photo courtesy of ALLSPORT / Gary Newkirk*
Mark McCumber: *photo courtesy of ALLSPORT / J. D. Cuban*
Larry Mize: *photo courtesy of ALLSPORT / David Cannon*
Jack Nicklaus: *photo courtesy of ALLSPORT / David Cannon*
Arnold Palmer: *photo courtesy of ALLSPORT*
Jerry Pate: *photo courtesy of ALLSPORT / David Cannon*
Calvin Peete: *photo courtesy of ALLSPORT / Mike Powell*
Gary Player: *photo courtesy of ALLSPORT / MSI*
Nick Price: *photo courtesy of ALLSPORT / Stephen Munday*
Chi Chi Rodriguez: *photo courtesy of ALLSPORT / Gary Newkirk*
Hal Sutton: *photo courtesy of ALLSPORT / David Cannon*